Understanding Information Policy

Also available in this series:

Effective Use of Health Care Information
Peter Merry

Quality Management and Benchmarking in the Information Sector: Results of Recent Research
edited by John Brockman

Modernizing Research Libraries: The Effect of Recent Developments in University Libraries on the Research Process
Bob Erens

Information and Business Performance: A Study of Information Systems and Services in High Performing Companies
Ian Owens and Tom Wilson with Angela Abell

Electronic Publishing and Libraries. Planning for the Impact and Growth to 2003
edited by David J. Brown

Project ELVYN: an Experiment in Electronic Journal Delivery. Facts, Figures and Findings
edited by Fytton Rowland, Cliff McKnight and Jack Meadows

Networking in the Humanities
edited by Stephanie Kenna and Seamus Ross

National Information Policies and Strategies: An Overview and Bibliographic Survey
Michael W. Hill

Changing Information Technologies: Research Challenges in the Economics of Information
edited by Mary Feeney and Maureen Grieves

Teaching Information Skills: A Review of the Research and its Impact on Education
edited by Rick Rogers

Decision Support Systems and Performance Assessment in Academic Libraries
Roy Adams, Ian Bloor, Mel Collier,
Marcus Meldrum and Suzanne Ward

Information Technology and the Research Process
edited by Mary Feeney and Karen Merry

Information UK 2000
edited by John Martyn, Peter Vickers and Mary Feeney

Scholarly Communication and Serials Prices
edited by Karen Brookfield

Scholarship and Technology in the Humanities
edited by May Katzen

Multimedia Information
edited by Mary Feeney and Shirley Day

Understanding Information Policy

Proceedings of a Workshop held at Cumberland Lodge, Windsor Great Park, 22-24 July 1996

Edited by Ian Rowlands

BOWKER SAUR

London • Melbourne • Munich • New Providence, NJ

British Library Cataloguing in Publication Data
A catalogue record for this book is available from the British Library.

Library of Congress Cataloging-in-Publication Data
Understanding information policy : proceedings of a workshop held at Cumberland Lodge, Windsor Great Park, 22-24 July 1996 / edited by Ian Rowlands.
p. cm.
Includes biographical references (p.) and index.
ISBN 1-85739-179-9
1. Information policy--Congresses. 2. Information policy--Great Britain--Congresses. 3. Information science--Congresses. 4. Information science--Great Britain--Congresses. I. Rowlands, Ian.
ZA3153.U54 1996 97-30014
020--dc21 CIP

Published by Bowker-Saur, a division of Reed Elsevier (UK) Limited
Maypole House, Maypole Road
East Grinstead, West Sussex RH19 1HU, UK
Tel: +44 (0) 1342 330100 Fax: +44 (0) 1342 330191
E-mail: lis@bowker-saur.com
Internet Website: http://www.bowker-saur.com/service/

Bowker-Saur is part of REED BUSINESS INFORMATION.

ISBN 1-85739-179-9

British Library Research and Innovation Report 49

Cover design by John Cole
Desktop published by Mary Feeney, The Data Workshop, Bury St Edmunds
Index compiled by Judy Batchelor
Printed on acid-free paper
Printed and bound in Great Britain by Antony Rowe Ltd, Chippenham, Wiltshire

Preface

This volume of Proceedings is the outcome of a British Library-funded Workshop, *Understanding Information Policy.* The Workshop was organized by the Information Policy Unit, a research group within the Department of Information Science at City University, and the event was held at Cumberland Lodge in Windsor Great Park in July 1996.

The Workshop brought together delegates from the research community (academics and consultants) and from the 'real world' of policy-making at corporate, national and international levels to discuss and reflect on information policy. A number of issues were identified as worthy of further study and are discussed at the end of this volume.

I would particularly like to thank Maureen Grieves for all her hard work in helping to ensure that the event was successful, Charles Oppenheim for his entertaining and informative after-dinner speech on the first night, and Michael Hill who acted as rapporteur throughout the event; his summary of the presentations and the ensuing discussion is included here. Finally, I would like to acknowledge all the contributors' work on this book which I believe will be a significant contribution to the literature of this very topical subject.

Nigel Macartney
The British Library Research and Innovation Centre
1997

Contents

List of Contributors

Francis Aldhouse	Office of the Data Protection Registrar
David Allen	University of Sheffield
David Bawden	City University
Harry East	City University
Tamara Eisenschitz	City University
Margaret Haines	Library and Information Commission
Michael Hill	Fédération Internationale de Documentation (FID)
Barry Mahon	Eusidic
Nick Moore	Policy Studies Institute
David Pye	PicaTEX / Advanced RISC Machines Ltd
Ian Rowlands	City University
Elspeth Scott	GlaxoWellcome plc
Janet Strachan	London School of Economics
Paul Turner	Centre de Recherches en Informatique et Droit (CRID), Namur
Tom Wilson	University of Sheffield
David Worlock	Electronic Publishing Services Ltd

GENERAL OVERVIEW

General Overview

Ian Rowlands

Background to the Proceedings

This volume is the outcome of an intensive two-day Workshop on information policy research held in July 1996 at Cumberland Lodge, a splendid residential conference venue in Windsor Great Park. The idea behind the Workshop was initiated by the Information Policy Unit (IPU), a research grouping within the Department of Information Science at City University. Thanks to the support and encouragement of Maureen Grieves at the (then) British Library Research and Development Department, the idea became a reality through the agency of a British Library grant.

The thinking behind the Workshop was not to justify 'why?' information policy should be studied and analyzed. The speed and extent of recent events had already legitimized that question for us. Instead the focus of the Workshop was on a rather more far-reaching and difficult question: 'how' should such studies and analyses be carried out and new knowledge and understanding in information policy be created? This remains a considerable task: there is little in the way of prior art in the library and information science literature to guide our endeavours.

The writings of Harold Lasswell (1970), an influential figure in the development of the policy sciences, provided much of the inspiration behind the Workshop:

> Sciences are policy sciences when they clarify the process of policy-making in society, or supply data needed for the making of rational judgements on policy questions ... if we rid ourselves of the standoffishness that has kept men of knowledge apart in our civilization, we can more conveniently come together in research teams that are capable of contributing the knowledge needed by the democratic polity.

Following this philosophy, the Workshop brought together academics, consultants, policy-makers and senior information managers. The aim was simple, yet ambitious: to arrive at a better understanding of the concepts, models and frameworks that we use when we undertake information policy studies or analysis, for, despite the rhetoric, relatively little attention has been paid so far to developing the theoretical foundations of the subject. Within this broad aim, three more specific objectives were identified:

- to explore current approaches to understanding information policy problems, from both theoretical and 'real world' perspectives;
- to encourage dialogue and closer links between the world of ideas (the research and consultancy communities) and policy-makers;
- to disseminate the findings to a wider national and international audience, in the form of published Proceedings.

The format of the Workshop revolved around twelve presented papers, given by academics and practitioners. The papers were (in most cases) made available and circulated before the event and (in all cases) discussed at the Workshop.

In an attempt to make the discussion as inclusive as possible, the structure of the Workshop reflected a 'stageist' model of policy-making, which reveals information policy to be a dynamic process:

SESSION ONE
Problem identification and agenda setting
Policy formulation and planning
⇓
SESSION TWO
Policy adoption
Policy implementation
⇓
SESSION THREE
Post-implementation evaluation of policy

This format transcended the more traditional division of information policy issues by scale (international–national–organizational–individidual), and it suggested an (unresolved) question in its own right: to what extent are there commonalities and differences in the ways that we think about information policy in organizational as opposed to more overtly political contexts?

In a further attempt to give structure to what might otherwise have been a loosely focused meeting, all delegates were asked to reflect on the following questions in advance:

- Session 1: Designing information policies

  What are 'information policies' and how do they evolve? From what traditions does information policy draw? How do certain ideas find their way onto the information policy agenda and not others? What kinds of information and research support are needed to design successful policy? Is policy-making a 'rational' process? Is information policy neutral or influenced by ideological values? How important are institutional factors in information policy design?

- Session 2: Implementing information policies

  What are the ingredients of a 'successful' information policy? Who is responsible for implementing policy? How do they secure the commitment of key stakeholders and ensure compliance? To what extent do different policies interact or even possibly compete with one another? What power structures underlie the adoption and implementation of information policies? Does information technology shape information policy, or vice versa?

- Session 3: Evaluating information policies

  How effective is policy X in relation to meeting its objectives? How can information policies be monitored and evaluated? What sort of feedback information and mechanisms are needed to generate better policy? What are the wider social and economic impacts? Who are the 'winners' and 'losers'?

In preparing these papers for publication, an editorial decision was taken to reverse the logic which drove the format of the Workshop in favour of a division into three main sections: Information Policy Concepts; National and International Perspectives; and Organizational Perspectives. One practical issue forcing this decision was the very evident lack of development of a body of theory or practice relating to the evaluation and delivery aspects of information policy: this is an important finding in its own right and it warrants further research. The lack of formal tools for evaluating the impacts of information policy may, perhaps, be rooted in a more serious problem; the absence, in many cases, of explicit aims and measurable objectives to start with. The polemical contribution of Barry Mahon in relation to information policy-making in European political institutions is well worth reading with this point in mind (this volume, p.101).

Each of the three main sections is preceded by a brief overview, offering some keys to the common threads and distinctive positions of the papers therein. I am deeply indebted to Paul Turner and David Bawden for their contributions here. A special word of thanks is due to Michael Hill who acted as the Workshop's rapporteur and who offered a uniquely personal and insightful summary of the presentations and discussion. His reflections are included towards the end of this volume.

Before turning to the first main section on information policy concepts, this General Overview will abstract itself from the detail of the various contributions to consider three higher order 'meta-level' questions which frame the contents of this volume:

- what are the characteristics of information policy as a field of studies?
- what are the unique and distinctive features of information policy?
- what is the normative structure of information policy?

Information policy as a field of studies

'Information policy' has become the subject of a great deal of attention in recent years. It is now possible to point to an extensive body of literature on the subject and to identify a community of information policy analysts and scholars employed in academia, in think tanks, and in government. The emergence of this new discipline, if indeed it is such, accompanies a much higher public profile for information issues and a vigorous debate about the role of information in economic, social and cultural settings.

While progress in the field of information policy is being made, it is widely agreed that the subject is presently at an early stage of intellectual maturity, with little consensus or agreement on what precisely the field comprises. Kajberg and Kristiansson (1996) crystallize the problem very well:

> A detailed examination of the published record of information policy reveals a variety of definitive and analytical approaches to the concept of information policy. There is an evident lack of consensus of what constitutes the core of information policy. An array of classificatory approaches in the field are offered but what is missing is a coherent theoretical framework.

Browne (1996) goes even further in arguing the need for a critical re-examination of the philosophical and methodological foundations of the subject:

> ... there is a feeling of discomfiture in a field in which its researchers are unable to even broadly indicate the substance of what it is they desire to study.

She points out that there are significant definitional problems in relation to the terms 'information', 'policy' and 'information policy' and how they are used (and abused) in different contexts. This means that its proponents have to battle to communicate both the need for and the parameters of information policy.

Information policy is frequently asserted to be a field of study which is highly interdisciplinary: Braman (1989), for example, claims that more than 40 academic fields deal with 'information policy', although she does not identify them. Burger (1993) argues that the core disciplines which inform information policy are economics, law, political science, public administration, sociology, public policy, management science and information science.

While the arguments of Braman and Burger are persuasive, there is very little empirical evidence to support or refute their assumptions. Some evidence that information policy draws from a number of intellectual wells is provided, indirectly, in the form of published bibliographies (Hill, 1994; Rowlands and Vogel, 1991) which identify relevant materials from areas as diverse as law, communications studies, public administration and telecommunications policy. The terms of reference of these works are internal to the library and information science (LIS) tradition, however, and no attempt to provide a coherent disciplinary mapping of the information policy construct is evident in the literature. The danger, of course, is that scholars within the LIS tradition are simply building a house of cards lacking in ontological or epistemological validity. Francis Aldhouse (this volume, p.114) notes perceptively that:

> ... as a stranger to the discourse of information policy, I have found some difficulty in identifying a unified set of topics which might be the subject of something called 'information policy'. Indeed if one considers the nine categories referred to by Rowlands (1996), the stranger might readily conclude that the only element unifying information technology policy, intellectual property, information disclosure, confidentiality and privacy, and the others, is that they are all of concern to librarians and information scientists.

To which one might add that these issues are also of direct concern to their suppliers (i.e. the information industries) and their user communities, a not insignificant coalition of interests. Aldhouse does, however, indirectly raise some important questions. Where does information policy sit in relation to library and information science? Is the natural home for information policy within the LIS tradition or does it share more features in common with broader public policy? Or are there unique characteristics of information policy which justify treating it as a field of studies in its own right?

In a comprehensive and wide-ranging pair of articles, Mairéad Browne (1997a,b), one of the Workshop delegates, suggests that the concept of the information life-cycle provides the strongest clue to the substance of information policy studies. In this conception, information policies are those which impinge on 'the production, collection, distribution / dissemination, retrieval and retirement of information' (Hernon and Relyea, 1968). Similar thinking informs Weingarten's definition of information policy, as 'the set of all public laws, regulations and policies that encourage, discourage, or regulate the creation, use, storage, and communication of information' (Weingarten, 1989).

These ideas neatly create a bridge between public policy, core information science values, and users. It suggests that it might after all be possible to find a more unified conception of information policy located within an information transfer paradigm. Or, possibly, within a knowledge hierarchy paradigm. In his contribution to this volume (p.74), David Bawden introduces the concept of a 'knowledge hierarchy'. In this model, information is seen as occupying a location on a continuous scale, lying somewhere between data and wisdom:

DATA⇒INFORMATION⇒KNOWLEDGE⇒WISDOM

Broadly speaking, as we move from left to right, we move from the decontextualized to the contextualized, from the meaningless to the meaningful. The most important point to be made about the model in this discussion is that it provides a rationale for library and information science both as a craft and an area of academic research. The ultimate goal in any given situation must be to effect or at least to facilitate a shift towards the right hand side of the model (for example, converting 'dirty' data into 'clean' data; turning raw statistics into meaningful indicators; providing a new interpretation of an existing body of facts). There is no other justification for what we do.

The sorts of activities which are involved in shifting the model to the right will be very familiar to those engaged in information work: checking and verifying, collating and analyzing, compressing and evaluating. These skills comprise the craft of information work, and they can be seen as offering different ways of adding 'value'. Adding value is a fine and noble aim, but something of a luxury item, perhaps. Effecting a shift along the knowledge hierarchy will happen only if two conditions are satisfied: (a) enough resources are committed and, (b) any barriers or obstacles can be overcome.

Information science lays a stronger claim than any other discipline to helping us understand the processes of adding value. For the sake of argument, it is accepted here that information science has traditionally sought to understand these processes from two broad perspectives:

- Information Systems
- Information Management

To which perhaps should now be added a third:

- Information Policy

In reality, of course, there is considerable overlap between these areas. While conceding that they are intimately linked, this Overview seeks to locate Information Policy within the mainstream of Information Science. It is not difficult to see how Information Systems and Information Management may contribute to a rightward shift in terms of the model.

- Information Systems
  - » better navigation tools to identify and exploit relevant sources
  - » more intuitive user interfaces
  - » more relevance, less redundancy

- Information Management
  - » best practice in information handling procedures
  - » quality assurance (e.g. Total Quality Management (TQM) approaches)
  - » user education
  - » effective system design

The immediate applications of Information Policy concepts to this equation are less immediately evident, but equally important. The transformation of data to information, knowledge and wisdom involves certain activities (compression, selection, etc.) applied in a given set of circumstances towards a particular goal. So information becomes not just compressed data, but data compressed *for a purpose.* In other words, information has to admit context in order to become meaningful.

Information Policy is precisely concerned with the nature of the contexts within which data⇒information and information⇒knowledge transformations take place. These contexts are much broader and wider than current Information Systems and Information Management paradigms can embrace, each of which tends to view information as a neutral object in social, cultural and economic terms. Information Policy seeks to understand the implications of these wider contexts in terms of how these shape meaning. It is hoped that this volume will provide many examples of those wider contexts. In the next section, I will explore some of the unique characteristics of information policy.

Some unique characteristics of information policy

It would be quite possible, if premature, to enter here into a long debate about the relationship between information policy studies and the wider policy sciences. Browne (1996) has argued that the information policy literature is isolated from the mainstream of public policy research and that this is unhelpful. Others would certainly agree, perhaps going a stage further by noting that the information policy community has also missed the boat in relation to some important developments in the wider social sciences. Paul Turner touches on some of these issues in his Overview to the next section (p.19), as does Janet Strachan in her review of the information-seeking behaviour of policy-makers (p.61).

Whatever the way forward might be, it has to be acknowledged that the roots of information policy studies are planted firmly in the library and information science tradition. In raising the question of what is *different* about information policy, I am in fact raising two sets of issues: not simply, is it different in kind from, say, welfare policy, but, in thinking about information policy issues, to what extent are we currently drawing on models from within information science as opposed to the policy sciences? What might be the contributions that these two very different traditions could bring to a unifying approach to information policy studies?

It is useful to turn at this point to the writings of Sandra Braman, one of the most consistently rewarding authors on information policy. In a 1990 paper, Braman identifies the factors that for her differentiate information policy from other policy issues. Information policy, she argues, is 'different' because:

- it is a relatively new area of policy concern;
- it involves an unusually large number of diverse groups of players;
- decisions about information can have an enormous impact on events and policies in other areas—the reverse is true to a much lesser extent;
- information does not fit into the traditional categories employed by policy analysts;
- information policies made at very different levels of the political and social structure, from the local to the global, are remarkably interdependent.

These differences are all, of course, relative. They may not be unique (i.e. exclusive) characteristics, but they certainly seem to be atypical of other areas of public and organizational policy, where the issues tend to be relatively more clearcut and the affected parties less numerous.

Consider, for example, the recent trend towards the electronic delivery of public services. Local government in London has been quick to embrace electronic communications, using e-mail, the Internet and the

World Wide Web. Thirteen London boroughs now have e-mail, and more than twenty boroughs have or are planning their own official World Wide Web sites. These borough Web sites contain a wide range of information, including 'What's On' guides of borough activities, council reports and plans, tourist information, and links to local community and voluntary groups. Many boroughs use innovative forms of electronic communication to provide information about local services. Examples include: public libraries with computers hooked up to the Internet; electronic kiosks displaying pages of local information in public places like supermarkets; and videotelephony for hearing impaired people.

It is possible to see these developments, simultaneously, as: informing and empowering local communities; extending democracy; instruments to reduce administration costs and head count by re-engineering local government services; providing a stimulus to the information industry; a new weapon in the councils' public relations armoury; or merely as gesture politics, pandering to the IT fetishists. The truth probably lies somewhere (everywhere?) on this list, but it is not immediately evident, especially as the waters become clouded by practical, legal and ethical issues arising in the implementation of these services.

Braman, like Bawden, and Rowlands and Turner later in this volume, suggests that complexity is a fact of life in information policy. Braman (1990) generalizes her argument to suggest that four general characteristics of information policy, regardless of setting, are major sources of confusion. These are: conceptual, informational, structural and orientational.

Conceptual problems arise from the fact that the rate of technological change is so fast that it is outpacing our ability to keep up (see David Pye's paper in this volume (p.191) for a graphic picture of the problems of runaway technology); that regulatory structures and values sometimes conflict (see Tamara Eisenschitz (this volume, p.128) and David Worlock (this volume, p.146)); that policy goals and regulatory goalposts are not static and may shift considerably (see Aldhouse (this volume, p.114) on the evolution of data protection policy). Throughout this volume, conceptual problems and dilemmas, over even the interpretation of basic terms like 'policy' and 'strategy' abound (see David Allen and Tom Wilson in this volume, p.178). Ominously, there appears to be neither consensus nor even much in the way of recent debate about the meaning of the term 'public interest'.

Braman argues that two types of problems emerge from the roles that information *itself* plays in the policy-making process: those that stem from a lack of information, and those that stem from the effects of skewed information. As the paper by Janet Strachan (this volume, p.61) intimates, information policy is quite often made in spite of the fact that the knowledge needed to support the decision is unavailable. Braman, quoting many examples from US policy-making, finds that policy decisions are often based on 'bad, outdated, non-academic, unscientific studies' or are made in an 'informational vacuum'. More excusably, perhaps, she finds also that decision-makers repeatedly claim themselves to be 'incapable of understanding technological development well enough to regulate it'.

The other source of confusion arises from what Braman calls the 'informational deficit'. This argument says that the information available to policy-makers tends to be skewed in favour of what is politically and ideologically acceptable: she places particular emphasis on the conceptual slippage between the image of the marketplace and its reality.

Structural problems are those that arise out of conflicts or contradictions between different policies or between different elements of the policy-making machinery. This is a common theme in writings on national information policy. It may be resolved into two components. The first is that seamless coordination between, for example, government departments, may not be possible in information policy terms because the goals and world vision of the parties involved are distinct and not necessarily capable of being resolved. A second, related, point is that the sheer complexity of information policy results in a reduction of the capability of the state to make policy coherently and effectively. The fact that so much public information policy is latent rather than explicit (see, for example, Martyn, 1992) becomes a real structural problem: compared even with stated policy, unstated policy is capable of many differing shades of interpretation and realization.

Finally, Braman addresses the big question of what information policies are designed to achieve. Without a clear sense of orientation, such fundamental questions as—What kind of social organization do we want? What kind of informational organization best serves that kind of society? What kind of regulatory structures best build and sustain that kind of informational organization?—all become superfluous. These are clearly highly political issues, with a capital P.

The uniqueness of information policy seems to be a function of its complexity. The encouraging aspect of Braman's paper is the (implicit) suggestion that, at least in part, 'complexity' is simply a result of our confused thinking.

The normative structure of information policy

Perhaps one key to unlocking that 'complexity' is first to acknowledge our own positions as policy analysts and policy actors. In this final section, I will turn to the question of values and norms and their role in information policy. No-one involved in information policy can really believe themselves to be totally objective and free of assumptions and prejudices. Progress in information policy studies is critically dependent on finding ways to make those assumptions and prejudices more transparent and challengeable.

Returning to the theme of how information policy seeks to understand the contexts within which value is added to data and information, I will now turn to two important and problematic issues. Both are to do with powerful forces that shape the nature and extent of information flows: economic considerations and power structures.

Economic arguments over whether information should be regarded as a tradeable commodity or a public good abound in the library and information science literature. Sometimes, though rarely, both characteristics may be accommodated by means of differential pricing structures (see Harry East's paper, this volume p.221). The debate on this topic is extensive, but personal views tend to be fairly fixed and unmovable, as we found at the Workshop. The creation and development of information goods and services require that the investors be rewarded for their efforts. This means conferring property rights and enabling a marketplace to develop. The disadvantage is that these rights may potentially erect a barrier to the world of ideas for those who are unable to pay (see Eisenschitz, this volume p.128). This in turn necessitates a further set of public policies, such as universal service, investment in libraries, research and development, and education, which deliberately distort the information marketplace in favour of the wider public interest. Questions of this kind are ubiquitous in the LIS literature.

Aside from monetary considerations, access to information and knowledge is also a function of power structures. In fact, there is an inherent tension in the notion of access quite distinct from the economic arguments outlined above. In many situations, the widest possible access to information is seen as a 'good thing': health promotion, information about school performance, consumer information, access to local government records, being classic examples. In other circumstances there are real problems in allowing unrestricted information access: examples include policy advice to ministers, personal information, and information which might be prejudicial to national security or a firm's commercial position. Restrictions on the free flow of information are sometimes essential, but there is always a danger that powerful forces in society will constrict these flows for their own advantage.

It is my contention that these two problematic dimensions of information—public good vs. tradeable commodity, access vs. secrecy—provide a useful tool for mapping the normative structure of information policy debates (see Figure 1).

Figure 1: Mapping the information policy construct

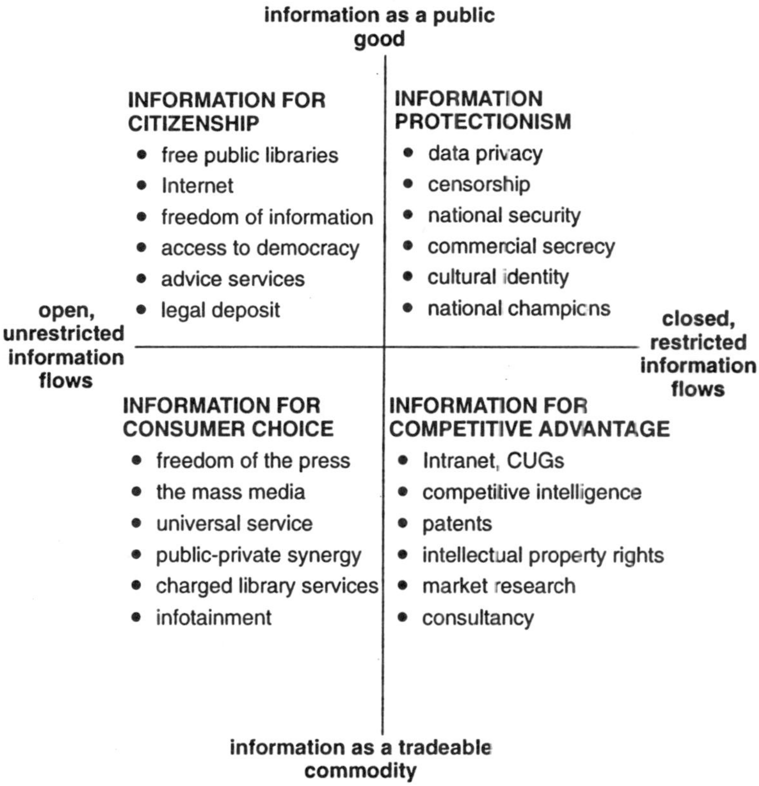

In Figure 1 these two sets of forces are displayed as a matrix. Within each quadrant I have included examples of information policy issues which seem to fall naturally into the boxes. In each case, the need to find a balance between these strong but opposing forces has direct implications for the day-to-day work of information professionals, and sets the boundary within which they develop systems and manage information. From this analysis it appears that four distinct areas, or traditions, may be differentiated within the information policy construct:

- Information for Citizenship;
- Information Protectionism;
- Information for Competitive Advantage;
- Information for Consumer Choice.

As I write, the model seems to be reasonably coherent, reasonably intuitive, and to embrace many information policy concerns. However, it is not my intention to try to locate the papers which follow rigidly into the quadrants of my model: it is far too blunt and unyielding a tool to allow that. I would, however, urge readers to use, and possibly reject, it as a tool to reconsider their own assumptions and prejudices about information policy.

INFORMATION POLICY CONCEPTS

Overview

Paul Turner

Introduction

This book contains the views, experiences and theorizing of some of the UK's leading information policy professionals and academics. The papers offer a range of perspectives on information policy, differentiated by scale—there are accounts of policy-making at international, national and organizational levels; differentiated by the roles of the policy actors involved—there are examples of scientific, professional and political policy-making; and differentiated by mode of inquiry—we find papers which provide analysis *for* policy-making and *of* policy-making. Some papers are descriptions of what happens in policy-making, while others articulate clear prescriptions.

This first major section of the book is concerned with conceptual issues. I hope to show that these are not just of academic interest; the way in which we approach the complex reality of information policy-making, whether as analysts or policy-makers, is an issue of far-reaching significance.

Information policy is a relatively young field of studies and many commentators have noted that the conceptual foundations underpinning studies in this area have not yet been clearly understood or articulated. Three particular concerns appear to run through the papers in this section, and indeed throughout the rest of the book, although much more explicitly in some than in others. These relate to the acute problems of definition of basic terms and concepts; the problem of appropriating the right models to help us make sense of the awesome complexities of information policy; and an even more fundamental question over whether we are even employing the most appropriate paradigms. In offering a context for the papers in this section, I will reflect on these concerns, and attempt to link some of the presuppositions that have underpinned information policy studies from within the library and information science (LIS) tradition with some of the 'isms' and 'ologies' that are dominant discourses in the wider social sciences literature. My purpose is to urge information policy researchers to be more sensitive to the historical and socio-political contexts of the concepts they employ. I also hope that the papers in this section demonstrate the need to be more explicit and critical about the basic presuppositions that inform their approaches to policy research.

Definitional dilemmas

The concepts underlying information policy studies exhibit a high degree of theoretical pluralism. Even a casual glance at the information policy literature reveals a surprisingly wide range of stances and interpretations (compare, for example, Machlup and Mansfield, 1983; Liebenau and Backhouse, 1990; Buckland, 1991). Some researchers seem more easily able to accommodate, even welcome, this theoretical pluralism (Braman, 1989, for example) than others for whom it creates confusion and a sense of unease at what really lies at the core of the subject.

The ambiguities associated with the term 'policy' hardly help matters. Hogwood and Gunn (1984), for example, identify ten distinct meanings for the term, nearly all of them in common usage and instantly recognizable to the non-specialist. To make matters worse, the definitional problem is compounded when the two terms are brought together: as Ian Rowlands puts it in the first paper (p.27), 'there are at least as many definitions of "information policy" as there are writers on the subject' (if only they would write them down!). The limited vocabulary available to the information policy specialist and the potential for its misuse is a problem which recurs throughout this book (see, for example, the later paper by Allen and Wilson (p.178)).

Problems of definition are not to be dismissed as being of purely academic interest; they run much deeper and are not just concerned with semantics. They are important in the 'real world' where, implicitly, information has tended to be discussed and approached in a very narrow way, as an object/commodity, something that can be measured in bits, bytes or dollars. In turn, policy is generally taken to imply purposeful action directed towards a set of identifiable goals; and policy research as the analysis of these actions by objective scientific criteria. In these highly pragmatic working definitions of the core vocabulary of our field of studies, objectivity is emphasized and subjectivity, value judgements and power relations played down.

Underlying the ways that these terms are used in practice are two interrelated and highly problematic assumptions: first, that social facts can in the end be reduced to a basic question of truth or falsity; second, that as a result, there will be one single 'correct' answer (the one perhaps with the fewest dis-benefits) to any particular policy problem. These basic assumptions must be traced to the positivist paradigm of the natural sciences which holds that a basic set of truths underlie all social phenomena, with truth existing in the same unambiguous way in the social world as it is presumed to apply in the natural world (Robertson, 1988). In revealing these assumptions it becomes clear how questions over the influence of individual values and judgement can be ignored and how questions of information meaning can be bypassed by the assumption that a direct correlation can be made between the demand for information and its utility and significance (Turner, 1994).

Each of the papers in this first section should offer much food for thought for those who retain unswerving loyalty to logical positivism. Strachan's review of the published research on how policy-makers use information (p.61) concludes with the thought that information systems designed 'rationally' to support the policy-making process often fail because the design does not take account of the highly 'irrational' ways in which research information is actually used. Research may be used as a weapon to neutralize the opposition, to present an image of careful decision-making, to legitimize rather than influence; sometimes further research is commissioned as a spoiling tactic, to postpone a final decision.

Clearly the different ways in which 'information policy' is defined and discussed, in what circumstances, and for what purposes, have received too little attention. What information policy is, is still hotly contested. However, despite a range of positions, it is apparent that most writers assume information policy is something that can be distinguished from other types of policy. It is dangerous to assume at the outset that the different definitions employed are simply the result of examining different aspects of the same phenomena or the same aspects from different perspectives. Initially perhaps, there is a need to problematize another basic assumption—that information policy is a coherent phenomenon.

For the time being at least, definitional dilemmas appear here to stay. But despite our discomfort they can play a positive role; by uncovering the different assumptions underpinning these definitions it becomes easier to accommodate different ways of understanding and representing information policy. These may complement, compete and sometimes cancel one another out, but in adopting such an apparently relativist stance we would, however, do well not to neglect the differentials in power that exist and contribute to the legitimacy of one definition over another.

It is hoped that by positioning ourselves and our definitions in this wider context an opportunity is provided to compare and contrast differences and similarities, to generate common ground and clarify our own perspectives.

A problem with models

> Descriptions are never independent of standards, and the choice of such standards rests on attitudes which because they can be neither logically deduced nor empirically proved are in need of critical evaluation. (Habermas, 1972)

A second theme emerging in this section relates to models and how we use them. In a paper reprinted from the *Journal of Information Science* (p.27), Rowlands identifies the main conceptual tools, frameworks and methodologies that have been applied to the creation of knowledge in information policy. He examines the strengths and weaknesses of the existing tools for understanding information policy and some of the reasons for the fragmentation of research effort. He concludes that the current approaches to its analysis within the LIS community are severely limited by the paucity of concepts, frameworks and research tools. In the following paper (p.46) Rowlands and Turner attempt to offer a way out of this *cul-de-sac* by addressing two highly confused and confusing areas: questions of complexity and scope delimitation. They offer an (untested) approach to information policy studies which involves three re-interpretations of a basic and well-established process model of policy-making. Finally, Bawden (p.74) opens up new vistas by peering into the realm of semiotics. He asks a very fundamental question: what kind of information do information policies deal with? He concludes that we have to appreciate the meaning and significance of knowledge in its context.

Just as there is a range of definitions, so too there is a range of models, methodologies and frameworks for conceptualizing information policy. While the purpose of these frameworks varies (ideal type, descriptive, prescriptive), the basic task they fulfil is the same—they enable us to simplify reality. Models achieve this by being highly selective about those aspects of reality they project and emphasize and those which they play down or ignore. Each policy model encapsulates a particular way of seeing the world and makes a set of assumptions that are rarely if ever made explicit. Models are representations of reality. But representations do more than simply aid us in comprehending reality, they actually construct that reality by attributing relationships between aspects of our models that may be only partially reflected in the real world.

While helping us to come to grips with reality there is a danger that they may actually displace it. At a more social level, there is a danger that researchers will find it easier to interact with, analyze and investigate their models than to deal with the messiness of the real world. Without care and attention our models begin to undertake ideological work by enabling us to ignore or marginalize extraneous data that do not fit. Analysts and policy-makers alike must beware the capacity for models to enable us to see what we want to see (Parsons, 1995). We must be critical about the models we use and the claims we make for them. The choice of models and the criteria used to evaluate them must themselves also become a visible part of the field of study of the information policy analyst.

The conceptual issues raised so far point up the need to approach policy-making and policy studies as a set of social practices in their own right. This emphasizes the need not only to be critical and self-reflective about the definitions, models and frameworks used by ourselves and others, but also to reflect on paradigms which support the assumptions upon which these different approaches are based. More critically, it implies being explicit about the influence and impact of the positivist paradigms that have underpinned most of our work so far.

Relocating positivism: paradigms in research

> Any statement can be held true, come what may, if we make drastic enough adjustments elsewhere in the system ... Conversely, by the same token, no statement is immune to revision. (Quine, 1964: 43)

Even if we leave aside problems of definition and the pitfalls often associated with our inadequate attempts to model reality, a further conceptual issue needs to be considered: the paradigms that underpin the definitions and models we use.

The positivist paradigm is dominant within the library and information science (LIS) tradition (Saracevic, 1992). Hoel (1992) has argued that the existing approaches within information science rely on a substantialist view of information and a subject/object divide. This tradition has clearly had an influence on the approaches adopted in information policy studies, especially as many senior writers in the field are scientists by training. Why this is an issue of concern for information policy studies links directly to criticisms of positivism. Ironically, these criticisms arose from investigations into the theory and practice of science and highlighted how far from scientific, science often is.

Popper (1959) argued that facts exist in the context of theories, values, beliefs, not independently of them; the implication being that scientists do not engage merely in passively describing pre-existing facts about the world, but in actively formulating or constructing the very nature of that world (Woolgar, 1996). Kuhn (1962), whilst agreeing that science was a constructed discourse, rejected Popper's claim that science proceeded by falsifying its theories and argued instead that it proceeded by a cycle of 'normal science' followed by revolution. In this sense, then, it was not only the theories but also the methodologies employed which participated in the construction and re-enforcement of the normal science view of the world. These critiques shook the foundations of science, and it became problematic to assume that reality could be explained in terms of cause and effect, that inquiry could be neutral, objective and value-free. The result of these criticisms was to reposition positivism as a powerful way among many to look at reality.

Having acknowledged that the criticisms of positivism reposition it as one of a number of paradigms, it is useful to consider what other ways there are of viewing the nature of reality, knowledge and ourselves. In approaching these newer paradigms it is helpful to be able to navigate between them. A useful, if rather personal, overview of the range of paradigms that have emerged since the critiques of positivism, has been provided by Egon Guba (1990). Guba proposes that the current state of social science can be understood in terms of four paradigms which are differentiated by contrasting their approaches to ontology (the nature of reality), epistemology (the relationship between knowledge and the knower) and methodology (how knowledge should be established). Guba's paradigms are summarized in Table 1.

Table 1: Guba's paradigms (Table adapted from Parsons, 1995).

Paradigm	Ontology	Epistemology	Methodology
Positivism	Reality exists. It works according to the laws of cause and effect: these laws can be revealed.	Objectivity can be achieved. Inquiry can be value-free.	Hypotheses can be empirically tested.
Post-Positivism	Reality exists. It can be neither fully understood nor explained. There are multiple causes and effects.	Objectivity is an ideal, but it requires a critical community. Subjectivity is acknowledged.	Critical of experimentalism, it emphasizes qualitative approaches, theory and discovery.
Critical Theory	Reality exists. It can be neither fully understood nor explained. There are multiple causes and effects.	Values mediate the inquiry. Requires selection of value system.	Proposes the elimination of false consciousness and facilitates and participates in transformation.
Constructivism	There are multiple realities. They exist as mental constructs and are relative to those who hold them.	Knowledge and the knower are part of the same subjective entity. Findings are the result of the interaction.	Identifies, compares and describes the various constructions that exist: hermeneutical and dialectical.

The critics of positivism showed that there is not one correct way to comprehend reality but rather a number of versions of that reality. Of course in problematizing our notions of reality there is the danger of going so far as to lose a sense of our ability to analyze or explain anything. But this would be to forget that, while different paradigms can be characterized as providing multiple versions of reality, they have differential access to power to enforce or support the view articulated. Positivist theories and methodologies are currently dominant in information policy studies, the result of historical, socio-economic and political forces.

If we accept that knowledge is contextual, mediated and rarely value-free, we must also recognize that so is our analysis of it. There are many different ways of looking at the information policy issue: from seeing it as a purely technical problem at one end, to a reality constructed in the minds of the participants at the other. There is a need for a sophistication in information policy studies to acknowledge that there are radically different theories over the nature and construction of knowledge and over what knowledge means. Thus we must accept a broad church of opinion, from quantifying cost-benefit analysis at one end, to discourse analysis and critical theory at the other.

As an overview of a section on concepts it is has been appropriate not only to acknowledge the good work that has already been done, but to try and build on this to take the debates and the discipline as a whole forward. A crucial perspective throughout is that in conducting information policy studies we must be capable of adopting techniques and tools that are contingent on the circumstances as we find them, not as we have theorized.

Understanding Information Policy: Concepts, Frameworks and Research Tools[1]

Ian Rowlands

Abstract

This paper considers the need for a more systematic and critical approach to the academic study of information policy at national and international level. It reviews the complex, multifaceted nature of large-scale information policy problems and considers some of the main sources of confusion in the journal literature. It is argued that while information policy has been largely technology-driven, the consideration of information policy issues has, for historical reasons, typically been discipline-bounded. This has contributed to a fragmentation of research effort and a lack of consensus on the most appropriate home discipline for the study of information policy. In a search for a more critical scientific understanding of information policy issues, a brief review is made of the strengths, limitations and applicability of the broad theoretical and methodological approaches which have been adopted, often implicitly, by writers reporting in the library and information science literature. The paper concludes with a consideration of some desirable characteristics for the design of information policy studies.

Introduction

Information policy is currently receiving a quite unprecedented degree of exposure in (and beyond) the library and information science literature. The information community's renewed interest in policy issues is

1. This is an edited version of an article published in the *Journal of Information Science*, 22(1), 1996, and is reproduced with the permission of the publishers.

not entirely surprising given the high-profile political discussion currently taking place in relation to information superhighway and related developments. Two factors in particular are motivating new approaches and experiments in information policy: the convergence of media, technologies and services (Garnham, 1994) which is increasingly challenging the established policy and regulatory order; and a widely accepted article of faith which suggests that information policy has the potential to make a positive contribution to economic and social well-being (CEC, 1994). At a time when the significance of 'information' is being emphasized in contemporary debates, it is ironic that so little has been written about the study of information policy itself; to date, relatively scant attention has been paid to the theoretical foundations of the subject; indeed, the lack of commonly accepted frameworks, tools and methodologies for information policy analysis is a source of difficulty and frustration for the serious academic researcher.

This paper identifies and comments on some of the main concepts, frameworks and research tools which are evident in, or can at least be inferred from, writings on information policy in the library and information science literature.

Many analysts have argued for more 'rational' approaches to the study of public policy, pointing to the need for more sophisticated indicators of economic and social impact, better forecasts, clearly expressed hierarchies of objectives and improved definition. As will be seen in this paper, these are some of the areas where the currently available tools for information policy analysis appear to be less than wholly adequate.

Complexity is a *leitmotiv* running throughout the information policy literature. Information supply, transfer and use take place within an environment which is in a constant state of flux, shaped by the often unpredictable interaction of commercial, economic, technological, social and demographic forces (Hawkins *et al.*, 1992). One of the most difficult and fascinating problems in information policy research is that public policy has an influence, directly or indirectly, on each of these sets of forces; hence, even such broadly horizontal policies as those relating to education, open government or the funding of civil science may have quite dramatic implications for information availability and use. The complex and rather abstract nature of information policy means, however, that public understanding and consensus on such key issues as trading in government information or data privacy are less than they might be. The popularization and wider dissemination of information policy research may have a useful role to play here in raising awareness of the issues and contributing to a more open public debate.

This paper is concerned primarily with the study of information policy from an academic perspective, motivated chiefly by curiosity and the desire for greater understanding. It does not claim to provide specific insights into the 'black box' of policy formulation within the executive or legislative branches of government. It certainly does not conclude with recommendations for what national or European information policy *should be*. Its intention is directed instead towards a better understanding of what information policy *is* and what tools, frameworks and methodologies are currently available for its systematic and critical analysis. The material for this paper is drawn primarily from a review of the journal literature, much of it North American in origin. For reasons which I hope will become clear, it has also been necessary to look beyond the boundaries of the library and information science literature in a search for potentially applicable models and frameworks.

Some dimensions of the information policy problem

Before looking in more detail at some of the concepts, frameworks and research tools which have been applied to the study of national and international information policy, some preliminary remarks are called for in relation to the object of study and its highly problematic nature. First of all, what is information policy? There are at least as many definitions of 'information policy' as there are writers on the subject; in this section a few broadly representative examples will be used to illustrate some important points about the characteristics of information policy. Weingarten (1989), for example, defines information policy as comprising 'the set of all public laws, regulations, and policies that encourage, discourage, or regulate the creation, use, storage, and communication of information'. This is a broad and inclusive definition and one which suggests that the fundamental role of policy is to provide the legal and institutional frameworks within which formal information exchange can take place. It implies that information policy addresses both political and bureaucratic goals (an interesting point, as these may not necessarily be congruent) and since public information policy emerges out of the machinery of government, its formulation, implementation and evaluation may be expected to be accompanied by the production of various documents—discussion papers, legislative drafts and memoranda. To a greater or (usually) lesser extent these may be available for purposes of study; an idea which will be returned to later in the section on tools and methodologies.

Another valuable insight into information policy is offered by Hernon and Relyea (1968), who underline its complex nature by noting that 'although the literature often refers to information policy in the singular, there is no all-encompassing policy—rather information *policies* tend to address specific issues and, at times, to be fragmented, overlapping and contradictory'. Certainly, the emergence of information processing as a significant force in society has been accompanied by an extraordinarily wide and diverse range of public policies; from the regulation of value-added and data services to the licensing of government datasets for commercial exploitation and legislation to protect personal data privacy. The extraordinarily complex and diverse nature of information policy is a common theme in the literature (Malley, 1988; Gray, 1988; Suprenant, 1987; Moore, 1992) and one which poses serious difficulties for research design. Faced with what sometimes appears to be at best a 'fuzzy set' or at worst a set of unconnected or contradictory laws, regulations and policy statements, issues of scope and definition in the field of information policy enquiry become highly problematic. The situation may be messy, but it is inevitable given that the practical realities of information policy are much to do with the art of compromise: there are neither 'good' nor 'bad' policies but maybe there can be effective compromises between competing interests. Galvin (1994) states this idea with admirable clarity, noting that information policy-making comprises 'a fundamental enduring conflict among or between objectives, goals, customs, plans, activities or stakeholders which is not likely to be resolved completely in favour of any polar position in that conflict'. This suggests that another feature of information policy is that it is, or at least that it should be, flexible, dynamic and responsive to changing circumstances. It also implies that the impact and outcomes of information policy decisions are difficult to predict with any certainty, and that a key objective for information policy research might therefore lie in trying to set some kind of bounds and limits to that *uncertainty.*

Given the complexities and uncertainties associated with information policy, how widely should the scope of academic studies be drawn? A wide range of forces other than public policy are relevant to a consideration of the issues affecting the supply and use of information goods and services in society. These include, *inter alia,* the commercial strategies adopted by publishers and database providers, the behaviour of consumers, the influence of pressure groups, and the structure and patterns of ownership within the information industry. One of the characteristics of public information policy is that it both *shapes* and *responds* to events and so can be regarded as either an independent or a dependent variable in scientific policy studies. As an *independent* variable, information policy can be analyzed in terms of its impact and outcomes, both on the wider environment and on the political process itself. When it is viewed as a *dependent* variable, our attention is drawn to the environmental, cultural, economic and other factors which shape and guide policy and its implementation. This insight leads Burger (1993) to define information policy even more broadly and inclusively as those 'societal mechanisms used to control information, and the societal effects of applying those mechanisms'. Clear differentiation between the treatment of information policy as an independent or a dependent variable in analysis should be an important consideration in research design, but my observation is that little is made of the distinction in the journal literature.

There is an understandable tendency for writers on information policy to define the scope of their work narrowly and in a self-referential way; to discuss issues surrounding intellectual property rights or public library policy solely in terms of their implications for information professionals. In reality, however, it is impossible to detach information policy from its wider social and political context, a point which the Secretary of State's speech to the Library Association Umbrella Conference on 9 July 1993 underlines (DNH, 1993):

> ...there are many major challenges facing the library world at the moment. To take a few of the more prominent ones: local government reorganization; new further education funding arrangements; competitive tendering for public services ... all these issues stem from government policies originating outside the Department of National Heritage's field.

These remarks suggest that there is, in effect, an *information policy hierarchy* comprising three levels:

- *infrastructural policies* such as tax or employment law, freedom of establishment, and education policy, which apply across society and which affect the information sector directly and indirectly, providing a social and economic context for its activities;

- *horizontal information policies* with specific application and impact across the whole of the information sector, such as the statutory provision of public library services, zero-rated VAT on books, or data protection law;
- *vertical information policies* which have specific application to a particular information sector, such as the geographic information community.

This hierarchical model is useful in that it locates information policies in the broader context of public affairs. This may be productive in itself, but it further extends the scope problem: it becomes very difficult to conceptualize information policy in its most inclusive and comprehensive sense, since this would need to include, as well as an analysis of narrow sector-specific policies such as intellectual property rights and information access policies, the wider contexts of educational, social and industrial policy. However, all three levels must be of interest to the information policy analyst because of the inevitable degree of interaction between them. Indeed, the overlap between the three levels can sometimes seriously obscure our understanding of what 'information policy' means and what it actually consists of. Martyn (1992) makes the point that the absence of horizontal policies (in the above sense) does not necessarily mean that there is 'no policy'. Rather, information policy may be subsumed by infrastructural policy: '... in effect, there is no real policy for the information industry, electronic or otherwise, *other than that which conforms to the general Government policy towards industry,* which is to allow free market forces to operate within a lightly regulated environment, the regulation being put in place when the need becomes evident and pressing'.

An implication of the hierarchical model of public policy is that power, influence and decision-making in relation to information policy are inevitably scattered across different parts of government. A major conceptual problem therefore lies in defining an overall set of policy values and a framework for specific information policy actions. In other words, there is a need for the establishment of an *information policy regime* which is comprehensive, sensitive to new technology and responsive to the implications of the 'information age'. The lack of such a coherent framework is a relatively new theme in the information policy literature (J. Gray, 1989; R. Gray, 1993).

Theoretical approaches to the study of public policy

Political and social scientists have developed a number of models, frameworks and theories for analyzing public policy, although few of these have been explicitly applied and tested in the context of information policy analysis. As well as lacking theory, we lack a sound basis of empirical data relating to information policies and their outcomes: indicator data relating to their impacts are either very difficult to obtain or simply not available. Yet without the appropriation and development of a body of explicit theory it is difficult to see how a more rigorous (possibly more quantitative?) approach to information policy analysis can be forthcoming: it has often been observed that there is nothing more practical than a good theory! Burger (1993) notes that information policy is 'complex because we have not yet developed ways of understanding it that are widely accepted and broad enough to encompass its range: we now rely on existing disciplines to inform us about the soundness of information policies'. This may be an honest appraisal of our current difficulties in defining the scope and boundaries of the subject, but it offers little practical comfort.

Broadly speaking, there are three sets of motivation for studying information policy problems: for scientific, professional, or political reasons. The scientific rationale is motivated primarily to gain a greater understanding of how they originate, how they are developed and implemented, and what their consequences are for particular interest groups or for society as a whole. The scientific motivation seeks to understand policy, not to suggest what that policy ought to be. Clearly, however, information policy studies undertaken for professional or political ends have a different emphasis: here analysis has an applied orientation and is concerned with determining the most efficient or 'best' alternative—the one that will yield the largest net benefit for dealing with a particular problem. This approach is concerned with achieving the 'right' goal, with what policy *ought* to be, and cannot therefore be arrived at without reference to an ideological ('the market should decide') or a normative ('the preservation of our cultural heritage is paramount') position. As such, it is a value-oriented approach and should be located outside the scientific policy studies tradition, which asserts itself to be rigorous, objective and value-neutral.

A useful working definition of the scientific approach to policy studies is offered by Dye (1972), who suggests that it comprises: 'a description of the content of public policy; an assessment of the impact of environmental forces on the content of public policy; an analysis of the effect of various institutional arrangements and political processes on public policy; an enquiry into the consequences of various public policies for the political system; and an evaluation of the impact of public policies on society, both in terms of expected and unexpected consequences'. Within this tradition, Anderson (1990) identifies four dominant theoretical approaches: political systems theory (Easton, 1965); group theory (Latham, 1965); elite theory (Dye and Ziegler, 1990); and rational-choice theory (Downs, 1957). The applicability and potential value of these theories in the specific context of information policy is unclear (and beyond the scope of this paper) but they possibly represent a fruitful line for future enquiry.

One of the features of information policy research is the number and diversity of academic disciplines which have, with some justification, laid claim to being the home discipline for studies in the area: such is the fragmentation of the field that Braman (1989), a researcher from a communications studies tradition, identifies more than 40 academic fields that deal with 'information policy'. Braman does not offer a list, but Burger (1993) suggests that the core information policy disciplines comprise economics, law, political science, public administration, sociology, public policy, management science and information science.

In trying to understand the highly distributed nature of information policy research, it is worth considering three factors: the multiple interpretations of the term 'information' by policy-makers in different economic, social and cultural contexts; the way in which information policies have developed over time as pragmatic solutions to specific problems; and the highly institutionalized nature of policy studies.

Traditionally, information policies have evolved in direct response to the emergence of specific technologies, such as print, telephony, radio or value-added and data services. Not surprisingly, the analysis of these policies has tended to fall within the domain of whichever professional information community was most directly concerned with the particular technology involved (as librarians, computer scientists, broadcasters or information scientists). In other words, while information policy has been *technology-driven,* policy research has typically been *discipline-bounded* (Trauth, 1986). The fragmentation of information policy research is mirrored by a fragmentation of policy-making institutions. In Britain, for example, the Department of Trade and Industry is the lead agency for developing policy in relation to tradeable information, standards and intellectual property; while data protection is under the jurisdiction of the Home Office; legal deposit under the Department of National Heritage; and public records under the Lord Chancellor's Department.

If information policy studies are discipline-bounded, they are also to some extent institutionally-bounded; just like the policies themselves, research emerges from bureaucratic institutional settings which have their own distinctive goals, perspectives and agendas. Sometimes, academic studies are carried out directly to support the efforts of those engaged in policy formulation, DG-XIII of the European Commission, for instance. Such research is likely to be highly prescriptive and goal-oriented, designed to meet the immediate needs of policy-makers. Other studies are undertaken to meet the needs of the information industry, perhaps in the form of market studies and assessments, or (occasionally!) funded by a research council where longer-term, more fundamental objectives are sought. The linkages between research and research funding are important because they reinforce the process of fragmentation; information policy develops along different research fronts, informed by very different theoretical approaches—factors which have not been conducive to establishing consensus and agreement on central information policy issues and values.

While most observers would agree that there is currently little consensus over where the boundary lines of the information policy discipline should be drawn, there are others who actively resist such an approach. Braman (1989), for example, argues that 'theoretical pluralism' is the most appropriate way to deal with phenomena and processes which unfold in different ways at different levels of the social and economic structure. Her argument offers two challenges to those engaged in information policy research: firstly, the need for a high degree of self-awareness of the assumptions and paradigms being brought to bear from within one's own disciplinary tradition, whether library and information science, telecommunications policy or media studies; and secondly, a reminder to beware of the sweeping generalizations which inform much writing (and, dare one say, public policy) in this area. We should not simply accept that broad statements of policy intent, such as 'the protection of national security' are in themselves a sufficient justification for information control, particularly since these are too often only a guise for economic protectionism or the censorship of press freedom.

Tools and methodologies for information policy research

Methodological problems exist in all disciplines, but information policy has more than its fair share. Despite all the difficulties and complexities surrounding information policy as an object of study, a considerable amount of material continues to be published on the subject. Whether this is an entirely healthy situation is open to question since, more often than not, its authors fail to make explicit either their methodology or their underlying assumptions. This is a particularly unfortunate state of affairs on those occasions when research is commissioned by the policy-making community as an input into decision-making.

Consideration of the methodological basis of information policy research is conspicuous by its absence in the journal literature. One of the few authors to tackle the issue is Trauth (1986) in a paper published nearly ten years ago which offers a highly generalized description of the information policy literature, locating studies in a two-dimensional matrix.

This matrix indicates the *scope* (vertical axis) and the *intent* (horizontal axis) of individual policy studies, regardless of their methodology. In this scheme, 'descriptive studies' are those which describe the current status of a policy or which highlight issues that should be addressed in its implementation. 'Prescriptive studies', on the other hand, are those which explicitly set out to make recommendations and to have an influence on the formulation of policy. As well as differing in their intent, information policy studies have different scope characteristics. In Trauth's framework, the scope axis (particular-integrative) expresses both the breadth of coverage and the degree of interdisciplinarity reflected in a study; 'integrative studies' being those which go beyond the usual boundaries of a single discipline. Trauth concluded that the biggest gap in the information policy literature (at the time of writing) was for studies falling into the top left-hand quadrant of the matrix: research which is both highly integrative and focused on the immediate needs of policy formulators. Published studies sharing both of these properties are still rare; a function, perhaps, of the fact that they need, ideally, to be conducted on a large scale by multidisciplinary teams yet within the restricted time horizons of decision-makers.

This section reviews some of the predominant modes of investigation which can be inferred from an examination of the literature; it is by no means comprehensive but I hope it will help us to draw some tentative conclusions for future, and possibly more productive, lines of enquiry. It is argued that five broad methodological strands can be inferred from a review of policy-related articles in the library and information science literature: approaches based on (1) classification; (2) the identification of policy issues and options; (3) reductionism; (4) forecasting and scenario-building; and (5) process-oriented research and case studies. Each approach serves different purposes and makes different sets of assumptions; and they are by no means mutually exclusive.

Classification-based approaches

It is hardly surprising that, faced with the enormous problems of scope and definition noted earlier, and given the natural predisposition of authors from the library and information science community, one methodological approach has been to identify and categorize the information policy literature. Bibliographies are not uncommon (Bennett, 1987; Julien *et al.*, 1992; Dahlin, 1990) and they provide a very useful key to the growing body of official reports, policy guidance, statutes, books and journal articles. This bibliographic approach confers several advantages. It means that policy documents and studies are reasonably well documented and described, and it facilitates access to a considerable amount of primary material for research purposes. As a tool for demonstrating the wide range of issues which fall under the general rubric of 'information policy', classification schemes fulfil a useful secondary role in drawing attention to the breadth of the subject.

The most traditional approach to categorizing information policies and issues is to develop a classification which reflects *policy goals and objectives.* Chartrand (1986) and Milevski (1986) use the same scheme, which neatly reduces the scope of information policy to nine broad categories:

- Government information resource management policy
- Information technology policy
- Telecommunications and broadcasting policy
- International communications policy
- Information disclosure, confidentiality and privacy
- Computer regulation and computer crime
- Intellectual property
- Library and archives policy
- Government information dissemination policy

Other authors, notably Hill (1994), derive hybrid literature-based classifications which may include a categorization by institutional source (e.g. the European Commission), by document type (e.g. UK Acts of Parliament) and by policy goal (e.g. jobs and education). An alternative approach, adopted by Rowlands and Vogel (1991) blends a chronological description of policy events with goal-based subject access in the form of 'chronological trails'. These different approaches raise an interesting methodological question: to what extent is it possible to derive an understanding of information policy from a reading of the 'cold' policy literature as set out in White Papers and statutes or recorded in the form of administrative or court decisions? Information policy exists at two layers: that which is *explicit* and recorded in documentary form, and that which is expressed *implicitly* in the form of habits, received wisdoms, unwritten codes of behaviour, expectations and societal norms. As the influential US Rockefeller Report (SATCOM, 1969) observes:

> ... to debate whether there should be a national information policy is pointless ... There will be such a policy ... arrived at consciously or unconsciously, by commission or omission, carefully or haphazardly, in a comprehensive or piecemeal fashion.

While there may be some practical benefits in a classification-based approach to information policy, there is little to recommend this approach from a theoretical standpoint: classification can only deal with policy in a very superficial way, obscuring the political, social and institutional contexts within which policy is shaped and implemented. A more fundamental objection is that by classifying policies into mutually exclusive categories we risk losing a sense of the inter-relationships between groups of issues. Burger (1988) overcomes some of these objections by applying content analysis to the recommendations in the SATCOM Report, the result of a three-year long deliberation of the status and future requirements for scientific and technical information in the United States. In effect, Burger used content analysis systematically to categorize and classify not just the policy goals for each of the Report's recommendations, but also their rationale and the actors involved in their implementation.

In an interesting recent paper, Sillince (1994) has developed a *paradigm-based* (rather than a goal-based) categorization as a means of demonstrating some of the ideological and institutional factors which he argues are responsible for the fragmentation of information policy at

European Union level. Whether this represents a new lease of life for the classification-based approach is still questionable: perhaps classification is best regarded as a tool for the initial exploration and perception of pattern in complex policy data.

Issue identification and options

Without any doubt, the most prevalent methodological position to be encountered in the information policy literature (Moore and Steele, 1991; McIntosh, 1990; Rowlands, 1995) is the 'issues and options' approach, although few authors are honest enough to make this explicit. This is an approach which seeks to identify the issues and concerns raised by the adoption (or potential adoption) of a specific policy, and then to suggest a range of possible actions to resolve potential conflicts and mitigate any foreseeable negative impacts. This style of research is often commissioned by policy-makers in government or industry as an input to the early stages of policy formation and it is typically activated by a notable legal or public policy event (e.g. the publication of the Bangemann Action Plan (CEC, 1994)) or a technological advance or new application (e.g. video-on-demand).

The function of 'issues and options' is primarily an information-gathering one. Its strengths lie in its currency and in its ability to map the policy terrain and scope the dimensions of the problem under consideration. Whereas classification-based approaches tend to focus on documents as the primary object of study, 'issues and options' typically draws on a much wider range of inputs, notably interviews and questionnaires directed at policy-makers and other stakeholders. This approach is therefore more integrative (in Trauth's sense) than the classification-based style of research, although it almost inevitably lacks the former's very explicit articulation of assumptions. Examples of the 'issues and options' approach are pervasive in the journal and grey literatures. The methodological limitations are serious: most notably because the approach fails to provide a coherent framework within which policy-makers can properly evaluate the options open to them. There is a further danger that this style of research, while implicitly (or openly) appropriating values of independence and objectivity, is in fact methodologically vacuous and its results *sui generis*—neither robust nor amenable to verification. Furthermore, the results generated are often heavily value-laden. Unfortunately, and despite all its evident weaknesses, the issues-based approach emerges as the dominant methodological construct in the information policy literature.

Reductionist approaches

Earlier in this paper, reference was made to the normative basis of public policy. An argument was put forward which stressed the desirability of a more theoretically pluralist approach to information policy problems, drawing on multiple perspectives and traditions. As a call to arms to the policy studies community, this seems a reasonable proposition but it is a call to which few individual researchers can respond with any conviction or intellectual credibility. The reductionist approach is one which, while (sometimes) acknowledging that a policy problem is inevitably multi-faceted, seeks to reduce ambiguity by constraining data collection, analysis and interpretation within the framework of a specific discipline. Bushkin and Yurow (1981), for example, argue that 'aspects of United States domestic information policy can be divided into two broad categories: (1) the legal foundations of information dissemination and access; and (2) the economics and management of information'. This framework is one which seems to have received the endorsement of a number of researchers who have adopted deliberately narrow legal (Braman, 1988; Burkert, 1992) or economic (Porat, 1977; Greenstein, 1992) perspectives.

The reductionist approach is inevitable, given our need to make sense of extremely complex phenomena and, in many ways, it is highly desirable if it leads to a more rigorous consideration of information policy. Reductionism overcomes the vagueness of the 'issues and options' approach and enables underlying assumptions to be made much more explicit. Whether reductionist analysis leads to good policy, however, is a much more difficult proposition: given the complexity of the forces which drive and shape policy, to what extent can exclusively legal, economic or other single disciplinary models predetermine an overall 'optimal' policy regime? This is a fundamental problem of the reductionist approach: how can the parts be related to the whole? An analyst may get the organizational and economic aspects right, but ignore other factors that can be a decisive factor in the success or failure of a policy. Burger (1993) observes that:

> ... there may be several reasons why information policy does not work. Specific policies may have overlooked

> certain contextual factors in the implementation of a policy; the initial premises in the formulation of the policy may be incorrect; the policy may not be implemented as designed; or there may be unforeseen problems or situations about which no one has thought. Almost all of these reasons for a failed policy, however, have a common denominator of knowledge. Do policies fail because of ignorance or because society is too complex and things do not turn out as they were intended?

Scenario-based approaches

Forecasting studies and scenario-building represent another, quite different, methodological construct and one which is widely reported in the library and information science literature (Bates, 1990; Bezold and Olsen, 1986). A notable recent example of the species is the British Library's Delphi-style *Information UK 2000* study (Martyn *et al.*, 1990). Scenario-building allows the construction of several alternative 'visions' of the future which policy-makers can use to develop appropriate strategies for reacting to events. Scenario-building is a particularly attractive tool in the context of information policy problems because of the very high levels of uncertainty which are inherent, especially those associated with the adoption and use of information technologies. Large uncertainties can lead reasonable people to quite different judgements about information policy issues and the best ways of dealing with them. The central objective of scenario-building should therefore be to reduce those uncertainties to manageable proportions. It is also one very effective way of accommodating the notion of stakeholders and the possibility of differential effects occurring in relation to various social and economic interest groups (Kiesler and Hinds, 1993).

Almost by definition, these futures-based approaches need to be highly inclusive (as advocated by Trauth) in their scope: Burke (1994) notes that scenario-building is commonly based on the STEEP framework, which embraces Social, Technological, Economic, Ecological and Political perspectives. On the other hand, the limited effectiveness of forecasting and scenario development is often mercilessly exposed under the glare of hindsight. Two of the more obvious reasons for their comparative repeated failure are the extreme difficulty of capturing sufficient data from a broad enough base to make reliable extrapolations, and the use of conceptual models which are too deterministic, in terms of the power of either technology or public policy to shape events.

Does the inevitable uncertainty which results from even the most meticulous forecasts imply a need for greater frankness by governments about the uncertainty of the environments in which they operate and their ability to deliver policies to precise targets? The study of forecasting raises questions of how decisions are made, not just an understanding of the techniques available.

Process-oriented approaches and case studies

Despite the frequent assertion that information policy is enormously complex and multifaceted, it can be argued that at least some of that 'complexity' derives from confusion and lack of definition. Hogwood and Gunn (1984) note that there are many different uses of the word 'policy' in circulation. These include policy as a label for a broad field of activity (a government's overall 'economic' or 'industrial' policy); as a specific proposal or decision of government; as a programme or legislative outcome; as a theory or model; or as a *process*. Conceptualizing public policy as a process, rather than as an outcome or an event, is the dominant theoretical approach in the general policy studies literature. The reasons for this emphasis are not too difficult to understand: it enables us to understand how the complexities of the policy-making process unfold over time and thus raise some fundamental questions, such as who are the 'policy-makers' and how do institutional factors bias policy-making?

Anderson (1990) has developed a highly generalized model of the policy process and argues that it provides a fairly realistic map of the events which underpin public policy-making as well as offering a useful analytical framework:

Stage I : Problem identification and agenda formation
Stage II : Policy formulation
Stage III : Policy adoption
Stage IV : Policy implementation
Stage V : Post-implementation evaluation

From the point of view of our search for methodological tools and approaches to information policy problems, this framework appears to offer a number of potential benefits: it represents an antidote to the narrowly reductionist approach by allowing us the possibility to build 'rich pictures' of information policy and its evolution. There are few examples of a process-driven analytical approach to information policy in the literature, however. One notable exception is Karni who, in a paper on the formulation of information policy within organizations (1983), suggests that a framework for understanding policy formation should comprise four elements: information policy objectives; measures to determine how well these are achieved; policy actions and alternatives; and a consideration of the information services system itself.

Closely related to the process-oriented approaches and partially overlapping is research based on case studies. Several detailed case studies (Burger, 1988; Dawes, 1991; Jacobson, 1989; Stewart, 1990) of the history and evolution of (US) public policies are available, and they demonstrate the importance of institutional, historical, cultural, political and human factors in determining information policy, throwing further doubt as to the usefulness of the narrow reductionist approach.

The particular value of case studies is that they can reveal much about the policy-making process that might otherwise be hidden from historians or other researchers who rely primarily on printed documents. Guiding philosophies about government and information are not the only determinants in the policy debate; policy formation and implementation may also be shaped by staff-level government workers in the legislative and executive branches of government. A major limitation of case studies is that they do not permit generalization. They can be used, however, to test existing theories; to develop new theories; to provide detailed contextual analysis of particular events; and to help provide an 'intuitive feel' for the subtleties and nuances of the policy process.

Journal articles by Bearman (1988) and by Hammond *et al.* (1983) indicate that information science methods can be applied to advantage to the study of how policy-makers use and filter information inputs during the early stages of the policy process (problem identification, agenda setting and policy formulation). Their findings suggest that there are fundamental obstacles to the effective use of scientific information in public policy-making and that 'rationality' in this context may be subservient to other factors such as bureaucratic goals and political expediency. One of the least explored aspects of policy-making is how certain issues manage to get onto political 'agendas' for discussion and action while others do not. There may be a need for more scientific and objective inputs into the early stages of policy formation, possibly including the development of a broader range of indicator data than policy-makers currently have access to.

Conclusions

The picture which emerges from this brief review of the methodological tools employed by writers on information policy is not a flattering one. Compaigne (1988) notes that the information policy debate is a highly political one and that whether we are discussing issues such as ownership, copyright, equity, or literacy, the 'right' answer is (and should always be) subject to legitimate debate. There is considerable value, therefore, in reminding ourselves that a truly open and democratic debate should make explicit the variables which go into determining the 'right' answer. What assumptions are being used? Is there another set of reasonable assumptions that would yield different answers? What is the agenda of the policy-makers? Do they state their agenda explicitly, or is it hidden? What is needed and what does not yet appear to exist is a body of knowledge and research tools that can provide a *value-critical* and *paradigm-critical* approach to the study of information policy. The methodologies for policy analysis are themselves rarely 'value-free'. Many techniques have unstated but built-in assumptions about values. This means that, in some cases, a particular technique may be chosen for 'political' purposes, to advance a cause rather than in a genuine spirit of scientific enquiry.

I have deliberately not set out in this paper to offer a blueprint for undertaking information policy research; we are a very long way yet from developing a robust box of tools and methodologies. Nonetheless, the limitations of much of the current reporting in the library and information science literature suggest to me some fairly urgent desiderata for the design of information policy research:

- greater recognition of the need for a more *value-critical approach* to information policy problems;

- the need to distinguish more clearly between *descriptive* and *prescriptive modes of policy analysis*: between what policy is and what it ought to be;

- greater awareness of the dangers of confusing the treatment of information policy as a *dependent* or an *independent variable* in analysis;

- the need for a broader range of *more sophisticated indicator data* on the social, cultural and economic impacts of information policy;
- greater clarity in terms of describing the *scope* of information studies and the *definition* of terms used;
- the need to make assumptions, methodologies and working hypotheses *more explicit*;
- greater awareness of the *hierarchical* nature of public policies ('no policy' does not necessarily mean no policy);
- a more imaginative and *catholic* approach to the appropriation and testing of research tools from other policy disciplines;
- a more creative approach to information policy analysis and a greater willingness to develop *explanatory models*;
- the need to retain a *multidisciplinary integrative perspective*, even in small-scale studies;
- greater recognition of the *discipline-bounded* and *technology-driven* nature of much information policy research;
- greater awareness of *context* and the factors which influence the formulation, adoption and impact of information policies.

Models and Frameworks for Information Policy Research

Ian Rowlands and Paul Turner

> Practical men, who believe themselves to be quite exempt from any intellectual influences, are usually the slaves of some defunct economist. (Keynes, 1936)

Abstract

The notion of 'information policy' is currently generating considerable interest across the public, corporate and academic sectors. While there is little in the way of formal definition of what the notion actually means, there does at least seem to be a broad consensus (a) that information policy is highly complex, and (b) that it presents considerable difficulties in terms of scoping meaningful studies. Borrowing a phrase from Charles Handy (1994), information policy might well be described as a slippery 'low-definition concept' which defies easy analysis.

The main theme of this Chapter is an argument that the related problems of complexity and scope limitation in information policy studies are best dealt with by conceptualizing information policy as a process (a verb), rather than an object (or noun). Drawing on ideas from the policy sciences, a process model of information policy is presented. The process view of information policy is shown to be helpful in drawing attention to the temporal and dynamic aspects of information policy-making. This basic process model, which determined the overall structure of the British Library Workshop, is open to a number of re-interpretations ('rational actor', 'bureaucratic imperative' and 'garbage can'). It is argued that these interpretations are highly applicable in the context of information policy studies and offer a useful triangulation tool with which to begin to isolate some of the main sources of complexity surrounding information policy.

Complexity in information policy research

In his analysis of the library and information science (LIS) literature presented in the last Chapter, Rowlands concluded that the concepts, frameworks and research tools currently available to support information policy studies are limited. This conclusion arose out of a belief that the LIS literature tends to pay lip service to the complexity of its subject matter.

Information policy issues certainly are complex and multifaceted. This complexity, however intractable it may at first appear, needs to be taken seriously by the academic LIS community and incorporated into research design. In this Chapter, we argue that a new research approach is needed to deal with the contradictory, interrelated and unpredictable (the incidental and the accidental) factors that characterize information policy-making in the real world.

The fact is that information policy is a hard nut to crack, both epistemologically and from a research design perspective. But does that justify the temptation conveniently to push 'complexity' to one side or to retreat into sterile arguments over definitions? Researchers often acknowledge the complexity of information policy, but then proceed to use that as a justification for ignoring its analysis. This means accepting wider social, political and cultural forces as somehow a series of 'givens'. This is unfortunate because it homogenizes the wider context for information policy in such a way that denies it as contested territory. It removes the researcher's own assumptions and opinions from the field of analysis. Tacit agreement to accept that things are 'complex' neatly avoids more difficult issues such as analyzing how and why they are complex and what differences and disputes may exist between analysts. There is also a real danger that the notion of 'complexity' will be used by policy-makers as a rhetorical smokescreen to disguise the real policy agenda.

Rather than ignoring complexity, changing the subject matter, or trying to explain it away, we will argue in this Chapter that an attempt can be made to study complexity in a systematic way.

Scope limitation in information policy research

Closely related to complexity is the problem of scope limitation. What are the boundaries of an information policy problem? How do we know when we have cleared away sufficient undergrowth to see the trees clearly without losing a sense of the forest?

Public policy is particularly difficult to draw lines around, but the issue of scoping our research needs to be taken seriously. There is otherwise a danger that we will fail in our research because we recognize the wrong problem. We therefore need methods that yield 'an approximate answer to the right question, which is often vague, rather than an exact answer to the wrong question, which can always be made more precise' (Rose, 1976). This is not easy, especially within the limitations of the existing LIS research toolbag.

Information policy in Britain at the national level is highly decentralized. The motivation for policy development and change comes from many quarters and, as a consequence, 'national information policy' is an amalgam of statutory law, common law, social norms, administrative practice, market forces and international agreements and treaties. Pragmatists will argue that information policy is essentially a tool for problem-solving. It is goal-based. The boundaries of a policy are defined by the problem at hand. This is true up to a point but it fails to recognize that different actors involved in policy-making will perceive different boundaries (consumer interest groups, regulators and industry lobbyists, for instance) and within those boundaries view the problem with different attitudes, motivations and values.

In the last Chapter, Rowlands argued that there is a general failure in the information policy literature to identify the models and assumptions being employed. All policy researchers distinguish between the aims and results of their research, but only rarely do they identify the specific limitations of the tools they employ in relation to the conclusions they draw. This raises a series of questions, including: the role we attribute to the analyst (as an impartial observer, biased agent or ideologist?); the type of analysis being undertaken (whether describing what a policy *is* or telling us what it *should* be?); and the stage of policy development being considered (policy design, implementation or evaluation?). These fine distinctions are more of a problem for academics than for 'real-world' policy practitioners, but this observation does reveal a worrying deficit between policy formulation and the information and research feeds into policy design.

The role of a scientific approach to information policy must be to unravel these assumptions and make them explicit. Ideally, a conceptual framework is needed that can account for specific problems yet allow for more generally applicable hypotheses to be formulated and tested.

In the next section we will look at a widely accepted model of the policy process and show how that model can be developed to deal with the issues of scope and complexity in information policy research.

Modelling the dynamics of information policy

This Chapter does not offer a 'magic bullet' for addressing complexity and scope issues in information policy research. The approach here is at least to acknowledge them and suggest that they can and should be studied systematically. As Turner (1994) argued, information policy is too often conceptualized simply as a 'thing', as an object. This notion is particularly evident in the LIS literature where many writers draw our attention to a specific legislative proposal, Select Committee Report or executive decision. There is a lack of good case study material in the information policy literature, and little illumination of the human, organizational and dynamic aspects of policy-making.

The policy sciences literature does offer a choice of research frameworks for trying to understand the dynamics of policy-making. Some writers view policy-making as a series of choices: choices of scope, of policy instrument, of distribution, of restraints and innovation (Jenkins, 1978). Some view policy-making as the reaction of a political system to external stimuli (e.g. Easton, 1979). Others view policy-making as the result of bargains struck between agents or flowing from existing organizational processes and procedures (e.g. Dye, 1972; Burns and Stalker, 1961).

A review of all the frameworks potentially available for use in the context of information policy studies is beyond the remit of this Chapter. We argue here that an immediately useful and productive way of trying to understand information policy is to employ a systems approach. This recognizes that policy-making comprises a series of inputs (people, ideology, expediency, information, research, investment) and outputs (wealth creation, better health care, access to democracy). By conceiving of information policy-making as an INPUT–PROCESS–OUTPUT (I–P–O) model for organizing our thinking, we shift to the view that information policy governs a *process* (such as the storage and transmission of information) rather than a *thing* (such as technology). 'Information policy' might therefore be better thought of as a verb rather than a noun. Just as the I–P–O model can be used to describe how data are transformed into information and then knowledge, so it can also offer insights into policy-making. So, rather than addressing policy issues relating to a specific advance in software or data communications (i.e. technology-driven), we can switch our attention to the underlying functional aims and objectives of policy (Trauth, 1986).

Conceptualizing policy as a *process,* rather than a specific outcome or event, is very useful. It helps us to understand how policy develops over time and how policy is shaped by (and, in turn, shapes) organizational and social factors. Policy is not an abstract ideal, it takes place in an imperfect and sometimes confusing world. A typical representation of the policy-making process is the 'functional staged model' (Lasswell, 1970). A simplified version is illustrated in Figure1.

Figure 1: Staged model of the policy-making process

Identify problem and set agenda	→	**Formulate and plan policy response**	→	**Adopt policy**	→	**Implement policy**	→	**Evaluate policy outcomes**
DESIGN				**IMPLEMENT**				**EVALUATE**

As we move from left to right, a problem is first recognized and defined and then finds itself on a decision-maker's agenda. Alternative 'solutions' are developed, presented and rejected in favour of the option which offers the maximum net benefit (or is the most convenient, expedient or cheapest). This is then officially adopted. Implementation begins and evaluation or monitoring procedures are usually invoked so that any undesirable outcomes can be identified and dealt with. In many cases, the results of that evaluation will require adjustments to be made earlier in the chain, perhaps resulting in a complete redesign of the policy.

To a large extent, once a policy-making process gets underway, it tends to be continuous. It has been said that policy-making has 'no beginning and no end' (Lindblom, 1959). This overstates the case, as it is possible to define reasonable starting and termination points in a pragmatic way. Within those bounds, however, the process can be regarded as continuous.

The power of the staged model is that it offers us a way of grouping a wide range of apparently disconnected decisions, phenomena, observations and data into meaningful units, and it has a certain intuitive appeal. It also has its limitations. Many critics would immediately point out that real life, with its rough-and-tumble of politics and 'horse-trading', is not nearly as tidy as the model suggests. Nonetheless this is how policy-making is most often presented in the media, and many policy-makers would still justify and defend their own actions, however apparently irrational at the time, in terms of this ideal framework. Clearly, theoretical models can be very powerful and may shape the course of events in the real world. Quite how different theoretical models interact and impact on the course of events has yet to be examined in the context of information policy studies but it might well prove a productive research topic.

One aim of this Chapter is simply to extend the current vocabulary of information policy studies. The social sciences are already heavily preoccupied with debates on the nature and the definition of models, and we do not intend to enter into the realms of philosophy. We do suggest, though, that the process model of policy-making can be of real value in facilitating a deeper understanding of information policy problems.

Lasswell's simple basic model can be re-interpreted in a number of ways. In the next sections we will look at three such re-interpretations: 'rational actor', 'bureaucratic imperative' and 'garbage can' perspectives on policy-making. These three perspectives or dialects of Lasswell's 'mother tongue' are not proposed as exclusive, alternative methods for analysis. They should be considered as a single overall framework for generating value- and paradigm-critical research strategies. We hope to show that the three re-interpretations are sufficiently distinctive to enable us to clarify at least some of the complexity surrounding information policy.

Re-interpreting the process model: the 'rational actor'

A 'rational actor' interpretation is perhaps the one which most closely fits into Lasswell's original conception. Here the model is presented as an (unattainable) ideal, unencumbered by external events, and policy-making the result of a series of wholly rational decisions.

Under this interpretation, policy design takes place in the context of explicitly stated goals which are pursued relentlessly and consistently and brought to an intellectually satisfying conclusion. The choice of which policy option to adopt from the many considered is determined by a cold assessment of costs and benefits based on analytical criteria.

Rather akin to the British jury system where the assumption is that any group of 'Twelve Good Men and True' drawn from the population are likely to reach the same conclusion based on sufficient evidence, the rational actor view of policy-making draws heavily on objectivity, impartiality and a sense of fairness.

This interpretation is the one which is most intimately related to the notion of policy as a planning activity. Here *ends* (policy goals) dictate the choice of *means* (tools and methods). The most prominent writers to develop an ideal type interpretation of this kind are Simon (1983) and Lindblom (1959) who differ in respect of the importance that they attach to this means-ends schema. Lindblom stresses the importance of specifying policy objectives in advance and then searching for options, while Simon argues that by specifying policy objectives at the outset there is a danger of foreclosing too quickly on possible alternative courses of action. This may seem a relatively small point, but it does suggest that there are strains and tensions within the classical artifice of the rational actor interpretation.

It would be difficult, if not impossible, to find 'real world' examples of the rational actor approach in its purest expression. Yet the interpretation is a powerful one and the assumptions that underpin it can still be seen in many press and media accounts of policy events. It has a great deal to offer, even if only in the negative sense of drawing our attention to deviations from the ideal in the real world. We may never be able to approach or even approximate to the rational actor model in real life, but the conceptual framework it provides does allow us to isolate some of the sources of complexity in information policy.

What are those sources of complexity? A difficult question, to be sure, but perhaps a few ideas will be suggested by challenging some of the assumptions that underpin the rational actor interpretation. For instance, take the assumption that policy-making is somehow synonymous with planning. In real-world situations it is usually very difficult or even impossible to reach agreement on policy goals and objectives. There are likely to be many conflicting views, values and assumptions held by the various stakeholders, so too rigid an approach to 'planning' from the start may simply lead to open conflict. This raises the important issue of who, precisely, are the policy-makers? Just those with the legal authority to engage in the formulation of policy? Research organizations? The media? Consumer interest groups? Industry lobbyists?

The rational actor interpretation of policy-making is particularly interesting from an information science viewpoint. If totally rational, then policy-making must take place in information-rich environments where there is unimpeded access to comprehensive, reliable, timely and objective sources of research.

This ideal is unattainable for reasons of time and the availability of resources alone. But what happens when critical information is unavailable? Does the policy-making process *really* stop in its tracks? There is a balance to be struck between the potential benefits of having comprehensive information available versus the potential costs in terms of time and cost of seeking the missing information (see, for example, Walsh and Simonet, 1995). Given that the equation will not always tilt in favour of seeking the missing information, policy will sometimes proceed on inadequate information or research which 'satisfices'.

There are perhaps other more fundamental issues in relation to the quality of the information feeds to policy-makers. Are the information systems and services which they use attuned and sensitive to their needs? How do you constantly update a 'perfect' knowledge base? To what extent can (usually generalist) policy-makers be expected to understand and interpret complex scientific information? Do we have useful metrics for evaluating the effects of particular policy choices? Consider, for example, the problem of justifying corporate investments in information technology. Many recent studies have failed to show a direct correlation between IT investment in companies and measurable benefits. Is that because there are no benefits, that there are disbenefits, or that we are simply unable to find the right metrics? These are pertinent questions in the context of a view of policy-making based on rationality.

Even the assumption that careful planning makes good policy may be challenged since even the most carefully planned policy will meet with unforeseen snags or give rise to unintended consequences. This is an inevitable possibility given the complexity of social and organizational environments. Careful planning and analysis are doomed to be only partially adequate as a means of selecting between policy alternatives. There is no way of fully knowing what the practical effects will be, other than through pilot projects and experiment. Policies may generate knock-on second order effects which may be desirable or undesirable and which may assist or inhibit the realization of the original aims and objectives. Ignoring these effects is itself dangerous, risky and irrational, yet responding to them is costly and may rely on *ad hoc* improvisation—the antithesis of a wholly rational approach.

Before turning to the other two re-interpretations of the process model examined here, it is important to qualify what we mean when we use the term 'rational'. We need to be aware of the distinction between rational decisions, as defined by the ideal described above, and decisions that are rational to actors in the given contexts as examined below (Hill, 1993); since rarely can it be argued that actors take decisions that are at the time irrational to them, even though for the (often distant) analyst this may appear to be the case.

Re-interpreting the process model: the bureaucratic imperative

In the real world, a wholly rational approach to policy-making is impracticable and probably misguided. The limits to rationality in policy-making are obvious, the notion of 'perfect knowledge' being possibly the most difficult aspect to accept. The rational actor interpretation does not embrace the fact that values and beliefs (whether personal, organizational, professional or ideological) have a major bearing on the priority which human beings attach to particular choices of action. It requires an enormous act of faith to believe that policy-makers are always able to act independently of their values and beliefs.

Another 'bureaucratic imperative' interpretation of the policy-making process is possible. This assumes that, in spite of their best intentions and endeavours to behave in a 'rational' manner, powerful organizational factors come into play which sometimes make this impossible. Even if the individual could overcome his own personal limitations as a policy-maker, he would still face obstacles that were in his way because of the fact that he has to work as part of an organization. For instance, in the name of efficiency, modern organizations tend to involve a high degree of division of labour and specialization, but this often gets in the way of being able to see the big picture clearly. Instead, the individual tends to perceive problems through narrower departmental 'spectacles'. A truly rational policy would be based on the *widest* possible field of vision. It would avoid the kind of sub-optimal policy-making that confuses a sub-system (such as a department in a local authority) with a larger system (local government). This, of course, still begs the question of how values at the largest relevant scale can be set and articulated.

Institutional settings are also a significant source of values, norms, procedures and accepted wisdoms which may influence or override 'rationality'.

Burger (1993:19) observes that:

> People within the system make decisions on the basis of clearly established rules and modes of conduct. Any policy that is to be implemented by a bureaucracy must be transformed in such a way that whatever the intent of the policy-makers about the implementation of the policy, the bureaucratic rules of the implementing organization will be more powerful.

The bureaucratic interpretation conceptualizes policy-makers as reacting to immediate short-term problems rather than planning for the future. It assumes that even though agreement on policy objectives or values may well be impossible, pragmatic agreement on what can be done to solve a problem is nevertheless within reach. For many people, policy-making *is* a problem-solving activity. A 'good' policy is one which forges agreement between people with different values and interests. The bureaucratic interpretation accepts that reality is too complex ever to be understood completely and that there are too many variables to control. Policy-makers therefore get by as best they can in circumstances of uncertainty and ignorance. They operate on the basis of experience, by trial and error, adopting flexible but cautious approaches to the complexity of the social and organizational environment. Their behaviour is characterized by an incremental, step-by-step approach.

The bureaucratic imperative shifts the focus of policy process away from planning to the business of doing something now rather than looking to the future. Policies are evaluated quickly in terms of the marginal benefits they offer in improving the *status quo*. This highly pragmatic approach can be summed up as 'the art of the possible'. Consensus rather than a rational exposition of the problem and possible remedies becomes the key determinant of policy choice. This tends to favour gradual or piecemeal change. This approach admits no strategy, it simply 'muddles through'. It prioritizes experience, intuition and feeling and plays down the role of analysis. Here *ends* become subservient to the *means* available (Jenkins, 1978).

The assumption that consensus is the mark of a 'good' policy implies a view of society as highly pluralist, where people are free to pursue and protect their interests, where all interest groups are equally articulate at expressing their views, and where government is open, sensitive, impartial, unbiased and evenhanded. Yet society is far from this ideal: differences in power, skills, financial and other resources exist. Consensus, if reached at all, tends merely to be compromise and is often skewed towards the needs and desires of the powerful. Another problem is the tendency for consensus to promote forces of conservatism and inertia, to be cautious and to discourage innovation.

Ironically, the concept of bureaucracy is one which tries to make administrations more rational and more neutral. Max Weber's ideal construct of bureaucracy is of an impersonal, hierarchical system of authority where rules, procedures and regulations form the basis for actions. While these formal characteristics are supposed to lead to efficiency, objectivity, consistency and predictability, they also deeply affect the way that the members of a bureaucracy behave.

The hierarchical structure and authoritarian character of bureaucracies are essential to control the activities of their members and coordinate efforts towards a common goal. There is, however, a tendency to institutionalize conformity. This is reinforced by such factors as socialization into the bureaucratic culture, the desire to belong, peer pressure and self-interest (anxieties over job security, for instance). This in turn leads to situations where people clearly define their sphere of responsibility and stick to it, become unwilling to use personal initiative, search for approval before doing anything and generally 'pass the buck'.

These are significant points for a consideration of how policy is designed, implemented and evaluated. Rules and regulations have a tendency to become more important than the goals themselves (goal displacement), because abiding by the rules and regulations itself becomes the primary goal. At its most extreme, the protection and survival of the bureaucracy and its members override its original goals and becomes 'bureaucratic pathology'.

The bureaucratic model may appear to be a good description of the way organizations make policy decisions, but it is not necessarily a good model for *how* they should make decisions! The bureaucratic interpretation contrasts strongly with the rational actor approach outlined above. Its value lies in drawing our attention to the specific organizational factors which shape and constrain policy-making. It is important because analysts and commentators have certain assumptions about how policy is made in government or in commercial enterprises. These assumptions are often not explicit but they certainly affect the conclusions which are drawn. One way of testing the credibility of a policy analysis is to ask the author what assumptions were made about the organization's room for manoeuvre. If these assumptions are in doubt, then the entire evaluation may be brought into question.

Re-interpreting the process model: the garbage can

Despite their differences of emphasis, the rational actor and bureaucratic interpretations share one thing in common: an assumption that policy-making is essentially orderly, continuous and linear. Both proceed from gaining an initial understanding of a problem to the application and evaluation of measures designed to bring about a resolution.

The question of how that problem is recognized by policy-makers in the first place is itself worthy of attention. Information policy studies tend to devote little attention to the nature and definition of problems. Instead, problems are taken as 'givens' and the analysis moves forward from that point; but why is it that some problems are acted upon while others are neglected?

The definition of problems is itself a political activity. At any given time, many problems and issues will be competing for the attention of the policy-maker. Only a relatively small number will have any reasonable chance of being seriously considered; and only a very few will gain more than short-lived support within the policy environment. This is a particularly difficult aspect in many areas of information policy where the ultimate policy goals are themselves often unclear and ambiguous (take, for instance, the European Union's Information Society initiative).

Kingdon argued that a major limitation of both the rational and bureaucratic interpretations of the policy-making process is that they are too clearcut. In neither interpretation do such anarchic (but instantly recognizable) concepts of disorder and chance happenings and sheer bloody-mindedness sit very comfortably.

In developing his own interpretation, Kingdon (1984: 104) depicts policy-making as:

> ... a garbage can into which policy goals, organizational rules and constraints, the 'right climate', and other often unexpected variables are thrown together. The resulting policy outcome is often unpredictable and because of the ambiguous nature of the policy goals themselves, often unrecognizable.

Kingdon sees the policy-making environment as being made up of a constantly shifting network of interested parties and strategic alliances (consumer groups, industry lobbies, executive and legislative branches of government, the media). In the nature of things, these different groups pursue their own objectives in their own time and at their own pace. The policy consensus which finally emerges from this process can be seen as the output of a network of 'organized anarchies'.

Why anarchies? Kingdon identifies three sets of characteristics that are common to all organized bodies and decision-makers and argues that these constitute powerful reasons why we should regard aspects of the policy-making process as being essentially chaotic and non-linear (Figure 2).

Figure 2: Sources of non-linearity in policy-making processes

Problematic preferences	In the early stages of the policy-making process it may be very difficult for the individual participants to grasp what their preferences really are: these may have to be 'discovered' as the process rolls out and as more information becomes available.
Unclear technology	Individual participants in the policy-making process may not necessarily fully understand the needs or the goals of the organizations they 'represent' nor appreciate some of the finer points of protocol. They may instead operate largely on the basis of personal initiative, of trial and error, of doing what seems right at the time.
Fluid participation	The composition of the participants in any large-scale decision-making process may change over time. Sometimes capriciously, as they lose heart or move onto other things, or by design, as their power and influence are neutralized. On the other hand, previously 'dormant' participants may suddenly become active.

It would be unreasonable to characterize policy-making processes as being inherently chaotic all the time. But the garbage can interpretation is useful in that it suggests that at some points, especially perhaps in the problem identification and agenda setting stages, policy-making is associated with disorder.

From our new perspective inside the garbage can, policy-making can be seen as the result of political bargaining or 'horse-trading' rather than the result of carefully considered analysis. This interpretation draws our attention to the actors involved rather than the issues at stake: powerful elites emerge and act strategically as 'policy entrepreneurs', taking advantage of temporary 'windows' or opportunities.

Under the bureaucratic interpretation, organizations are seen as mechanisms which coordinate the deployment of resources and technology in pursuit of clearly defined goals. But if the policy goals are hazy, the participation fluid and decision-making disorderly, then the basic assumptions behind the bureaucratic interpretation soon become redundant.

The 'garbage can organization' has been characterized by Cohen *et al.* (1972) as comprising a set of:

- choices looking for problems;
- issues and feelings looking for decision situations in which they might be aired;
- solutions looking for issues to which they might be the answer;
- and decision-makers looking for work!

The garbage can interpretation admits spontaneity and chance into the study of policy-making processes. Fundamentally, it argues that policy-making is first and foremost about politics and power structures, not rational argument. Ultimately, the garbage can interpretation offered here may be too indeterminate to provide fully satisfactory explanations of what happens in policy-making. It does, however, provide a sufficiently distinctive perspective (especially from the rational actor approach) to suggest that triangulation of the three perspectives might provide some useful insights.

Some implications for information policy research

So far, we have argued that academic information policy studies should take greater account of the process dynamics of policy-making. By developing a simple process model and opening up that model to three radically different (but overlapping) interpretations, we suggest that the framework offers a tool for beginning to isolate and understand some of the main sources of 'complexity' surrounding information policy.

We suggest that the framework developed here offers a useful mapping tool for locating case study findings in a rigorous scheme and feel that the framework is flexible enough to allow for the extrapolation of such findings in a more highly generalizable form. A crucial perspective throughout has been that in conducting information policy studies we must be capable of adopting techniques and tools that are contingent on the circumstances as we find them and not as we have theorized: 'the fact that alternative frames of reference [may] produce quite different explanations should encourage the analyst's self-consciousness about the net he employs' (Allison, 1971). In developing any model a process of abstraction, selection and simplification is going on.

An obvious danger is over-simplification and distortion, or the development of over-elaborate models which are too complex to use or understand. The analyst clearly has to beware of his own political and ideological biases and the presuppositions and assumptions which influence his view of the way things are. Whether he is operating in the academic arena or in the world of consultancy, the analyst has an important role to play as an identifier, exponent and interpreter of relevant policy models (Hogwood and Gunn, 1984).

Figure 3: Comparison of the three interpretations

INTERPRETATION	Type	Goals	Stage at which interpretation is most useful
Rational actor	prescriptive—says how policy-making *should* take place in an ideal world	driven by rationality and 'perfect information' towards well-defined goals—strong affinity with planning activities	policy evaluation
Bureaucratic imperative	descriptive—shows organizational goals and values sometimes take precedence over rationality	driven primarily by the need to achieve consensus within the constraints imposed by the institutional setting	policy implementation
Garbage can	descriptive—says *what happens* in policy-making	essentially non-linear policy goals emerge through bargaining and social processes	policy design (especially agenda setting)

Each of the interpretations focuses attention on different aspects of policy-making and may be more useful for some purposes or some situations than others (see Figure 3). Generally, one should not permit oneself to be bound too rigidly or dogmatically to a particular model. Indeed a deep analysis of information policy can only be achieved by linking a number of differing perspectives.

Information for Policy-Making[1]

Janet R. Strachan and Ian Rowlands

Abstract

This Chapter reviews some of the research carried out and reported in the LIS and policy sciences literature into the information needs, information seeking behaviour and preferences of public policy-makers. It concludes that a broad frame of reference needs to be brought to bear in developing an understanding of how policy-makers use (and 'misuse') information and research inputs. It reflects on some of the situational, cognitive and scientific barriers which impede the use of research by policy-makers. Finally, it suggests a role for the information community in bridging the gap between the 'two communities' of policy analysts and policy-makers, by intervening in such a way as to make information flows more transparent and balanced.

The information needs of policy-makers

There are few references in the library and information science literature which address directly the information needs and information-seeking behaviour of public policy-makers. Information needs in the context of decision-making tasks and roles are examined in a number of cases, though, (see, for example, White and Wilson's 1988 study of the information needs of managers in industry) and are clearly of interest. One reason for the lack of studies may be that defining 'policy-makers' as a coherent user group presents considerable difficulties: policy decisions, especially in the information policy arena, are typically influenced by a wide variety of actors. Furthermore, by its very nature, areas of public policy draw on information from a broad sweep of disciplines. It may also be that policy-makers are not the principal users of the kinds of

1. This paper was not presented at the Workshop.

information services that are the focus of classic user needs studies. These typically deal with bibliographic information, either in the form of databases or information services. Collections of this kind are most often used by professionals, academics and other groups undertaking directed research. We will show later in this paper that policy-makers seek and use information of a quite different order, sourced through different channels.

In order to examine actual information needs, rather than information-seeking behaviour, it is necessary to ask why the user decides to seek information in the first place, what purpose s/he believes it will serve, and to what use it is eventually put. Wilson (1981) suggests that interviews about information-seeking need to be structured around the idea of problems experienced in everyday life, whether or not these can be addressed by 'formal' information systems. An even broader view of the information needs may be required when examining policy-makers.

Aiyepeku (1982) found that among the most important factors which influenced the use of information by policy-makers were the activities of powerful interest groups, political considerations, public opinion, and the position of a given policy-maker in the hierarchy. Other aspects of the policy-makers' environment are important, too. Changes in the policy environment can trigger information-seeking activities. These may include shifts in the client profile (for example, an ageing population), new problems such as child pornography on the Internet, or new potential solutions offered by advances in technology (Hogwood and Gunn, 1984).

We argue in this paper that the information community has paid insufficient attention to analyzing the policy process; that is, the context in which the information needs of policy-makers arise. More case studies are needed to analyze the dynamics of the policy cycle and to show how policy-making really happens: who the policy-makers are, how they interact with one another, and what are the information dimensions of the policy cycle, especially in relation to how information is organized, managed, distilled, interpreted and used (Ballantyne, 1995). Work by Bearman and Hammond indicates that information science methods can be applied to advantage in studying how policy-makers use and filter information during the early stages of the policy-making process, when tasks such as problem identification, agenda setting and policy formulation are being undertaken. As a point of caution, it should be noted that there are multiple interpretations by policy-makers of the term 'information', depending on the economic, social and cultural context. It is very important to clarify the policy-makers' own understanding of this term in any user needs study.

The world of the policy-maker

In a given policy environment a number of factors are likely to shape information need and information-seeking behaviour. The prevailing political culture is obviously a major issue and traditions may be subtly transmitted from one generation of policy-makers to another by a process of socialization. For example, a comparative study of groups of legislators showed that nationality affects the way in which policy-makers integrate information into the policy process (Pierce *et al.*, 1987). Institutional factors also impact on the ways in which information is disseminated, the media and channels that are used, ease of access, and the degree to which decision-making is decentralized (Davies, 1994).

Political values and the policy-making structure play a major role in determining the use and acceptability of information. Legislators are highly sensitive to the political implications of a given piece of information and will break down most legislative issues into their technical and political components. How the policy-maker perceives policy issues will be addressed in the legislature, and his or her perceptions of the legislative structure are also important. Both legislators and bureaucrats must constantly look over their shoulder to their constituents; indeed, they often define their jobs in terms of constituent services and contacts (Webber, 1987). The need to seek re-election is a strong motivating factor to ensure that the political impact of their decisions is acceptable, and that they remain responsive to their constituents, or at least true to their own myths about societal problems and crises. All of this too often translates into short-range attention being given to specific issues (DiMento, 1981). Interestingly, local policy-makers appear to be more sensitive to policy information than those at the national level. This may be because they are in greater proximity to the issues and impacts (Pierce *et al.*, 1987), or it may simply be that politicians at the national level service a broader constituency.

Sometimes, bureaucrats are instrumental in making and developing policy. They often have considerable discretion in terms of how policy is implemented. Bureaucrats develop policy through rules and guidance which make flesh of the bare provisions. They may also undertake adjudication, law enforcement and compliance activities (Anderson, 1990). They are subject to many of the influences outlined, but the nature of the bureaucratic system itself is also an important factor. Departments tend to behave in such a way as to protect their own budgets (see the Chapter by Barry Mahon in this volume, p.101). They tend to be preoccupied with process rather than results, and the personal ambitions of individuals can sometimes be placed ahead of achieving policy goals (Lindblom and Woodhouse, 1993). In agency policy-making the hierarchy is of critical importance to the decision-making process. This enables decisions to be coordinated and disputes to be settled among lower officials. However, hierarchy also affects the free-flow of information and ideas within an organization. In comparison to legislatures, decision-making is relatively hidden in bureaucracies: this can be both a positive and a negative factor (Anderson, 1990). White (1986) found that in bureaucratic structures, individuals reported great dissatisfaction with their information supply. However, Grant examined in detail the process of making a policy choice in US local government and found that a degree of secrecy in negotiations centred around the siting of a General Motors plant had been critical in permitting a level of rationality to prevail in the policy process (Grant, 1990).

The information policy-makers use

Practical approaches to policy analysis include formal information collection and analysis, particularly statistical analysis, and the use of task forces such as Royal Commissions and the deliberations of Parliamentary Committees. Some governmental agencies are created partly or wholly to carry out policy analysis. Specialist research organizations may be contracted by the government to undertake policy tasks. Academic and research institutions also play a key role in gathering facts and processing them. Businesses, non-governmental organizations (NGOs) and other interest groups all generate a strong flow of unsolicited policy studies (Lindblom and Woodhouse, 1993). Government agencies, industrial firms, political parties, trade unions, political pressure groups are all involved in 'intelligence' work of one kind or another.

Grant (1990) found that the types of information used in making policy choices include formal policy studies, statistics and indicators, expert advice, use of consultants, studies and commissioned reports, negotiations (open or in secret) and public hearings. It should also be noted that in the policy cycle, the product of one process may often be used as an intermediate information input to another process.

How policy-makers use information

Crain (1994) identifies three core information strategies in policy-making:

- information gathering, including information storage and retrieval;
- interpretation;
- information use/decision-making.

Similarly, the literature identifies three key information roles undertaken by individuals in the policy process (Kochen, 1975):

- the compiler/organizer;
- the preparer of decision-related assessments;
- the maker of final policy decisions.

Combinations and overlaps in these roles are not uncommon but a broad summary can be made of the kinds of information sources associated with different groups of policy-makers (Table 1).

Table 1: Information roles and sources in policy-making

Policy-maker	Role	Information sources
Legislator	• make decisions • set policy direction • monitor issues	• public opinion, constituents, press, lobby groups • political parties system outputs (e.g. from the bureaucracy, Royal Commissions, etc.) • debates in the legislature sought-out opinions from individuals policy papers, considered expert opinion
Bureaucrat	• develop policy options • policy implementation • policy review	• system outputs (as above) • commissioned work (consultants, issue monitoring experts, etc.) • policy papers/considered expert opinion/ intelligence work (including analysis of indicators, data and trends, State-of-the-Environment reports, etc.) library/research data/ indicators
Interest group	• issue development • policy advocacy • lobbying /agenda setting	• published data and indicators • research results in the literature • own/commissioned research

Policy-makers and the information community seem to share the view that better use should be made of information in public policy-making. Both groups presume that the information generated through research can assist in making sound policy decisions. But despite a tremendous increase in policy analysis over recent years, governmental policy-makers continue to make little direct use of research (Webber, 1987). In examining the impact that academic social science has on the policy process, DiMento (1981) suggests that the influence may be of two kinds: instrumental or conceptual. Research may have an instrumental influence when social science findings are translated directly into programmes of action or legislation, or a conceptual influence when the results impact on the thinking of the policy-maker (without necessarily leading to an immediately identifiable impact on policy decisions). It is interesting to note that information providers may often be looking for evidence of instrumental influence in their studies on the usefulness of information services to policy-makers (see, for example, Menou, 1993). However, Webber's research (1987) suggests that information more commonly exerts a conceptual influence.

A related approach to understanding how policy-makers use research has involved looking at the attitudinal characteristics of policy-makers. The 'two communities' theory asserts that the direct use of policy research by policy-makers is unlikely because the two groups involved, academics and policy-makers, have different world views and belief systems. Each responds to different rewards, uses different technical language, holds different values, and is affiliated to different professional organizations. The two communities theory suggests that these factors create a fundamental barrier to the use of social science research by policy-makers. An overview of the literature and research in this field can be found in Nelson *et al.* (1987).

Another, more empirical, approach to the question has been to investigate scientific communication patterns and mechanisms (Kochen, 1975). In this context, Nelson *et al.* (1987) looked at the use of social science information by policy-makers. Their study illuminated the characteristics of and constraints to communication associated with different elements of the communications process: the *source* (internal sources are more likely to be used than external sources); the *message* (reliability and validity are important in facilitating use, as is the preference for 'soft language' rather than hard statistical data); the *channel* (accessibility, preference for informal communication and research synthesis); and the *receiver* (the need for the policy-maker to have a reasonable appreciation of the scientific and political aspects of the policy decision).

One other consideration should be mentioned—the relationship between information, knowledge and power. In public policy-making it is important to understand the political and economic context in which information is generated and used in the public domain because all actors generate and use information for their own gain. A particular concern is that no amount of improvement to data collection and information generation can improve information use unless the underlying power relationships inherent in information collection and access are understood and addressed. For this reason there have been many efforts to encourage what are seen as more appropriate, participatory techniques in research aimed at supporting policy development and decision-making.

What policy-makers use information for

Policy-makers require information for an exceptionally broad range of purposes and information providers should expect their needs to be equally wide-ranging. However, while a number of studies have looked at the information that policy-makers trust, much less is known about their more general information-seeking habits.

The limited findings that are available suggest that the purposes for which policy-makers acquire and use information are broader than those associated with framing policy issues and developing effective solutions to problems faced by society. Policy-makers may use information in the following ways:

- to develop general knowledge in a particular policy area, perhaps to create a niche political role;
- to help conceptualize and define issues;
- to gain recognition for successful programmes.

Policy-makers may also use information as political ammunition to neutralize the opposition, or they may insist that more information is required, simply as a spoiling tactic to delay decisions (Nelson *et al.*, 1987).

Policy-makers may use information to legitimize, rather than to influence, policy decisions. Information may be required in order to protect a governmental agency from a potential legal challenge, or for statutory reasons, for example if the law requires that all relevant evidence is collected. Information may also be used to promote an image of careful decision-making, which may not necessarily be acted upon (DiMento, 1981).

Factors influencing the use of information by policy-makers

There is a difference between the information, advice and research that policy-makers seek, and that upon which they act. The information that policy-makers trust has great influence (Pierce *et al.*, 1987). It stands out and rises above the overwhelming volume of data and advice that policy-makers are presented with and is more likely to generate a reaction. If professional communicators aim to procure voluntary changes in behaviour through information transfer (Roling, 1994), it is important for those who are targeting policy-makers to understand the factors which influence the use of information by policy-makers and to develop services that they trust.

Barriers to the use of information by policy-makers

Obstacles to the use of research information by policy-makers, as reported in the literature, may be summarized under the three categories (situational, cognitive and scientific), suggested by Hammond *et al.* (1983).

Situational barriers
Potentially, there is an almost inconceivable volume of policy-relevant data. Much of it will be collected locally for operational purposes that are far removed from the policy-making setting. For this reason, the information may not be directly relevant or presented in a format that is useful to policy-makers. There may be a tendency to collect information for its own sake and to create an illusion of knowledge through clever presentation and the use of statistics (Davies, 1994). Environmental and geographical information systems, for example, tend to emphasize the technical aspects of information management, rather than its use. They can be disconnected from the policy-making process and have relatively little utility in selecting and packaging information for easy digestion (Ballantyne, 1995). Indeed, technological barriers to the use of informa-

tion are rising, as equipment becomes a prerequisite for information access, and the outputs of information systems become increasingly complex (Davies, 1994).

Policy-makers do not lack advice, rather they are overwhelmed by it and need to filter the volume of information that they are presented with. This, in part, is achieved through the political process, but this may also have the effect of reducing the diversity of the debate (Lindblom and Woodhouse, 1993). Despite the apparent overload, the quantity of information available is rarely deemed adequate for decision-making. The quality and credibility of information, too, are often seen as a central barrier to its use (Davies, 1994).

Time and cost constraints often mean that the analysis of problems and their solutions may not be exhaustive. Time is often a more critical limiting resource than staffing or communications (Webber, 1987). Blagden contrasts decision-making in science, where an absence of information leads to a postponement of any decision or conclusion, to decision-making in management, where people operate with insufficient information when time pressures are critical. Here, individuals will often cease searching as soon as a satisfactory answer is available to them, rather than carry on until an exhaustive examination of the issues is completed, or an optimal solution found (Blagden, 1980). Policy-making often takes place in similar time-pressured environments, where legislators are required to react quickly to political situations as they arise. John Martyn (quoted in Slater, 1989) found that local government officials were subject to intense time pressures in their work. Faced with vast amounts of potentially relevant information, he found that they indulged in what he described as 'information gambling', using what ever information comes to hand.

Chambers (1994) suggests a set of barriers to the use of information which are essentially related to power and to the 'world-view' of the policy-maker. These include factors such as self-interest (political and personal), the fact that the ideas of dominant groups (those with power) are seen as more valid than others, and the influence of centralized decision-making systems which can result in a failure to take account of locally-generated information.

Cognitive barriers

The methods used to present scientific information may also discourage its greater use. Policy-makers may find the technical language off-putting, and they are often presented with far more research than they can possibly analyze or absorb. The information skills of policy-makers are important too—their ability to understand the technical concepts presented and their policy implications (Hammond *et al.*, 1983). At times, policy-makers may not be able to absorb information because they do not recognize it as being important (Kochen, 1975). At other times, the mind may not be able to grasp the complexity of social policy issues, even when it is extended by computers and written documents (Lindblom and Woodhouse, 1993).

Scientific barriers

Scientific information is, by its very nature, probabilistic, and it is difficult to make policies based on this type of evidence. For example, the Second Assessment Report of the Intergovernmental Panel on Climate Change concluded that the balance of current scientific evidence suggests that there is a discernible human influence on the climate (World Energy Council, 1996). However, building concrete policies and plans of action based on this kind of scientific evidence has not proved an easy task. In this matter, as in all other policy areas, bureaucratic goals, political prudence, political ideology and the need to maintain consistency, whatever the facts, play a determining role in the kinds of policy responses that emerge (Pierce *et al.*, 1987; Hammond *et al.*, 1983).

Another scientific barrier is that researchers may not have undertaken work in, and generated information on, a given issue (Lindblom and Woodhouse, 1993). It may have been ignored, or not recognized as being significant, or the concept of a given avenue of enquiry may only just have come into being. In some areas it may not be possible to perform experiments which produce the kind of information that can reliably be generalized to policy problems.

Factors promoting information transfer and use

Research indicates that there are a number of criteria that make information and research more acceptable to policy-makers, and that few of the traditionally recommended organizational changes are likely to succeed in improving legislators' use of policy information (Webber, 1987). Studies have shown that scientific information is more acceptable to policy-makers when it involves high-quality research on a specific subject that has been executed by prestigious scientists; also where there is general consensus on the goals to be pursued and the discussion on empirical questions is of moderate scientific complexity. Technical information is most likely to be used for legitimizing purposes when it is presented late, on controversial issues, and when there is little consensus over empirical questions (DiMento, 1981).

Webber's research (1987) showed that legislators see universities as useful sources of policy information and maintain frequent contacts with them. They also have contacts with interim study commissions, legislative service agencies and committee staff, though these sources are not primarily committed to, nor necessarily capable of, keeping legislators abreast of the most current information relating to policy issues. Legislators tend to have a positive attitude towards the more systematic types of policy information such as policy studies and research reports. They tend to use knowledge from research that is funded, or conducted, by government, and are more likely to use information which accords with their intuitive feel for a problem. Government officials are, on the whole, less favourably disposed to social science information than scientific information, which they perceive as being more objective (DiMento, 1981).

Policy-makers seem to find information with the following characteristics particularly attractive:

- clearly presented materials that avoid technical jargon and make limited use of statistical quantification (Lindblom and Woodhouse, 1993);
- synthesized and evaluated research which includes a discussion of the policy implications of the results (Nelson *et al.*, 1987).

Policy-makers also require information that is presented in a transparent manner so that they can assess its quality. On the whole, however, policy-makers prefer interpersonal sources over print-based sources and actively maintain the network of contacts that they routinely encounter in their jobs: colleagues, constituents, academics and members of interest groups.

Indications for further research

The literature suggests a number of avenues for further research which might help information specialists to better understand the factors underlying the information preferences of policy-makers. Work is needed to understand the underlying dynamics of these preferences and to provide greater insights into what might constitute better and more effective ways to provide information services to policy-makers. One example is person-to-person information exchange. Could it be that interpersonal contacts offer precisely the kind of information—concise, evaluated, synthesized—that policy-makers are looking for? It may be that because personal communication is an interactive activity, the volume and complexity of a given information exchange can easily be controlled. Policy-makers can ask for more details, clarify technical terms, rush through information that is not of interest, and explore the background or side-branches of a subject. It may also be that policy-makers can subjectively assess the value of the information that they are receiving, based on their perceptions of the individual supplying it. Understanding these dynamics could have radical implications for information services.

Other potentially fruitful areas for research include the impact of time pressures on the work of policy-makers and their patterns of information seeking and use. Further detailed studies are needed on policy-makers' actual information-seeking habits and the sources that they most frequently use, along with investigations into why they seem to prefer research that is funded or conducted by government (control of the research agenda, greater confidentiality, more control in terms of the publication of results—allowing for greater political flexibility?). Many of the efforts to explain policy-makers' limited use of policy research have focused on highly generic factors, rather than on the opportunities and constraints of specific decision-making contexts (Webber, 1987).

Information systems tend to be designed according to the information that is perceived to be useful in 'rational' decision-making. In developing services for policy-makers, information providers should begin with the real nature of the decision process and the information needs of the target group (Kochen, 1975; Davies, 1994). Effective information systems are derived directly from the needs of the particular system and people involved (Carley, 1994). One approach to setting the scope for a policy information system is as follows (Ballantyne, 1995):

- look at the policy process and the people engaged in it;
- know the intended purpose of the information and the context in which it will be used;
- take a systems view that accommodates the full breadth of the policy issue in question and map information resources, informa-

tion sources, institutional strengths and weaknesses, and likely participants in specific policy areas.

Three important factors that information providers should focus on in improving information resources for decision-making are quality, relevance and utility (Kochen, 1975; Ballantyne, 1995). In particular, it would be helpful to increase the transparency of the information presented so that policy-makers can gain a sense of its quality. An International Development Research Centre (IDRC) consultation on environment, development and information concluded that existing information systems could be improved through a meaningful participatory approach in their development, by using effective feedback loops on services and cost effectiveness approaches, and by developing the role of the information broker (IDRC, 1994).

It may be noted that all of the factors listed above can be taken account of by information specialists in their design of services for policy-makers. We suggest that there is indeed an opportunity for the information community to provide a bridge between the 'two communities' of researchers and policy-makers, by interpreting and synthesizing research in a transparent manner, and by presenting it in a format that is suited to the target group.

Information Policy or Knowledge Policy?

David Bawden

Abstract

Information policies are, self-evidently, concerned with information. But what kind of information? The answer 'all information' is misleading and can result in a paralysis of action, in an attempt to be all-encompassing. It is helpful to consider a spectrum of forms of information, from data, through information with varying degrees of structure, to knowledge and perhaps wisdom. Information with lower levels of structure, and raw data, may be managed by systems, technical and administrative, and by procedures. Knowledge, understood in this way, can only be managed by policies. There is, therefore, a close link between information policy formulation and evaluation and the emerging discipline of knowledge management. The paper concludes that information policy is (a) inevitably complex, (b) not concerned with technical solutions, and (c) dependent upon an appreciation of the meaning and significance of knowledge in its proper context.

Introduction

This paper deals with a fairly fundamental question. What kind of information are we concerned with, in discussing and formulating information policies? Only when this is explicitly understood can we see fully what the nature of an information policy—any information policy—must be, and how it can be rationalized and evaluated.

We will follow two general pathways. One, starting from a familiar distinction between data, information and knowledge, will lead to the concept of knowledge management, and the link between information policies and the complexity of information environments. A second, taking a semiotic viewpoint, will again lead to thoughts on the intrinsic complexities of information policy formulation. It will be obvious that I have drawn largely from the insights of others in developing these two themes, and no apology is necessary for this; as Bertrand Russell, albeit speaking of mathematical axioms, put it, 'theft has obvious advantages over honest toil'.

Information policies are, self-evidently, concerned with information. But with what kind of information? The apparently obvious answer, 'any and all information', is misleading. Though it is true to say that it would be folly to suggest that information policy formulation, in general terms, may sensibly be restricted to a particular kind of information, or to particular delivery media, the opposite is not necessarily valid. To insist on an all-encompassing view of information policy may simply lead to a paralysis, possibly of thought and certainly of action, as the policy-maker is overwhelmed by the diversity in volume, scale, granularity and content of the forms of information being included.

An informational view of information policy

To get one perspective on this, consider the 'traditional' representation of information and related concepts. Conventionally, a spectrum is considered from data, through information with varying degrees of structure, to knowledge and perhaps wisdom. T.S. Eliot's quotation, too well known to bear repetition, expresses this cogently. Very often, these entities are represented in the form of a pyramid, with the base composed of data, while higher layers of information and then knowledge support an apex of wisdom (Figure 1).

Figure 1

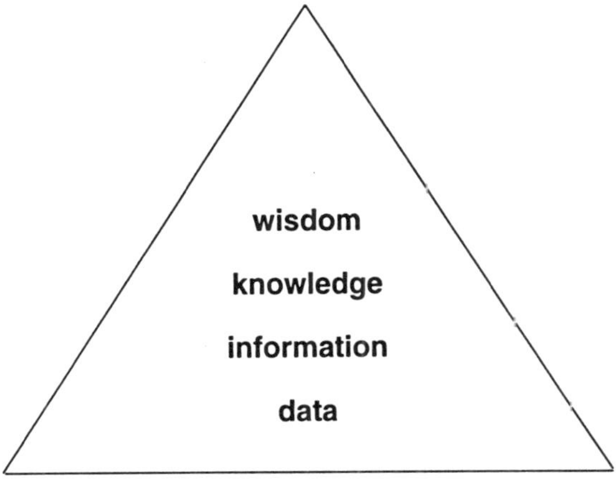

This is quite a useful representation, in that it suggests a reduction in volume of the entities at the lower levels as the more refined entities are constructed from them. An alternative picture simply presents a spectrum from data to wisdom, avoiding the awkward questions of just how much data it takes to make some information, and so on (how steep are the sides of the pyramid ?); and of just where the dividing line between the entities is to be drawn (at what stage exactly does information become knowledge?). It is perhaps better to adopt the view that these entities are all forms of information, with different characteristics. These simple pictures, however, useful as they may be, may reasonably be criticized on the grounds that they ignore context; one person's data element may be another's knowledge structure.

Nonetheless, these simplistic pictures have the virtue of reminding us of some fundamental truths about information entities, which is why they are widely used, and understood, by practitioners. Specifically, they remind us that moving along the data–wisdom spectrum is accompanied by—arguably caused by—value-adding processes: evaluation, comparison, compilation, classification, and so on (Bawden, 1990). Knowledge can then be understood as that form of information which is characterized by several resultant attributes, particularly compression, abstraction and categorization. It is thereby endowed with characteristics not associated with other forms of information, most notably with meaning and with significance. This lends this form of information a transformative power, such that it may bring about real changes within the organization or society in which it resides (in line with the original meaning of the Latin *informare*). Wisdom can be seen as an extension of this, incorporating judgement and informed action.

These qualities of the 'higher' forms of information lead to a distinction in the way they may be handled and managed. Information with lower levels of structure, and raw data, may be managed by systems—technical and administrative—and by procedures. Knowledge, understood in this way, can be managed by policies. (Wisdom is presumably beyond management by any conventional means.) Policies may, of course, have a natural extension into the more detailed levels of management of information and data, by policy-driven procedures and systems.

There is therefore a close link between information policy formulation and the emerging discipline of knowledge management. Policies, if they are anything, are about context, meaning and action, and these are the qualities of knowledge, as we understand it here. Though the term 'knowledge management' is somewhat over-hyped, and subject to very diverse understandings, nonetheless it is this aspect of the information management spectrum with which information policies are intertwined.

Information policy and complexity

There is another possible way of looking at knowledge, in this sense. Seen from the perspective of the developing sciences of complexity, we may regard knowledge as being a particularly organized form of information, an emergent property of a complex information environment. There is not space here to deal with the ramifications of these ideas: good, and comprehensible, accounts are given by Jack Cohen and Ian Stewart (1995), and by Peter Coveney and Roger Highfield (1995). Complexity is a multifaceted concept and is linked to the ideas of chaos theory. Where complexity theory tells us that simple systems produce complex behaviour, chaos theory shows that complex systems may produce remarkably simple behaviour. Emergent properties are those which transcend the sum of individual effects, and in particular exhibit 'organized complexity'—a good overall description of any non-trivial information transfer system. Indeed, one might say, in an informal way, that information policies are themselves inherently chaotic: policy formulation, like most interesting things, happens 'at the edge of chaos' where static order meets formless chaos, and patterns and organization emerge. Information policy formulation must deal with this complexity; indeed, the concept of information policy only makes sense in such a complex setting, with its diversity of meanings, significances and contexts.

The semiotic viewpoint

We may, alternatively, approach the whole question of the type of information addressed by an information policy from a different viewpoint; the viewpoint of semiotics. Here we follow the approach pioneered by Ronald Stamper, and cogently expressed by Jonathan Liebenau and James Backhouse (1990), and compared with related approaches by Soren Brier (1996). From this perspective, information in all its variety may be—indeed, for completeness must be—described at four levels: empiric, syntactic, semiotic and pragmatic. The empiric level deals with the mechanisms of transmission information: physical pathways and their information engineering consequences. The syntactic level is concerned with languages and codings, grammars and comprehensibility. At the semantic level, meaning predominates, and context becomes significant. The pragmatic level is concerned with the significance and purpose of information transfer.

Towards a holistic understanding of information policies

Information management, including information technology management, records and document management and so on, may in principle operate at any of these levels. However, in practice it generally involves no more than one or two levels together, often the lower levels. Knowledge management, and hence information policy formulation, since it is concerned with significance and purposes, must necessarily involve the pragmatic level, i.e. the highest level. (Failure to recognize this may lead to policies which are based solely on technological 'quick fixes', but these, in themselves, cannot address other than the empiric and syntactic levels.) However, in order to formulate and implement policies, it may be, and often will be, necessary to carry out an analysis at any or all of the other levels, or at least explicitly to appreciate their significance. The inevitable result is that information policy formulation has an intrinsic, and hierarchical, complexity. Failure to appreciate this can lead to policies which are literally not comparable, since they address different levels and granularities. The only solution, after recognizing the complexity, is to ground policy formulation explicitly in the pragmatic level of significance and purpose, which in turn imply meaning and context. From here, policies may be worked out to the other levels, ultimately generating systems and procedures. This is merely another way of saying that information policies are, in truth, grounded in the organized complexities of knowledge.

We may conclude that information policy formulation is:

- inherently and intrinsically complex;
- not directly or primarily concerned with technical solutions;
- dependent upon an appreciation of the meaning and significance of knowledge in its context.

This clearly implies that the evaluation of information policies must be the same: holistic and integrated over all its levels.

As we have already suggested, T.S. Eliot's words are over-used in discussions of these topics, so we conclude, in recognition of the inter-relations of complex environments, with Francis Thompson:

All things by immortal power
Near or far
Hiddenly
To each other linked are
That thou canst not stir a flower
Without troubling of a star.

(Francis, Thompson, *The Mistress of Vision*)

NATIONAL AND INTERNATIONAL PERSPECTIVES

Overview

Ian Rowlands

The papers in this section deal with various aspects of information policy formulation and implementation at the national and international level. Several common themes emerge. One is the provisional nature of information policies: there are inherent uncertainties connected with the policy environment, especially those to do with technological developments and economics, which mean that policy needs to be continually monitored, refined and sometimes re-conceptualized. Francis Aldhouse, for example, shows in his paper (p.114) how shifts in the wider policy and social environments have radically altered our perceptions of the nature of data protection over little more than a decade. With that thought in mind, it is somewhat disappointing to find that very little consideration is given in the literature to the evaluation (and termination, an even more difficult issue) of information policy. Perhaps the reasons for this lie in an incrementalist approach to policy-making, reflecting what Aldhouse sees as 'a common aspect of British political and legal culture: a reluctance to make grand gestures and [instead] an empirical [approach to the] development of policies'.

This is understandable, but whether it is good for democracy is another question altogether, placing as it does considerable room for manoeuvring on the part of non-elected officials. Information policy is inherently value-laden, especially so at national and international level. The question of values and their interpretation links each of the papers in this section. Policy-makers have daily to face a very difficult balancing act, negotiating an acceptable compromise between conflicting objectives, values and interests. These are often diametrically opposed, as in the following examples:

- market-led *versus* state-led visions of the development of the Information Society (Moore, p.89)

- freedom of expression *versus* rights of personal privacy (Aldhouse, p.114);
- the monopoly functions of patents and copyrights *versus* their informational aspects (Eisenschitz, p.128);
- the philosophy of open government *versus* retention of Crown copyright and restrictive licensing practices (Worlock, p.146).

Information policy, in common with all aspects of public policy, is deeply embedded in a political and cultural context from which it derives its values and its sense of direction. Some would even argue that information policy is fundamentally about the exercise of power by the state (Braman, 1990). In this context, information policy is just one strategy among many which the state draws upon to establish and consolidate its authority.

Browne (1997b) considers the values that underpin information policy and cites work by Overman and Cahill (1990) which presents a normative set of information policy values, as exemplified in US Federal legislative, executive and judicial decision-making over several decades (see Table 1 overleaf).

This value set provides a very useful tool for understanding what underpins information policy both as an area of scholarship and an area of practice. Seen from this perspective, information policy might be seen as a strategy for embodying and acting upon these fundamental values.

Values provide rather a slippery context for information policy, and they raise an important question: what is the nature of the overall framework within which information policy-making takes place? As Kristiansson (1996) points out, information policy-making activities have historically tended to focus *ad hoc* on specific issues and problem areas such as research and development, information market development, freedom of access to official information, legal aspects such as privacy, copyright and intellectual property rights. The legacy of this approach has been a fragmentation of policy-making responsibilities, institutions and discussion fora. The evident lack of coordination of these disparate but obviously related policy strands is something of a preoccupation among writers on national information policy. It may well be argued that information policy is so loose and broad a concept that it cannot and perhaps should not be accommodated within a single ministerial portfolio. What cannot be escaped, however, is that there appears

Table 1: Overman and Cahill's information policy values

Access and freedom	If democracy is to work, then people need to be well informed. Although rights to access information are enshrined in legislation in many countries there are significant tensions around the questions of access, security, and freedom of information.
Privacy	This is a widely accepted value in Western-style democratic societies although there are tensions which arise out of the needs of government and society on the one hand, and on the other, individuals' rights to privacy in their affairs.
Openness	This is about open government and the right of people to know about the processes of decision-making in government.
Usefulness	With the rise of the administrative state, governments began to collect records. 'Usefulness' refers to the idea that the worth of information is determined with reference to the use to which it is put. A key issue is who decides what is useful and, therefore, what is to be collected and stored.
Cost and benefit	This assumes that information has economic value, costs and benefits and raises problems of reconciling commercial interests and the public interest in the matter of the information collected by government.
Secrecy and security	Secrecy and security are two high profile values with significant issues around the question of the amount of latitude to be given to government officials.
Ownership	Intellectual property addresses not the ownership of tangibles but the form and expression of ideas through patents or authorship of texts of any kind. Here, issues of commercial interest can collide with the needs of individual users and society.

(Table adapted from Browne, 1997b).

to be no explicit overarching framework within which issues and conflicts may be resolved.

This is an important point so I will illustrate it by means of an example. Classically, the genesis of a public policy involves the recognition of a problem. Consider, for example, the following sequence:

Issue	People sleeping on the streets
Problem	Homelessness
Policy response	New forms of policing

What counts as a problem and how a problem is defined depend very much on the way that the policy-makers perceive it. A problem has to be defined, structured, located within certain boundaries, and given a name. The mechanics of this process prove crucial for the way in which a policy is addressed to a given problem. If we see people sleeping on the streets as a problem of vagrancy, then the policy response may be framed in terms of law enforcement and policing. We might also view the same issue as an indicator of social deprivation or a sign of failure in other policy areas such as community care; in which case, the policy response will obviously be very different (we might provide low cost housing, for example, or appropriate mental health care).

In his paper (p.114), Francis Aldhouse, the Deputy Data Protection Registrar, leads us through the series of events that led to the UK's Data Protection Act in 1984. He shows that the legislation was originally framed by the need to regulate international flows of automatically processed information pertaining to individuals. As he points out, its motivation was primarily commercial and the issue a largely technical one: 'it might as well [have] concern[ed] the thickness of plate for steam boilers'. Aldhouse then charts how perceptions of that issue have shifted, particularly in response to the intensification of computer power and new applications which are having profound social consequences. He concludes that 'the use of information technologies [has] become so pervasive an issue that information policy is not readily distinguishable from general social policy and notions of communitarianism and good citizenship'.

Several of the other papers in this section touch on various aspects of a grand design that politicians and journalists call the Information Society. Nick Moore (p.89) explores some of the concerns and motivations behind this concept. In his analysis of the underlying issues behind the Information Society ideal, Moore identifies fear as a major component: fears borne out of poor economic performance, globalization, structural employment, and North American cultural imperialism. He argues that Information Society policy is concerned with modernizing the telecommunications infrastructure, promoting industrial and commercial competitiveness, re-skilling the workforce, promoting social cohesion, extending democracy by making governments more open and accountable, and contributing to cultural development. This is a breathtakingly ambitious list of policy objectives and it is rather surprising that so little public or political debate has fastened onto the subject, in the UK at least.

Information policy invites a range of opinion and Barry Mahon (p.101) offers a more sanguine viewpoint, characterizing the Information Society as a convenient phrase for collecting together all sorts of issues and concerns in an apparently integrative framework so that politicians 'can create a warm feeling in audiences'. He suggests that in reality it has confused the debate which ought really to be focused on practical issues of information availability and access. Webster, a British sociologist, is even more polemic (1994):

> What I find most noteworthy is that Information Society theorists, having jettisoned meaning from their concept of information in order to produce quantitative measures of its growth, then conclude that such is its increased economic worth, the scale of its generation, or simply the amount of symbols swirling around, that society must encounter profoundly meaningful change. We have, in other words, the assessment of information in non-social terms—it just is—but we must adjust to its social consequences. This is a familiar situation to sociologists who often come across assertions that phenomena are aloof from society in their development (notably science and technology) but carry with them momentous social consequences. It is demonstrably inadequate as an analysis of social change.

While the problems which Nick Moore identifies as driving IS policy are real and pressing, there is a danger that the politicians are guilty of over-determining their ideas, based upon unsupported assumptions about the effects of information on society. As Braman (1990) points out, these assumptions may be 'so diffuse as to be inoperable ... The free flow of information, international cooperation, and peace are among the driving principles that have been offered to justify information policy'.

Tamara Eisenschitz (p.128) nevertheless argues that it is important that we work out commonly understood criteria for assessing policy in the information field: we currently have neither common measures nor common base-lines of assumption. If the Information Society concept is to become a reality, she argues, a more unified approach to information handling and a much more consistent regulatory framework will be required. Worlock (p.146) elaborates much the same point in his analysis of the ineffectiveness of UK tradeable information policy. He notes that there are real practical issues around the difficulty of defining precisely what is a source or primary document, and even more difficult, in defining precisely what constitutes 'value added'.

Towards an information policy regime?

Consensual approaches to thinking about a particular issue area in ways that provide a basis for decision-making are called policy 'regimes'. A regime may be thought of as a normative framework that is less rigid and formal than a legal system but nonetheless serves to provide a common understanding binding all parties together.

Since information policy is a relatively new area of public policy concern, an information policy regime may only just be evolving. While working policy-makers cannot put aside immediate problems until the larger theoretical issues have been resolved, it is possible to approach problems with an awareness of their theoretical context and large-scale socio-economic, political and cultural impact. The final thought goes to Sandra Braman (1990): 'to be "information-literate" in the twenty-first century will be to understand information technologies, messages, institutions, and effects within the context of ongoing explorations in both epistemology and the sociology of knowledge'.

Neo-Liberal or Dirigiste? Policies for an Information Society

Nick Moore

Abstract

We are undergoing profound change and countries all over the world are responding by developing policies intended to shape the development of Information Societies. The goals of these policies are remarkably similar, although it is possible to identify differences in the motivating factors. When considering the mechanisms that have been chosen to achieve the policy goals, it is possible to identify two broadly divergent models. One is based on neo-liberal economic philosophies and emphasizes the importance of market-led solutions, exploiting private capital. The alternative model can be described as dirigiste. It is based on a much greater degree of intervention and, consequently, places more emphasis on the role of the state as a participant rather than as a facilitator.

While it is too early to identify fully the effects of these policies, the author argues that neo-liberal policy mechanisms with their emphasis on narrow economic solutions are likely to be inadequate: the holistic approach that is characterized by the dirigiste model seems more appropriate.

Introduction

We are living at a time of profound change. The introduction of new information and communication technologies is having far-reaching effects on individuals, on organizations and on nation states. It is changing the ways in which we work, learn and play; changing the relationships between individuals and the state; changing the nature of business and commerce; and, in the long-run, it will change fundamentally the characteristics of cultures that have evolved over centuries.

It is not surprising, therefore, that governments are trying to find the most appropriate responses to deal with this situation. What is unusual is the fact that this has produced a flurry of information policy formulation, the like of which we have never seen before. Just five years ago, for example, Singapore was alone in having a clearly formulated set of national policies that were concerned with information and its use in society. Today, just about every country of significance has produced some form of information policy or is making an attempt to position itself as an Information Society.

Across the world, the goals of these information policies are surprisingly consistent. What differs are the mechanisms that have been selected to achieve the goals. Two dominant models have emerged in the last few years; each has different origins and characteristics and each is likely to produce different effects. It is now becoming possible to assess which is likely to produce the most successful and enduring model of an Information Society.

The goals of information policy

The goals of information policy are remarkably similar. The hopes and aspirations of Bill Clinton and Al Gore in the USA are, when it comes to the development of an Information Society, uncannily like those of Jiang Zemin and Li Peng in China. They are a set of aims that are shared by the G7 nations, by developing countries like Thailand, by newly industrialized countries like South Africa and by small but mature economies like Belgium or Finland.

Broadly, what all these states are trying to achieve is, firstly, cheap and efficient telecommunications infrastructures that will enable individuals and organizations to communicate with one another. Initially the need is to extend the reach of these networks so that there is universal service. Increasingly the pressure is on to expand the capacity to accommodate the larger and larger flows of digital information. An efficient telecommunications network is the single most important element in a successful Information Society.

The second goal is to improve industrial and commercial competitiveness and productivity by encouraging organizations to use information as a resource. The productivity gains can come in many ways: through better use of research to speed innovation; through the automation of administrative processes; or through the application of information-intensive management techniques. The secondary expectation is that, once individual companies and the overall economy become more competitive, it will be possible to make a fundamental shift in the nature of the economy by moving into more information-intensive operations that increase the value-added by each worker and, in so doing, bring about real increases in *per capita* incomes.

A prerequisite for this is a skilled workforce or, more properly, an educated and flexible workforce. The third policy goal is, therefore, to improve education and training. All citizens must have basic information and technology skills. Many need to develop these to a high level so that they can meet the needs of information-intensive organizations. What is more, the education and training system must accommodate the need for lifelong learning and a constant process of extending and enriching skills.

An Information Society is seen as a means of promoting social harmony and cohesion. In developed countries, this goal stems from a concern about the level of fragmentation that has developed in the last thirty years. Rising levels of crime, unemployment and social deviancy worry politicians and they see the creation of an Information Society as a means of halting the slide into chaos, although it is never made very clear how this will come about. In less developed countries, the same goal of social cohesion is identifiable but here the motivation comes not from rising levels of fragmentation, but from a concern to ensure that everyone benefits from economic growth. Thus the intention is to reduce the disparity between rural and urban areas, to lessen the gulf between the poor and the prosperous and, in countries like Malaysia, to ensure that there is racial and religious harmony.

This is closely related to a set of political goals. Al Gore sees the information superhighway as a means of promoting more informed democracy and a higher level of participation. It would be stretching the point to say that such aspirations are shared by Li Peng in Beijing, but even here there is a recognition that centralized planning is a brake on economic and social development and that it is necessary for the central organs of the state to become more transparent so that sensible and better informed decisions can be made in a devolved structure.

Throughout there is a concern about culture. There are those who perceive Hollywood and the American information complex as a means of exerting a new form of hegemony. Some of these reside in the USA and regard this as a good thing. Many more reside elsewhere and have a different point of view. What they have in common is a desire to ensure that the development of an Information Society enhances and strengthens the home culture and, wherever possible, promulgates it elsewhere.

Finally, most of the information policies seek to provide some form of support for the information services sector. This is seen as a key strategic asset for the future and most states are trying to do something to nurture it.

The underlying policy motivations

When we consider the underlying motivation for these policy aspirations the differences begin to emerge. Very broadly it is possible to identify two distinct clusters of motivation.

The first is dominant in the developed world and, in particular, in North America and Europe. It is motivation through fear. The dominant economies in the global economic system are seeing their positions eroded. New economies are emerging and changing the balance of power. This is producing a widespread concern about the loss of dominant economic positions and the consequent loss of influence on the world stage. At home there is a corresponding concern about social disruption brought about by high levels of unemployment and by other structural changes in society. All this produces pressure to exploit an economic opportunity in the hope that, by maintaining or, if possible, increasing levels of national income it will be possible to stave off social dislocation and, critically, bring more of the workforce into employment. The way out is seen to be a return to economic prosperity which will secure the country's standing in the world pecking order while tackling deep-seated social problems at home. Such a rationale is admirably set out in the recently published manifesto of Tony Blair's New Labour Party.

The alternative is a cluster of motivational factors associated with a similar desire for long-term economic growth and expansion. But here the starting point is different. In the less developed and newly-industrialized countries an Information Society is seen, not as a means of hanging on to an existing position, but as a path towards future prosperity through accelerated economic growth. This accelerated growth is, however, also seen as the key to solving long-term socio-economic problems, such as rural stagnation, urban blight, disparities in income, poor education and inefficient public services. All can be addressed, so it is thought, by better use of information. In this way it becomes possible to achieve a desired degree of social cohesion and, what is more, to bring about conditions where economic growth reinforces cohesion instead of weakening it.

There is also, in some countries, a desire to move towards a new socio-political order. In many of the countries concerned, democratic systems are relatively new and are settling down after a period of disruption. Clearly, information systems and the creation of an Information Society have a distinct bearing on the way in which the political system operates. Getting it right in a country like South Africa can be important!

The information policy mechanisms

The wide variations in motivation contribute to the diversity of mechanisms that are chosen to achieve the policy goals. Here it is possible to identify two distinct models which we might designate as neo-liberal and dirigiste.

Neo-liberal policy mechanisms

The neo-liberal model is, unsurprisingly, market-led. Private capital, operating through efficient markets, is seen as the driving force for the achievement of the policy goals. This carries the clear implication that the scope of the information policies is determined by what the private sector deems to be important, or profitable.

In this model the state acts as a facilitator. Its essential role is to create the conditions that will enable markets to flourish. It should intervene only in cases of market failure, and even then its intervention should seek to create the conditions where market mechanisms can operate. This approach is clearly enunciated in the G7 information policy documents and it is a strand that runs through the National Information Infrastructure policies of the Clinton administration and through the Bangemann approach to the creation of a European Information Society. It is an approach that found its purest expression in British Conservative policy.

If the state is a facilitator, then the private sector is the doer. It is the private sector that mobilizes the capital, makes the investment decisions, carries the risk and, if all works out well, makes the profit. In many developed countries this makes real sense. In Britain, for example, the privatized British Telecom generates very substantial flows of income and can channel these into infrastructure investment in ways that benefit both the nation and the company. Similarly, if foreign companies can be persuaded to invest their funds in a national infrastructure, then the nation is a net beneficiary. A similar rationale applies to the development of multimedia products. To create these investment conditions, however, it is necessary to place due emphasis on competition. Markets must be opened up, state-owned companies must be privatized and competition must be encouraged. The key to this, so the orthodoxy goes, is to deregulate. But, as the British government is discovering, introducing competition into an industry previously dominated by a state-owned monopoly is not an easy business and calls, paradoxically, for a high degree of regulation.

The emphasis on markets tends also to create a perception of people as consumers. Companies need to direct their products at these consumers and, if they are sufficiently powerful, to shape individuals' consumer preferences. There should be little need to educate the consumers so that they can use the information products; rather, the emphasis is on ease of use—what Peter Cochrane of British Telecom calls the 'three clicks maximum' approach.

Education and training are not neglected altogether. The private sector needs to be able to draw on a skilled workforce, and ensuring that there is an adequate supply is one of the state's most important roles as facilitator. The educational reforms are, therefore, determined primarily by the requirements of the employment market.

Clearly, this approach to information policy draws on neo-liberal, post-Keynesian economics. It is, therefore, most evident in those countries that advocate such economic philosophies. In the USA the approach underpins the information policies, although it is tempered and alleviated in a characteristically pragmatic way. In Britain the market-led approach predominates, with the government conceding only reluctantly that it even has a role as facilitator. Working from this extreme, it is possible to identify a range of countries which have basically the same approach but which is moderated to a greater or lesser degree: Australia, Canada, all of the European Union member states and South Africa have moderated a basically neo-liberal approach to their information policies.

Dirigiste policy mechanisms

At the other extreme is the dirigiste or interventionist model. Far from being led by market forces, policy implementation is driven by the state acting in accordance with a pre-determined set of objectives. Clearly, in such circumstances the state is a—possibly *the*—key player. As such, it has many different roles. It can be the provider of investment funds; it can be a producer of information products and services; it can own major assets such as the telecommunications network; it can use its functions as facilitator, contributor, consumer, regulator, arbitrator and leader to advance progress towards the achievement of the policy goals. Above all else, the state is seen as the leader, setting the goals and writing the policy agenda.

But the private sector also has an important role to play. Many of the states that have adopted a dirigiste approach to their information policy are fiercely capitalist, and private sector companies play a major part in the present and future information societies. The critical difference lies in the perception that there is a partnership between the state and the private sector. The trick is to determine which functions are best left to the state and which are best delegated to the private sector. Many of the countries following a dirigiste approach are developing or newly industrialized. In some cases it makes sense for the public sector to lead investment in the infrastructure. In others it is inevitable. The large amounts of capital investment required are not sufficiently attractive for private capital: the returns may be too uncertain; the pay-back period may be too long; the investment may be required in areas that are never likely to show a profit; or the existing companies may be too short of capital resources to take on the high level of investment needed. So the state takes on the task of financing the building of the infrastructure, possibly introducing competition into the construction and operation of an asset that remains in state hands. It is worth noting that this was the strategy that was used by nearly all developed countries to create their infrastructures.

Where the private sector is deemed to be the appropriate player, the aim of policy is to create conditions where competition can be managed rather than left solely to market forces. This approach stems from two beliefs. First, there is the need to protect local industries until they are in a position to compete on equal terms with global players. This is the rationale behind the Korean industrial policy that produced world-class companies like Hyundai, Lucky Goldstar and Samsung. The second belief is that markets are not always the best allocators of scarce national resources like capital and skilled labour. The requirements of capital, particularly international capital, frequently call for short-term returns when a long-term approach is needed. Markets are also not very good at determining the output of educational systems. In response to this, a system of managed competition has arisen. And it is being applied in the information policy arena, particularly in the telecommunications and broadcasting markets. Entry to certain markets is restricted. Local companies are offered licences as monopolies, duopolies or oligopolies so that they can build up a strong home base without having to worry too much about obliteration by powerful multinationals. Even in mature markets like the USA competition is managed so that entry by foreign-owned companies is restricted and controlled.

In such circumstances, regulation is seen, not as an evil to be eradicated, but as a policy instrument that can be used to achieve certain policy goals. The most obvious example is the need to achieve universal service. Open, unfettered competition will never ensure that telecommunications are provided universally, other than, perhaps, in a compact city-state like Singapore. It is, however, possible to achieve the universal service goal through regulation and by placing conditions on the companies licensed to provide telecommunications service.

The other striking difference in the dirigiste approach is that it views people as participants in the Information Society of the future rather than simply regarding them as consumers or as potential workers in information-intensive organizations. There is, therefore, a much greater emphasis on education at all levels. The aim is to create a whole population with the skills and abilities needed to function in an Information Society. This dirigiste approach to information policy reflects, as we have noted, the general political economy of the countries concerned. As such, it draws on a wide range of influences, including Confucius, Marx, and Keynes. The theories put forward by these and other individuals have been reinforced by the practical example of countries like Singapore, Korea and Japan which have rapidly grown strong through dirigiste economic policies. There is little reason to suggest that they will not continue to do so.

The information policy rollout

It is still very early to say with confidence what the effects of the different policy approaches will be. We are, however, reaching the stage where it is possible to venture some observations.

First, there is the speed of change. The technology is developing rapidly and, riding on this, dramatic changes are taking place in national economies as well as in individual organizations. The challenge is to restructure national economies so that they can take better advantage of the opportunities presented by an information-intensive world. The structural change that has taken place in the economies of countries like Korea, Taiwan, Singapore and, more currently, China is, frankly, breathtaking. Within a very short space of time they have made a transition which is every bit as fundamental as that which took place in Britain in the 200 years since 1780. Contrast that with the very slow pace of structural change that is taking place in Britain and in our European partners.

Within individual companies there is an even greater degree of change. In a short space of time, for example, IBM changed from being one of the world's most prosperous and stable companies to a lame duck, and then back again into prosperity. New industries have emerged and with them have come powerful new multinational corporations. Which policy approach seems better able to accommodate such rapid changes? The neo-liberals would say that competition creates the conditions that are most amenable to rapid change. And, given the relatively inflexible and inefficient political systems of the West, they may be right. But the dirigisme of East Asia seems to have produced companies that are much better equipped to cope with major structural change. There is, it seems to me, greater stability, allied with rapid expansion, in companies like Lucky Goldstar, Samsung, Fujitsu and Mitsubishi, than there is in comparable Western companies like Compaq, Intel, Apple or even Microsoft. It is this combination of stability linked to rapid expansion that is, I believe, the key to successful organizational development. Markets may provide one means of responding to changing conditions. An interventionist industrial policy, backed by a clear government vision, certainly seems to offer an effective alternative.

Closely related is the question of relative rates of economic growth. Here the neo-liberal approach seems to be out-performed by the dirigiste economies of East Asia and, increasingly, those of Latin America. During the last 25 years, in the neo-liberal economies of the West we have achieved modest rates of growth, of around 3 per cent a year. In Britain the long-term growth rate is much lower, closer to 1.5 per cent. Over the same period the dirigiste economies of East Asia have achieved average growth rates that are closer to 10 per cent. As they pass Western levels of GDP per capita, they show few signs of slowing down. Within those rapidly expanding economies, information-related organizations will flourish. The demands for information will grow; the ability to pay will increase; and there will be sufficient capital to invest in new products and services. There will also be a sufficient national surplus income to finance the needed investment in education, in social and cultural information services and in the overall development of an information-intensive society.

We have noted that in both neo-liberal and dirigiste philosophies, one of the aims is to achieve stability and cohesion. How have the two systems performed? Market forces seem to be doing little to increase social cohesion. If anything, levels of alienation and isolation are increasing. The dirigiste systems are also under stress. The promised reductions in rural isolation, for example, have yet to materialize in countries like China, Vietnam and Thailand, although in Malaysia the differences between rural and urban areas are being reduced. What is, perhaps, the most notable achievement of the last 25 years is the high level of stability that has existed in the dirigiste systems. Rapid change, dramatic growth, racial and ethnic imbalances, all exist within the dirigiste economies, yet there has been remarkable stability. A major challenge lies ahead in testing whether the political systems that have evolved are sufficiently robust to survive the increased transparency that will come as the societies become more information-intensive.

Finally, we should consider what is becoming known as the 'cultural ecology' of the Information Society. That is, the impact on cultures of the information and communication technologies. Broadly, will the shift towards a global Information Society mean that national cultures become subsumed within a world culture shaped in Hollywood and controlled by Rupert Murdoch? Or will we be able to use the technologies to enrich the diversity of global cultures? A neo-liberal approach, leaving such questions to the market, would almost certainly result in an American cultural hegemony. The alternative is to resist such incursions so as to protect and nurture local cultures. Already countries like China, India, Indonesia, Malaysia, Singapore and Vietnam are developing policies that will constrain the impact of undesired cultural influences and I feel sure that the pressure to protect indigenous cultures will grow in the years to come.

Lessons for the future

What lessons can we learn from this analysis? The first thing that strikes me is that we are dealing with a pervasive phenomenon, one that will have a significant impact on the social, economic, political and cultural life of a country. Information is a key element in the whole fabric of a society and the changes that are taking place in the technologies used to manipulate information will have a profound effect. For this reason, if for no other, I believe that policies that are derived from narrow economic philosophies are inadequate. The neo-liberal approach which attempts to subject all issues to resolution by market forces may be an acceptable way of dealing with industrial and commercial policies, but moving us towards an effectively functioning Information Society requires more than changes in the economic system. Information policies need to address a wide range of social, political and cultural issues in ways that both accommodate and facilitate economic change.

The dirigiste approach, in marked contrast, emphasizes an holistic approach and, it seems to me, is almost certainly a more appropriate means of developing an Information Society. It is, therefore, encouraging to note that it is possible to identify a more interventionist approach emerging in Europe as concern moves away from information industries towards information societies. The interim report from the Commission's high level group of experts sets out a policy agenda that goes way beyond a reliance on market forces and private capital, although it has to be acknowledged that the overall thrust of European Union policy is still essentially neo-liberal. I am not at all sure how long Britain and Europe will be able to hold the line. We do not have an information market that is as big or as homogeneous as the United States. We also lack the dynamism and impetus of growth that exists in the Asia-Pacific Region. We therefore face severe competition from both the East and the West. And, as a consequence, we have an information services sector that is steadily losing out to American competition and that is failing to capitalize on the rapidly expanding East Asian market.

We have yet to crack the difficult task of introducing effective competition into the monopolistic telecommunications industry, with the consequence that our telecommunications infrastructure is expensive and inadequate. Yet we continue to follow the dogma of deregulation. We are very slow to introduce information-intensive working practices into our organizations, whether in the public or private sectors, and so we are slipping down the world competitiveness league tables. We are failing to make the quantitative and qualitative changes in the education system that will produce people with the skills and abilities needed by information-intensive organizations. We are not even able to produce an acceptable basic level of information literacy in our school leavers. And we are proving to be very slow at reforming our social and political systems to accommodate a new information-intensive social order.

The neo-liberal approach does not seem to have served us well. Success is not obligatory and the price of failure will be high. The time has come, I believe, to develop a different approach, one that does not rely wholly on market forces but that recognizes the need for a clear vision and for a radically different approach to the achievement of the goals.

European Information Policy: the Role of Institutional Factors

Barry Mahon

Abstract

This paper offers a critical perspective on thirty years of European information policy development, tracing its origins in OECD (Organization for Economic Cooperation and Development) policy and bringing the story forward to the current debate over the Information Society. Throughout this period, institutional factors rather than purely rational considerations are seen to have been instrumental in shaping the policy outcomes. The author argues that there has been a regrettable tendency within the European political arena to conflate the terms 'policy' and 'expenditure'. He concludes that European information policy is too reactive to technological forces and developments and insufficiently grounded in the social and cultural fabric.

Introduction

The term 'European information policy' is almost an oxymoron. This may seem a harsh statement in view of the large amounts of money spent by various European institutions over recent years on information development, but the apparent harshness is designed to challenge a belief, still held in some quarters, that expenditure on information product and service development can be equated with 'policies'. In the case of the European Union, my personal experience would be that this is not so, at least not in recent years.

I first became acquainted with European information activities in the 1970s, a period when the OECD was deliberating the topic, and the European Community (EC) just beginning to address the issue. In my opinion the OECD really was dealing with policy, examining the consequences of various options for the OECD countries if certain scenarios were followed. As a method of policy-making this might not have been perfect (what method is?) but it did open up discussion on the matter. It can be said that the OECD work declined in direct proportion to the increase of European Community activity during the '70s and had all but finished by 1980. The work of UNESCO (United Nations Education, Scientific and Cultural Organization), which had been attempting to use the European and American discussion on policy as a framework for less developed countries and regions, followed a similar course. This process was derailed somewhat by the McBride Report which essentially dealt with the mass media, and by the policies of the then Director-General of UNESCO which led directly to US and UK withdrawal. All this is by way of an introduction to my main theme, that European information policy in recent years is essentially European Union policy. I will concentrate on this issue and its consequences.

The early policy developments

Briefly, and to set the scene, I will review European information policy development since the late 1960s. As noted earlier, the European Community (from 1973 a community of nine nations—the original six plus Denmark, Ireland and the UK) had become the focal point for policy discussion. There was a degree of continuity with what had gone before since many of the participants had also been involved in the previous discussions in the OECD.

It might be said, although there is no evidence to my knowledge to prove it one way or the other, that the EC discussions awakened a sense of 'policy xenophobia' which tended to sharpen up the differences between European and US developments. It might even be said that European policy began to diverge, or at least that a certain lack of coherence became evident, coincident with the tendency to see Europe as a different policy *milieu* from the USA. What is certain is that two countries of the EC were developing policies for their own national information development, while most of the others were not. The two countries, France and Germany, were developing policies based on the need to maintain a presence in the information sector in the face of increasing US dominance, especially in science, technology and medicine (STM), and in view of the potential threat of Cold War politics leaving them isolated from US sources. However, these policies diverged markedly in their implementation. Germany developed the FIZ (Fachinformation Zentrum) concept, a series of speciality centres each devoted to an area of scientific and technical information, which would be responsible for the management of information in their territory. Meanwhile, France was developing competencies in information manipulation, typically in structural chemistry, and in ensuring the survival of the French language as a vehicle for scientific communication. As stated earlier, the other countries were not really creating policy, certainly not at the same level of detail nor with the expenditure commitments of France and Germany.

Into this environment stepped the European Community in 1974/75 with the first Action Plan in information. This had been initiated in 1971 as the first Council of Ministers Decision on information policy, essentially founding the concept of a common European Information Network, although lacking in detail. As a keystone of European policy this first Decision and the Action Plan deserve more detailed examination. They serve to illustrate some of the institutional factors that still influence the policy discussion today.

The early policy decisions and their subsequent influence

During the 1960s the EC had a significant role in nuclear research and development and operated several research centres. The outputs from these centres, together with the results from other work in the Member States, created a significant information store which was managed, at least in part, by the EC itself. There was also close collaboration with the UN in this sphere. By the late 1960s the EC's role in nuclear R&D was being scaled down and, with it, its direct involvement in information activities. Necessity being the mother of invention, the need to find new fields of activity led directly to the concept of developing a European level of information activities. This idea developed naturally out of the recognition that, as the EC developed, the pooling of information resources would become an important economic element for the future. Even at that time the prospect of decline in the traditional industries was mooted and the changeover to service industries was underway. The intention was that information, the product of a well developed and organized education and R&D sectors, would be the *leitmotiv* for future expansion. The 1971 Council of Ministers resolution was an agreement to implement such a policy.

However, in the years immediately following the decision, perhaps actually influenced by the discussion which led to it, France and Germany began to examine the national implications of a future information-dependent economy, although it was not obviously referred to in those terms. Viewed from the perspective of the late 1990s it might be seen as the first stirrings of the Information Society policy discussion which so preoccupies us today.

In parallel, new countries were joining the Community, including the UK, which was an active information sector participant with the particular advantage of the English language.

By 1973/74, when the first plan was being developed, the EC Directorate with prime responsibility for the information sector, DG-XIII, had a British Director-General and a new (French) Director who took the bold step of basing policy on the as yet untried technology of remote access to large computerized information stores. This aligned closely with the German FIZ concept (the FIZs could be seen as major future suppliers) and also accorded with French policy. The UK, as the other major player, had no declared policy but rapidly announced the development of a number of 'hosts' to be connected to the shared resource of the network. The UK, because of the English language, was perceived to be in a less vulnerable position than France or Germany and this was illustrated by the active collaboration between US and UK information interests and the progress of UK information products in the US marketplace.

Note that the only online information centre actually operational in Europe at that time, the European Space Agency (ESA), was not directly involved in these developments. Some of the personnel who represented EC countries on the committee which supervised ESA's information activities also served on the EC's own policy committee, but national development was given priority. So, the illustration of institutional influence begins. The EC was seen by some as a threat, by some as an opportunity, and by others as an impediment to their own developments. The EC had wanted to liaise closely with ESA, a policy that was welcomed in principle but not approved in practice.

Again, this assessment may seem harsh, but as an illustration of how, in reality, policy was implemented its essential accuracy has been borne out by subsequent events. Today ESA represents an information activity which is outside the mainstream of European policy, however defined, managed separately and not party to the day-to-day process of what passes for policy-related discussion at the EU level.

Later developments, funding mechanisms and the concept of Framework programmes

Moving rapidly forward, the policies of the 1970s were still being implemented in the period up to 1980 or 1981. They had not had a smooth path. In the early stages, particularly, the smaller Member States resented the concentration of 'new' information services in the larger countries. Although compromises were discussed, the reality was that the smaller countries secured no support for their own development and were only marginally involved in, for example, the shared creation of databases, a concept which was central to some aspects of European policy.

Around this time, when the larger countries were allocating moneys to national actions, and the European Community itself was spending almost 100 million ECU, US suppliers were beginning to market their services within Europe with some success. Indeed it has been suggested that EC actions to publicize online information succeeded only in boosting US market share, since at that time they were the most effective suppliers. Their products were in English, a language which was well known and understood by professional users, especially in Scandinavia. Early Eusidic (European Association of Information Services) papers illustrate the serious conflict between EC policy and the requirements of the advanced information seekers, the high technology industries.

By the early 1980s the EC's policies in the information area were undergoing change, coincident with a change of personnel in DG-XIII and the implementation of EC-wide research and development programmes, the first of which was ESPRIT.

ESPRIT introduced a major policy change—the availability of a large fund to be administered directly by the European Commission, to provide subsidies for research projects. In parallel, the information programmes introduced the concept of calls for proposals, a scheme to make money available for the development of new or improved information products and services which would be offered on the (by then) widely available data communications networks. It was at this point that the explicit and direct relationship between the expenditure of money and the development of policy arose. It has clouded policy development ever since.

The ESPRIT programme was based on a policy of spurring investment in research and development to ensure Europe's survival in IT. Representatives of the major European IT companies participated directly in the programme's management to ensure the relevance of the work. It may have succeeded, although it is perhaps too early to judge. What is clear, however, is that it has not ensured the survival of a major European force in the production of IT equipment. Perhaps this was inevitable given the nature of global cost competition in this sector, but nonetheless it represents the loss of a significant base upon which to develop software: the major mass market software products and associated revenues are certainly not European. However, the ESPRIT programme has probably allowed Europe to develop active niches in the market.

The influences of ESPRIT thinking on information policy are twofold. First, and as already stated, the relationship between EC money and policy, together with the pervasiveness of IT thinking, created overlaps in the management of activities which have a significant information content. As another illustration of institutional influence, the major IT programme developments took place in the European Commission's Brussels locations, while the information programmes remained centred in Luxembourg where they had begun. This may not of itself seem significant until one realizes that the political centre of EC activity lies firmly in Brussels with no serious input from Luxembourg.

The ESPRIT programme spawned a whole series of related actions, in education, medicine, transport, telecommunications and other sectors, all working under a common policy framework. The word 'framework' is now enshrined in the name of the overall programme of development of the EC's capabilities, infrastructure and application in information technology. The current Fourth Framework programme for research and technical development has been allocated a budget of over 14 billion ECU over five years.

During most of this period the EC's information policies and associated programmes were strictly segregated from developments in the IT area. It is clear that the information programmes were developed without a policy framework, being mere continuations of existing actions with small additions, such as the discussion of legal issues, together with some actions in relation to the less developed parts of the Community and the ever present mention of small and medium-sized enterprises (SMEs) (without any real actions for the latter). It was not until the early 1990s that information-related actions were specifically added to the Framework Programme, the first being the Libraries Programme and later Information Engineering. It should be noted that neither ended up in the R&D programmes as a result of a policy discussion involving the Member States at anything other than civil servant level.

While this was underway, national information programmes waxed and waned. The French programme was effectively diverted by successive changes in the surrounding administrative structure and by the decision to build a new National Library, while the German programme only just survived an extremely critical assessment of its effectiveness by the Federal audit office. A direct consequence of this latter event was the establishment of STN International, a joint US/Japanese/German online facility mainly in chemistry. This cut directly across the discussions which were then underway outside the EC framework, between French and German interests in chemistry, to create a joint activity.

The situation today

In analyzing the situation in Europe today, I am struck by three elements: the movement towards 'market' solutions in public policies generally; the predominance of grant-giving as a means of implementing policy; and the confusion caused by the introduction of the term 'Information Society'. I will deal with each of these in turn.

Market philosophy

The movement towards market philosophy can be said to have started in the UK in the early 1980s, especially in relation to the privatization of telecommunications. While it is true that the removal of the worst features of the monopoly positions of state controlled entities has been largely beneficial, it is not necessarily also true that it has improved information distribution. It is becoming increasingly clear that the policy of telecoms deregulation is currently at very different levels of development in the different countries of the EU. As a result, in European terms, the market for information services dependent on telecommunications is still distorted.

From the beginning the EU telecommunications policy debate has been isolated from the primary function that telecommunications provides: a means of distributing information. The failure of policy properly to separate the carrying from the carried has created a set of anomalies at the EU level that the Information Society (IS) debate is now trying to resolve. While the policy on telecoms has, in many cases, inhibited the carriers from wholesale involvement in information content, it has not been consistent. These inconsistencies have been aggravated by technical developments which make control, in the old sense, difficult, if not impossible. In addition, the policy has not clearly separated infrastructure provision from service provision and has thereby slowed the emergence of an Information Society in Europe.

In a bizarre way the Internet, which has been so beneficial to the information community, has contributed to the confusion of EU telecommunications policy. In the early days of R&D networking, European public telecommunications operators (PTOs) were quite happy to allow researchers to use leased line networks as 'closed' facilities between universities. In some countries the PTOs inhibited facilities such as IBM's European Academic Research Network (EARN), in favour of national alternatives. The Internet is the operational result of the research community's need for seamless e-mail, for example, which opened the floodgates, spurred on by the early deregulated operators, such as British Telecom, who ignored the 'old' rules, with consequences that are now well-known. The Internet, used as a generic term for data communications offering access to multimedia information, is in fact a network which uses 'non-PTO' standards—nothing more—but its availability has launched the greatest period of development the information sector has ever seen.

In a general sense privatization has influenced policy thinking throughout the world. However, it is highly selective. In the USA, for example, policy on government-owned information is clear. If the government paid for the data to be collected then the citizen has the right to the data in that form, free of charge. In the USA, private sector information suppliers may obtain public data on the same terms as individuals and then add their value. In the UK, in the case of company information or statistics, for example, the government competes with the private sector in supplying the data. In France, the government has published an elegantly worded statement on the subject of publicly-owned data but has not yet defined a policy in clear terms. In Germany, each of the Länder jealously guards its right to exploit public data, or not, as it sees fit.

Anomalies in the application of policy principles and political determinations have resulted in the EU's 1998 date for telecommunications liberalization being anything from a start date, to a mid-point on a move towards total freedom, to a point on a time line that runs to 2003 and beyond.

In the case of telecommunications the political debate was rushed. The Commission of Jacques Delors, imbued with the *dirigiste* mentality of that time, pushed the Member States to stare the issue of deregulation squarely in the face. The inevitable foot dragging and special pleading that follows such an approach has led to the present policy stalemate. The new debate on the Information Society has complicated matters further; there are too many anomalies in the basic policy framework (mainly in telecoms, but also those concerning content ownership, intellectual property and others) for the Information Society debate to be coherent. The result is a move away from formal policy to a situation where 'laissez faire' *is* the policy. This is justified by having a 'privatization policy' and is associated with concepts such as 'the modernization plan for the public enterprise sector' to quote the recent 'policy' of the new Spanish Minister of Industry.

The High Level Group of Experts, set up to advise the EU's Commissioner responsible for social policy on the Information Society, have taken a different view (CEC, 1996):

> In this report, we focus our attention on ways in which information can be converted into useful knowledge, so that the 'information economy' may become a 'knowledge-based economy' and the technology be put at the disposal of all.

They continue:

> Obviously, in an increasingly information-dependent society, a notion of universal service guaranteeing some level of equal access; neutrality with respect to users; continuity; availability; and adaptability to needs will remain essential. Communication will more than ever be of 'general interest'. The current notion of universal service has been defined as the 'basic service offered to all in the Union at affordable tariff conditions and at a standard quality level'. Such a service is of course much more difficult to identify when confronted with the wide and increasing array of complex and competing ICTs [information and communication technologies] associated with the Information Society.

Grant giving as policy

The structures for managing R&D in Europe are dominated by the EU programmes, as has already been mentioned. Increasingly in recent phases of the programmes, insufficient time has been allotted to assess or reassess what progress has been made, or not made, as the case may be. For example, the Oakley review of the EU's Libraries Programme and the various reviews of IMPACT and preceding programmes have never been the subject of widespread debate amongst the participants in the sector. The review process is itself part of the political process, designed to satisfy administrators. They are often undertaken by unsuitable or less than wholly qualified people for the task in hand. It is widely reported, for example, that the reviewers are subject to considerable pressure to ensure that they are not too critical. Furthermore, there is an internal dynamic within the various departments with responsibility for programme management to 'keep going', based on a fear of losing budget allocation in the next round if there is any slow down in spending.

The methodology of calls for proposals, now homogenized in the rush to submit proposals on four fixed dates per year, has created a commodity approach to project work and precluded a serious examination of policy. What was intended as a manifestly fair way of ensuring that all proposers had the same chance has instead developed into a primarily bureaucratic procedure in which proposal brokers become key players. The calls procedure requires considerable editorial skill in designing proposals which catch the eye of evaluators, who in many cases are also proposers, although not necessarily in the same field. The evidently artificial nature of the process is accentuated by schemes (using the same selection procedure of submission and evaluation) to provide money for the purposes of proposal creation and partner finding. Evaluation of proposals has become an incestuous process, and has developed into a race, where efficiency in processing the submissions is better rewarded than identifying innovative ideas.

According to Arnoud de Meyer, Professor of Technology Management at INSEAD, 'the danger of the Brussels strategy is that it can lead to R&D projects being grant-led rather than being developed in the best interest of the country or company in question' (*Financial Times*, 26 June 1996). To which one might add: 'or of the community of nations'.

The evolution of the EU processes of grant-giving has led to a diminution in national involvement. Not altogether apocryphal stories are told of projects being advised to 'go to Europe' for their money; and what started as a valid exercise at the national level in helping potential participants to make proposals has turned instead into a process of 'sieving' the ideas to ensure a good result. This is accompanied by nationally funded 'how to' guides, designed to prepare proposers for the handout of moneys and guide them to 'suitable' programmes. This process becomes ridiculous when, as has been observed by those assessing the proposals, the same project is submitted to different programmes, sometimes at the same time, but more often having been disappointed in a previous round of assessment in another programme area.

One of the strangest anomalies created by the EU programmes is the separation of naturally related areas of the information sector. For example, the newly approved Info2000 programme, the Telematics for Libraries programme and the Information Engineering actions are dealt with separately, albeit in the same administrative division. Info2000 is funded outside the Fourth Framework budget; Libraries and Information Engineering are within the 'Telematics' section of the Fourth Framework programme but are dealt with by separate administrative units, different again from the unit dealing with Info2000. It can be countered that administration and policy should be separated. But, in EU terms, administration relates directly to budget availability, and budget is allocated to units on an individual basis following higher level decisions which are supposed to be based on policy.

Compounding these anomalies is the diffusion of efforts to deal with the issue of intellectual property rights. Intellectual property rights are discussed in the Legal Advisory Board of DG-XIII in Luxembourg; at the same time, they are the subject of hearings under the aegis of the Directorate of the European Commission which deals with single market questions; research, in a number of projects, is funded under the IT part of the Fourth Framework programme; and finally, they are treated as part of the international discussions on trade in another section.

It might be assumed that such anomalies are acceptable, since the Member States have control of the policy issues. If the Member States *did* have such control, it would indeed be acceptable. However, decisions on the programmes are made at a very high level and within a policy framework of vague proportions where broader Union policy is paramount, with the result that individual programmes are reduced to the dimensions of paragraphs in the final document. As is common with such activities, the final texts are agreed by senior civil service personnel who are subject to political principles laid down by their governments and the need to reach consensus in the international sense. Coherence of the national policies, if indeed there are such, inevitably suffers in this situation.

A single European-wide research and development programme dealing with 'information' is clearly unrealistic. It is, however, equally unrealistic that while the IT-dominated Fourth Framework programme is projected to spend 14 billion ECU in the period 1994-1998, information-specific actions such as Telematics for Libraries should have only 50 million ECU and Information Engineering about 30 million ECU. I am not arguing that the allocation should be based on numbers of libraries or information entities, but its role should be more clearly delineated in an overall R&D spend on 'information'.

The Information Society

Reference has already been made to the Information Society in the discussion on telecommunications and privatization policy. The 'Information Society' is a convenient phrase for collecting together all sorts of issues and it is one which politicians use easily. It creates a warm feeling in audiences and can appear to cover all the policy issues in the debate. In reality it has clouded the discussion.

Commissioner Bangemann's High Level Group of Experts have made laudable efforts to rationalize the matter. Their discussions have placed the Information Society within the context of a 'learning society'. However, they note that (CEC, 1994):

> ... appropriate emphasis on learning illustrates that, although access to the information superhighway is and will continue to be important, it is insufficient to ensure the rapid development of a knowledge-based economy ... it is the ability to use information and to transform it into knowledge that is important.

It is this latter aspect that should rightly be at the centre of the debate since it is crucial to the information sector.

Much of the discussion of the Information Society focuses on: the prospect of several hundred channels of television; the 'risk' of cultural domination by Hollywood; the manufacture and sale of devices by Pacific Rim countries; and the dominance of a few major media moguls. While these are real and important issues, they tend to dominate (and distort) the policy debate. If a knowledge-based economy is the primary objective, then we need to focus the debate on achieving that. In the information sector we need to concentrate our efforts on ensuring that Europeans have comprehensive, easy and cost-effective access to the information they need. That should be the central point of the debate and from it should flow the policies.

Conclusions

The (sad) conclusion of this review is that we have lost track of policy on information in the European context. I began with the assertion that European information policy is an oxymoron. I now tend to the conclusion that it is less an oxymoron than a very confused set of discussions and debates which are dominated at various points by the need to react to some wider global development; some technological breakthrough; media hype; or simply the appearance of being up-to-date. There are indications that some of the participants in the debate are beginning to look beyond this to the wider social and other issues. Unfortunately, at the European Union level, the information policy debate includes few, if any, professional participants from the information sector, much less policy researchers from that area. Is this because they have become too focused on 'projects' and short-term actions which don't fit into specified policy frameworks?

I have no answer to that question, but I do suggest that we need to debate it.

Implementing Information Policies: Some Data Protection Experience

Francis Aldhouse

Abstract

This paper concentrates on the specific area of data protection implementation, rather than attempting to cover implementation of information policy as a whole. The intellectual machinery to be used is problematic. How does one define the problems? In the 1970s there were concerns about the threat posed by computing power to personal privacy, resulting in the 1981 Council of Europe Convention and other international instruments. Pragmatic business concerns arose about the use of data protection as a non-tariff barrier. The legislative reaction to those concerns has created a new political climate and future legislation will address personal privacy as a human rights issue. Incremental pragmatism creates problems of unexpected consequences: a notable example concerns personal privacy and the media. There is a need to balance privacy and freedom of expression, but difficulties arise in securing consensus. Similar difficulties are found in securing compliance with new legislation when passed. Advice-giving and other procedures have been adopted to assist organizations to adapt to new patterns of behaviour, e.g. direct marketing opt-outs. Data protection implementation is to be seen as an exercise in long-term education and cultural change. The future promises an intensification of these issues: the adoption of 'electronic government' and adjusting the implementation of ubiquitous computing environments to conventional social protocols turns information policy into general social policy.

In this paper I shall seek to address, albeit indirectly, five of the questions raised for this Workshop session in connection with the implementation of information policy. They concern:

- the responsibility for implementing policy;

- securing the commitment of stakeholders and ensuring compliance;
- interaction and competition between policies;
- the power structures underlying the adoption and implementation of policy; and
- the relationship of (information) policy to (information) technology.

I shall try to illustrate these issues in the particular field with which I am familiar, but I do not seek to propound any overarching principles.

First, as a stranger to the discourse of information policy, I have found some difficulty in identifying a unified set of topics which might be the subject of something called 'information policy'. Indeed, if one considers the nine categories referred to by Ian Rowlands (this volume, p.37), the stranger might readily conclude that the only element unifying information technology policy, intellectual property, information disclosure, confidentiality and privacy, and the others, is that they are all of concern to librarians and information scientists. This empirical and pragmatic approach to identifying the concerns of information policy might be most practical, but as a consequence I shall confine myself to remarks about an element of the total scene in which I can claim some expertise, namely data protection. If these remarks have any bearing on what makes for a successful 'information policy', then it is to be understood that I speak of many policies relating to different information issues and I do not have in mind any comprehensive scheme.

This line of thought leads naturally to questions about how one should address topics as disparate as intellectual property and privacy. Even if there were a useful set of consistent analytical tools deployed by information scientists, it is not clear that those are uniquely the best ways of conceiving of and addressing particular problems. The intellectual framework to be chosen is not a trivial matter, because it will often determine how a problem is seen and shape the political debate about its solution. I hope that point will emerge from subsequent remarks about the history of data protection policy.

The Introduction to the Explanatory Report to Convention 108, the 1981 Council of Europe Data Protection Convention (Council of Europe, 1981) says the following:

> Compared with manual files, automated files have a vastly superior storage capability and offer possibilities for a much wider variety of transactions, which they can perform at high speed.
>
> .... 'Information power' brings with it a corresponding social responsibility of the data users in the private and public sector. .... some countries have built into their domestic law special controls, for example in the form of a licence for export. However, such controls may interfere with the free international flow of information which is a principle of fundamental importance for individuals as well as nations.

The Commentary in the Explanatory Report on Convention 108 tells us at paragraph 25:

> The preamble reaffirms the commitment of the signatory States to human rights and fundamental freedoms. Moreover, it acknowledges that the unfettered exercise of the freedom to process information may, under certain conditions, adversely affect the enjoyment of other fundamental rights (for example privacy, non-discrimination, fair trial) or other legitimate personal interests (for example employment, consumer credit). It is in order to maintain a just balance between the different rights and interests of individuals that the convention sets out certain conditions or restrictions with regard to the processing of information. No other motives could justify the rules which the Contracting States undertake to apply in this field.
>
> It is also underlined that the convention should not be interpreted as a means to erect non-tariff barriers to international trade or to restrain the exchange of scientific and cultural information.

At the same time as Convention 108 was being developed, the Organization for Economic Cooperation and Development was developing Guidelines (OECD, 1980) with a similar content to the Council of Europe Convention. The Guidelines are to 'apply to personal data, whether in the public or the private sectors, which, because of the manner in which they are processed, or because of their nature or the context in which they are used, pose a danger to privacy and individual liberties'.

The Guidelines recognize that transborder data flows of personal data contribute to economic and social development and that incompatible domestic legislation could hinder such flows. It would seem that the Guidelines and Convention 108 had a similar motivation. But what was that motivation?

Certainly there were those who took a legally-based human rights approach to the issue. That can be found in Convention 108 which expressly refers to such matters and can be seen as seeking to balance the rights to privacy found in Article 8 with rights to freedom of expression found in Article 10 of the European Convention on Human Rights (Council of Europe, 1981).

Another stream of thinking is technological-based anxiety, fear of the machine—a fear that has sometimes been amply justified by cases relating to bugging and hacking that have come to public attention. The Younger Report on Privacy (Cmnd 5012) in July 1972 dealt with these computer-based anxieties and, as Chalton and Gaskill (1988:1002) remind us in reviewing the history of data protection, '87 per cent of those interviewed during the Younger survey said that they would regard details of their private lives being recorded on a big central computer, with any of the information being available to anyone who asked for it, as an invasion of privacy and 85 per cent thought that such a possibility should be prohibited by law'. The British concern of this nature goes back some years. For whereas Alexander Lyon published a Bill in 1967 to protect individuals from invasions of privacy, by 1969 Kenneth Baker was proposing a Data Surveillance Bill to address these specific concerns of technological threats to informational privacy.

There is, however, a third stream of thought in these debates. Both the Council of Europe and OECD felt it necessary to produce an international legal instrument because of threats to transborder data flows. One could allege that data protection laws only purport to concern themselves with the protection of personal privacy, but are in reality part of a wider game to control international trade and particularly the new information and communication technologies. Ian Lloyd (1993:23) reminds us that American commentators have expressed just such views about Convention 108 and the US State Department seemed to comment adversely on the limited references in the Convention to privacy protection.

So what was data protection for? It is not necessary to find a unique answer to that question. Mixed concerns come together and a partial resolution has been found in various international instruments. On the adoption of Convention 108, the United Kingdom Government had to decide what course to take. The Government's reasons for promoting data protection legislation were given clearly by the then Home Secretary in the House of Commons on 30 January 1984:

> ... first ... reassure people that .... there are special safeguards for individual privacy... secondly ... membership of the European data protection club ... a very important commercial interest ... British firms not placed at a disadvantage ...

The UK must not be placed at a commercial disadvantage and data protection law protects individuals. The commercial motivation, although given second by the Home Secretary, might seem paramount in this thinking.

However mixed the motives, since July 1984, the UK has had a Data Protection Act. The Act requires data users (those who keep on computer information about individuals) to register with the Data Protection Registrar and to comply with eight data protection principles; individuals have certain new legal rights, of which the most important is the right of subject access (to obtain a copy of information kept about them). The eight principles are drawn from Convention 108 and can be enforced by the Data Protection Registrar. Those principles form a code of good information-handling practice:

The Data Protection Principles

1. The information to be contained in personal data shall be obtained, and personal data shall be processed, fairly and lawfully.

2. Personal data shall be held only for one or more specified and lawful purposes.

3. Personal data held for any purpose or purposes shall not be used or disclosed in any manner incompatible with that purpose or those purposes.

4. Personal data held for any purpose or purposes shall be adequate, relevant and not excessive in relation to that purpose or those purposes.

5. Personal data shall be accurate and, where necessary, kept up to date.

6. Personal data held for any purpose or purposes shall not be kept for longer than is necessary for that purpose or those purposes.

7. An individual shall be entitled:

   (a) at reasonable intervals and without undue delay or expense
      (i) to be informed by any data user whether he holds personal data of which that individual is the subject; and
      (ii) to access to any such data held by a data user; and

   (b) where appropriate, to have such data corrected or erased.

8. Appropriate security measures shall be taken against unauthorized access to or alteration, disclosure or destruction of, personal data and against accidental loss or destruction of personal data.

The Registrar is in a distinctive position, as a state official independent of Ministers and reporting directly to Parliament. The nearest comparable post is that of the Parliamentary Commissioner, although it is clear that he is more directly a servant of Parliament. Despite the reluctance of the UK to involve itself in privacy legislation, the enforcement structure in the 1984 Act is in some respects more powerful than that to be found in other countries. For example, in the private sector in Germany, ensuring compliance is largely the responsibility of in-company data protection officials with limited enforcement support from the Interior Ministries of the Länder.

The very existence of data protection legislation for twelve years and the caution with which the first and second Registrars have progressively established their authority have changed the nature of the political discourse. The 1984 Act makes no reference to personal privacy. It is 'an Act to regulate the use of automatically processed information relating to individuals and the provision of services in respect of such information'. It would seem to be purely technical regulatory legislation; it might as well concern the thickness of plate for steam boilers. Its motivation, as it seems from the then Home Secretary, was substantially commercial.

This approach to the policy of the legislation was reflected in the publicly cautious position of the Registrar. In 1991, the then Registrar, Eric Howe, wrote (1991:345):

> In the United Kingdom, the introduction of the Data Protection Act in July 1984 broke new ground. It was a novel and complex piece of legislation dealing with the rapidly developing information technology, which now touches on most aspects of human concern and endeavour.
>
> Its purpose was to create openness in the use of personal data in computing systems, to encourage good practice in using such systems, and to establish new rights for individuals. Implementation of this legislation calls for consideration not only of the Act itself, but also of other competing public objectives and policies.
>
> Two concerns are met by the Act:
>
> That arising from the threat which misuse of the power of computing equipment might pose to individuals. This concern derives from the ability of computing systems to store vast amounts of data, to manipulate data at high speed, and, with associated communications systems, to give access to data from locations far from the site where the data are stored; and
>
> That arising from the possibility of damage to the United Kingdom's international trade, which might have occurred if the United Kingdom had not ratified the Council of Europe Convention for the Protection of Individuals with regard to Automatic Processing of Personal Data. Countries ratifying this Convention might place restrictions on the transfer of personal data to countries which have not ratified it.

You will find no mention of personal privacy in that paper, but there is a clear statement that the Convention, which underlies the Act, was 'to protect individuals'.

Nevertheless, the Act exists and it also drew its life from concerns other than international trade: anxieties about informational privacy going back at least 30 years in the UK and expressed formally in the language of human rights in Convention 108 whose preamble recognizes 'that it is necessary to reconcile the fundamental values of the respect for privacy and the free flow of information between peoples'.

Those references to the origin of the legislation have given the courts the basis for declaring that the 1984 Act is privacy legislation. In *R v Brown [1996] 1 All ER 545,* Lord Hoffman stated that the 'Data Protection Act was therefore intended not only to protect the privacy of our own citizens'.

In that same case, Lord Griffiths said:

> The 1984 Act was enacted to implement ... the Council of Europe Convention ... article 1 of the Convention sets out the object of the Convention.
>
> The purpose of this Convention is to secure ... for each individual .... in particular his right to privacy ...

Thus in the UK we have moved on from a piece of pragmatic legislation enacted to adopt good information-handling practice so as to ensure that we remained part of the information trading club. We now, through the Courts, recognize that this legislation had a human rights background and that it exists to protect, at least in part, personal privacy. I suspect that this process reflects a common aspect of British political and legal culture: a reluctance to make grand gestures, and an empirical development of the policies to be applied. This whole approach is reflected in the legal theory underlying our statute law: that each statute is a modification of the Common Law and in the absence of the statute the answer to a problem (even a negative answer) may be found in the common law. This conservative but flexible pragmatism seems to have served us well, but can create unexpected problems, especially when it is used to address fast-moving technologies.

The Data Protection Act was conceived as dealing with a small problem area: the concerns about computer-handling of personal information. This was thought of as an exceptional or unusual departure from the normal ways of treating information and therefore warranted special rules. Any problems that arose as a consequence of the special rules could be avoided by adopting the normal manual handling techniques. That cast of mind does not work well when faced with all-pervasive automated information technologies. The Data Protection Act no longer sets out the rules for the manipulation of a relatively small number of databases containing highly-structured sets of selective information searched according to strict criteria. The world has changed and we are faced with the consequences of applying to it a piece of legislation which was not constructed as a set of rules to apply to the handling of all information about individuals.

It is important to illustrate this consequence of the changing world. Perhaps the most sensitive effect is in the media. The issue of privacy protection and the media has been politically sensitive for many years. The Government last year announced in response to the report of the National Heritage Select Committee (1993:294-1) that there would be no legislation to enact a privacy tort or criminal offences as had been variously proposed. Sir David Calcutt (1993:xiii) had said:

> I recommend (recommendation 4) that the Government should now give further consideration to the extent to which the Data Protection Act may contain provisions which are relevant for purposes of misrepresentation in or intrusion into personal privacy by the press.

The Data Protection Registrar has made clear her view (ODPR, 1996a). Modern automated systems used by both the print and broadcasting media clearly bring their activities within the scope of the 1984 Act. As a consequence, the servants and agents of broadcasters and publishers must comply with the eight data protection principles. So, for example, they must obtain information fairly. There are no exemptions for the media in the 1984 Act. Is it 'fair' to use deceptive means to obtain information which will reveal a public scandal, criminal misdoing or other illegality? Data must be 'fairly' processed. Is it fair to process data to produce in a newspaper an article on the sexual life of a weather forecaster?

These questions may have to be answered by the Registrar, but it is not clear that she should have to. There is a need to balance rights of privacy (and I recognize that I have made no attempt to define or identify what those rights might be) with rights to freedom of expression. How is that to be done?

Once again, the law has moved on. On 24 October 1995 the European Union adopted Directive 95/46/EC (European Parliament, 1995) which sets out general rules for data protection in order to achieve an approximation of such laws within the European Union. Its substance is very similar to the 1984 United Kingdom Act for the reason that both owe their origin to Convention 108. However, the Directive differs in two important respects: first, in Article 1 it recognizes that it is seeking to protect the privacy of individuals; and, second, in Article 9 it recognizes that there is a problem in reconciling privacy with freedom of expression especially for the media. Article 9 runs thus

> Processing of personal data and freedom of expression
>
> Member States shall provide for exemptions or derogations from the provisions of this Chapter, Chapter IV and VI for the processing of personal data carried out solely for journalistic purposes or the purpose of artistic or literary expression only if they are necessary to reconcile the right to privacy with the rules governing freedom of expression.

How is that article to be applied in the UK? The Registrar has proposed that it should not be implemented as such (ODPR, 1996b). Freedom of expression is the right of us all, not just of journalists. Article 9 of Convention 108 and Article 13 of Directive 95/46/EC give authority to grant exemptions from data protection law in order to protect 'the rights and freedoms of others'. That is entirely proper, but what should those exemptions be? The Registrar proposes a mechanism for the new data protection law which will be required as a consequence of the Directive. That mechanism would enable the Home Secretary to grant exemption by order from the duties to obtain and process fairly and from the right of subject access where the right of the data controller was so weighty or public interest grounds so great that the interests of the individual should be overridden.

Will this proposal receive wide support? That is difficult to assess. This issue is one of such sensitivity, and the media feel under such pressure because of what they regard—sometimes, in my view, correctly—as the oppressive use of the defamation laws, that anything other than a very wide exemption for the media is likely to receive a hostile reaction. A judgement will have to be made by the legitimate political machinery; that is to say in Parliament. A balance will have to be struck. But what is notable is that the political decision now called for is not to impose privacy restrictions on the media, but to take away certain data protection rights from individuals. Although in principle the issue is the same and the decision should deliver the same result, in practice the political machine probably finds inaction, the negative decision, easier. Do we therefore run the risk of our media being subjected to unreasonable restrictions, because of the past history of media activity and the difficulty of legislating in this area at all?

At some stage there will be a new law and the Registrar (or her successor) will be faced with securing compliance, as was her predecessor in 1984. How does one achieve compliance? It is reasonably clear that the Registrar still has some considerable way to go. There would seem to be substantial under-registration, for example. One might say that this is a bureaucratic procedure and, if all data users respected the substance of data protection by full compliance with the eight principles, then technical breaches would be of little concern.

It is, however, not clear that there is a complete consensus on what is required by the broad, but vague, principles. There has to be a means for narrowing the area of disagreement and finally for resolving disputes. The latter is a judicial process, but that works best the more substantial the area of consensus and the more limited the decisions it is asked to take. So it would be possible to leave the resolution of the balance between privacy and freedom of expression to the courts. That would be to entrust to the courts major political and social policy decisions. In the context of entrenching the European Convention of Human Rights in UK law, T.A.G. Griffiths (1977:214) wrote that:

> Far more than on the judiciary, our freedoms depend on the willingness of the press, politicians and others to publicize the breach of these freedoms ...
>
> Judges are concerned to present and to protect the existing order. This does not mean that no judges are capable of moving with the times, of adjusting to changed circumstances. But their function in our society is to do so belatedly.

I do not wish to adopt a position in this debate on the role of the judiciary, merely to indicate that it is contested and that at stake are important questions about how we decide issues in our society.

Let us assume that narrower decisions are left to the judicial mechanism, but that some data protection supervisory authority has to enforce broad principles much as at present. I suggest that it will act as the Registrar has previously acted. The practice has been, after thorough internal discussion, to examine industry practices with organizations in that industry and to debate, often for a protracted period, the more contentious issues. Sometimes those contentious matters have been pointed up by complaints from the public, sometimes by an industry practice which it wishes to enshrine in a code of practice. So the Registrar's primary mechanism is debate, publicity and persuasion.

Another example might be helpful. The Registrar from an early stage commended the use of opt-out notifications in promotional literature. These give individuals the opportunity to indicate that they do not wish their names to be used for direct marketing purposes. The Registrar always made it clear that he thought this was the best industry practice and mentioned British Rail (ODPR, 1988:11) as an example of those who followed the best practice. He also made it clear that he could only enforce a requirement to obtain fairly, and in most cases that would mean telling people that their details would be used for sale on the list broking market, not necessarily giving them the opportunity to opt out. However, he also added that continuing to send direct mail when someone had objected would amount to unfair processing of data. The result was, nevertheless, that the industry came to believe and accept that it should allow individuals this right to opt out of the future use of their information. Ten years ago the direct marketing industry would argue that this was an unreasonable practice that would threaten their commercial existence; today it is the required industry standard; tomorrow, because of the EU Directive, it will be a requirement of the law.

The Registrar has adopted a practice of seeking to persuade organizations to his, or now her, point of view and using formal enforcement as a last resort. That has also enabled the Registrar to learn about the practice and the needs of that industry. This approach is a calculated and deliberate strategy.

The underlying view is that data protection is about the ready adherence to the eight data protection principles. As Eric Howe put it in his Second annual report (ODPR, 1986: 11): 'The objective should be for data protection and compliance with the Act to become a normal part of organizational operations.

That is to say that the natural cast of mind of organizations and those they employ should be (when using information about individuals) not what maximum benefit can they obtain from the information, but what uses and disclosures are fair to the individual. This is a major long-term educational exercise. Data protection legislation has moved the social goalposts. Individuals are now entitled to a greater degree of control over their information, but to be effective this approach must be internalized by those who use the information. How is that to be achieved?

The Registrar expressly developed a long-term strategy. In his Tenth annual report in 1994 (ODPR, 1994: 51), Eric Howe wrote:

> ... an educational publisher was contracted to produce formal teaching materials for use in secondary schools and these are scheduled to be available for the new academic year in September 1994. The long-term objective is to see a new generation knowledgeable about data protection emerging to adulthood in a few years time.

A cornerstone of Data Protection implementation is therefore the Datawatch pack. Produced in 1994, this pack has been produced to fit into many elements of the national curriculum. The underlying notion is that by educating our teenagers to think in terms of treating individuals fairly, society can change its whole approach to the use of information about individuals and absorb the fundamental notions of data protection.

The second Registrar, Elizabeth France, has generalized this approach. In her first annual report (ODPR, 1995) she explained that she had identified three priorities, two of which were:

- increasing awareness and accessibility of the Act amongst both computer users and the general public;
- stimulating debate over issues of public concern regarding privacy and the use of personal information.

Consequently, the Office of the Registrar has adopted a mission statement which runs thus:

> We shall promote respect for the private lives of individuals and in particular for the privacy of their information by implementing the Data Protection Act 1984 and influencing national and international thinking on privacy and personal information.

The implementation of data protection is accordingly seen by the Office as part law enforcement and part education and political debate.

What does the future have in store for us? We are promised an Information Society with an all-pervasive intensive technology supporting the availability, use and exchange of information. It is difficult to judge the pace at which these developments will happen, and one can be sceptical about some of the more imaginative proposals (McCrone, 1994), but there are powerful pressures driving public administration to adopt forms of 'electronic government' and the private sector to find machine-based methods of collaborative working at a distance and means of service delivery. If technologies develop as some suppose, we will find ourselves in a world of 'ubiquitous computing environments' (Bellotti and Sellen, 1993) in which we can all look to intensification of computing power to provide us all with comprehensive access to information about ourselves and our needs.

I have elsewhere (Aldhouse, 1996:160) written about the concerns of data protectors raised by the power which new technologies give the state, and for that matter private organizations, to track individuals. Electronic government service delivery necessitates identification of individuals and we shall all leave electronic footprints as we use these services. In the development of multimedia workspaces and ubiquitous computing environments, we are faced with the task of implementing these technologies in a manner which delivers the undoubted benefits whilst reflecting socially acceptable methods of behaviour. At a seemingly trivial level, media workspace systems have been designed so that when a colleague looks into your room by video camera, you hear the sound of a door opening.

The future undoubtedly holds the prospect of informational privacy issues of which the Registrar has only yet experienced the first suggestions. Changing technology or its applications are bringing about effects which can have profound social consequences. In part, data protectors have reacted by saying that implementations of technology can solve some of the problems. Personal data can be pseudonymized in many cases, as proposed by my Dutch and Ontario colleagues. But the adoption of such privacy-enhancing technologies will not come about automatically. There has to be an understanding of the importance of protecting private space for individuals. System developers must find it unacceptable to develop invasive systems. At that point the use of information technologies becomes so pervasive an issue that information policy is not readily distinguishable from general social policy and notions of communitarianism and good citizenship.

Legal and Regulatory Frameworks for Information Policy

Tamara S. Eisenschitz

Abstract

This paper looks at those aspects of information provision where the content is regulated. The areas examined in depth are patents and copyright, both forms of intellectual property. The laws on the use of personal information controlled by privacy and data protection, and publishing laws are introduced to illustrate basically similar behaviour and to note the differences.

The main questions asked are what was intended to be protected or facilitated originally and whether electronic dissemination methods and the accompanying economic and political changes have altered the goals. In each area examined, we can identify the balance of interests and the pressures put upon this balance by electronic dissemination and global markets. A comparison of the laws of information regulation with more established forms of property law maps the evolution of the older forms onto the Information Society. This gives a new overview of the effects of broad policy decisions on society.

To summarize, there are questions one might ask of any policy initiative concerning its intentions and its likely effects. The most important concern use rights, as opposed to property rights, and the importance of the meaning of any piece of information in terms of its regulation. Finally, some research questions that arise out of these ideas are outlined.

The regulation of information content

Information policy is currently being applied in increasingly complex situations. We need to explore how we can regulate while recognizing that complexity rather than denying it and risking over-simplification. Rowlands and Turner also recognized complexity as a fundamental characteristic of information policy in the previous section (p.46).

I concentrate in this paper on the regulation of information content. Much effort has been directed towards regulating the equipment which forms the information infrastructure and the services which are to be offered on it. Content is currently taking centre stage as the perspective most urgently in need of attention.

I look at two main areas of regulation: intellectual creations, concentrating on patents and copyrights, and personal information. My focus is on the essential nature of these regulations and how modern society has shaped them. I then ask whether analogous problems have been encountered in other areas of law. By comparison we can begin to understand the long term consequences of the policies which our laws reflect. This understanding might help to identify and avoid some of the mistakes of earlier policies. I then consider the criteria for judging the effectiveness of policies in light of this understanding. Finally, I note some areas of further research suggested by this work.

Intellectual creations are the products of individual creative skills. If these result in an invention, this will be protected by a *patent.* If the product is broadly cultural, then this will be protected by *copyright* law. Both patent and copyright laws confer a property right on their holders, to prevent others from exploiting the market for their creations. However, a large part of the rationale for these laws when they were first created was to encourage the flow of information. Protection was against commercialization, while access to the information was encouraged, either to create better inventions or to absorb culture and knowledge.

Both patents and copyrights function as monopolies which are generally regarded as anti-competitive and therefore undesirable. The compromise is to have limited time monopolies. This works well for patents where the maximum protection lasts about twenty years (details vary from country to country). In many cases the period is less, as renewal fees are not paid unless commercial returns warrant them. With copyright, the terms of protection are so long as to be, in practical terms, permanent in many cases. Aggravating circumstances are the difficulties of finding out who the owner is, not knowing how long an author may live and therefore not knowing if copyright still applies or not and, as there are no renewals, there is no opportunity to reduce the period of protection for lesser quality work. More positively, these rights do regulate their respective markets and, since this is necessary, they have their place.

In general these intellectual property rights (IPRs) perform an important protective function for their owners and are developed for that purpose. However, there exists a continual tension with their problematic monopoly characteristics which tend to reduce the benefits to other parties and thereby obscure the information function. To rectify this and to facilitate access, national laws include exemptions. These exemptions are usually designed to allow for public interest in a particular type of access, but may also be granted to hinder the anti-competitive practices of information providers.

Personal information relates to the need to regulate information concerning individual people. This includes administrative personal records in many collections and also personal information that is published in the media. There is a need for privacy laws to protect personal identity. The need to use some personal information to provide services and run organizations acts as a counterbalance to privacy and requires a limited degree of openness. This needs to be kept in balance with any public interest in personal life stories carried by the media.

Personal information and IPRs are usually treated as two self-contained and separate areas of regulation, but there are many points of convergence and I contend that they need to be balanced if we are to have a society in which information is the central commodity and object of our labours. This so-called Information Society will require a more unified approach to handling different types of information. It is also useful to have consistency in our regulatory approaches. New laws are rendered more acceptable, and if they fit into a conceptual framework this helps to define their scope.

Laws concerning personal information have existed roughly as long as large scale printing has been available: 300–400 years. Intellectual property rights have been in force for about 200 years. Both performed more or less satisfactorily as long as the methods of reproduction were analogue and required a tangible substrate to carry them. These substrates included print on paper, audio, video and film. The introduction of the photocopier caused copyright problems but these were reasonably soluble without requiring the entire structure of protection to change. Alongside analogue technology went a capitalist economy based on the nation state or a discrete multinational entity.

Both the forms of information regulation and the structure of capitalism have been thrown out of balance by the electronic revolution. Forms of regulation must be expanded in order to respond to these changes. But these are so radical as to require a rethinking of the basic philosophy. The structure of capitalism is affected because of powerful trends towards globalization within the information industries and their knock-on effects on the fabric of related industries, on societies and on nation states.

I will examine these topics from two perspectives, initially from that of use and access to information, and then from that of the meaning of the information content.

The essential nature of patents

The granting of a patent for an invention creates a monopoly for the commercial development of that invention for a limited time, around 20 years. The invention must be new and infringement occurs if the operation of that invention is reproduced whether copied or re-invented. There must be a saleable product at the end of the process. However, the history and organization of the patent system points very much towards the free circulation of information being the prime motivating force, with protection of the patentee being a necessary adjunct. Indeed, the English Statute of Monopolies of 1624, the founding law of the modern patents system, declared that the purpose of patenting was to foster the introduction of new technical ideas (Eisenschitz, 1993).

The initial requirement was for local novelty, an invention new in the UK, and the patentees were to teach the technology to their apprentices. The model was the introduction of weaving and glass-making crafts which spread slowly as ex-apprentices moved away from their masters, licensed to practise these skills in their turn, and then freely able to practise them with their own apprentices. The initial patent grant was for 14 years, the length of two apprenticeships. The practice of writing the invention into a specification came about when the basic technologies were known and the inventions were incremental improvements which needed to be spelled out. It is arguable that the capacity for effective teaching was reduced noticeably by going from individual teaching to a written description, but that decision has long been made on the grounds of practicality and scale (Eisenschitz, 1985). As information provision and access have improved, countries have gradually moved towards the concept of absolute novelty and this is now the norm. There are to be no publications or use of the invention anywhere in the world (apart from any exceptions written into national laws).

Anyone can try out the invention in private to familiarize themselves with it and possibly to improve upon it. It is only commercial exploitation that is banned. This means that one invention could either trigger another, or that someone could see a use for it other than the use(s) already suggested. Use would be likely to require permission and payment to the original patentee unless a further invention were revolutionarily different, but there could still be an extension of knowledge. Also, the protection sought could not be used to bury the invention entirely. Provisions exist for 'local working' of inventions, but these are not very effective in practice. However, the knowledge is available and, apart from one or two very fast moving fields, would still be relevant at the end of the protection period.

There must be only strictly limited publication before an application is submitted or patent grant is invalidated. What is allowed differs from country to country. Dissemination to a few trusted colleagues is part of the discussion process required for creativity. It is not considered to be publication, but the boundaries are strictly limited. Publication at conferences or in academic journals may be allowed in some countries for up to a year before the first patent application is made. Any other publications destroy the state of novelty. This concentration on a new description indicates the importance placed on spreading new technology.

The increasing internationalization of trade has led to an emphasis in public policy on the exploitation of inventions overseas. Political interest is focused almost entirely on enforcement of the protection and the earning of foreign currency. Within the European Union this is modified by a concern to balance protection with competitiveness. This is also true, though less so, in the USA. The quality and contents of what is transferred have been relegated to the private interests of the parties. We see that current initiatives in patent law concern themselves with stamping out piracy and counterfeiting, courts to deal with infringers, and arrangements for technology transfer agreements to ensure that due payment is received without stifling competition.

This has led to the devaluation in relative terms of the information side of the bargain. At first sight this would seem to be not so. Patent information services are flourishing. But the true learning, in the sense of having available a tangible product one can make and experiment with, has declined. This is very much due to the vast complexity of modern day technology. In one case involving colour television, a court ruled that the 'expert in the art' intended to read the specification and implement the invention should be regarded as an entire research team since no single person could fully understand all the complexities.

What is becoming clear is that the concept of a marketable product, and of clear instructions leading to technology that can be manifested in a distinct product, is being eroded. There have been cases demonstrating this in two areas of technology, both in the USA which, as a technological leader, is likely to manifest difficulties earlier than most other countries. One case concerns software patents, the other the patenting of gene sequences.

- *Software.* The software case concerned programs for the digital compression of graphics to allow them to be transmitted over networks. The software had been patented, some time ago, although without any application in mind, and the patent was duly forgotten. This is possible in the US because patents, once granted, did not have renewal fees and remained valid for their entire lifetime of 17 years. When the Internet was developing this software became a very common tool for transmitting graphics. The patent was revealed only later when its use was well established. It is likely that the patentees had no idea of this application and there was probably no application at all, otherwise there would have been some indication of patent rights attached to the software or its documentation.

  The software had probably been patented just as a useful-looking sequence with no application in mind, i.e. not as a product. In the USA, many software patents are granted, but this is still controversial and rather less common in most other jurisdictions. Software expressed as text is protected mainly by copyright law.

- *Gene sequences.* The case of gene sequence patenting is similar. As the genetic code is unravelled, sequences become known. Some US research bodies began to patent sequences which coded for specific proteins or other chemicals. But they also applied for, and were granted, patents on sequences which did not correspond to any known chemicals in living cells and which had no known function, 'just in case'. Firstly, these are discoveries rather than inventions, patented because these are the sequences that occur in nature rather than because anything is being 'manufactured'. Secondly, these are not products—there is nothing at the end to be used and/or sold.

In both these cases we have a set of components patented in a particular arrangement because the arrangement fits together and 'works', not because a problem has been solved and something useful created, which was the original intention of patent systems. The central motivation now is simply that it might be possible to make money in the future, and that competitors, especially foreign ones, need to be kept off the patch. In the USA and EU competition is normally encouraged, but when this is foreign competition, it is still possible to invoke a protectionist stance.

Blanket patenting shifts the balance from the dissemination of information towards the protection of R&D investments. In the short term this may well improve profits, but in the medium term it will discourage the processes of experiment and improvement which generate new products. This is already happening in industrially-funded university research where researchers cannot discuss their ideas with outsiders during the creative phases.

Of course, one way to enable a useful technology to be exploited is simply not to patent it at all but to allow free access. Examples of this approach include the X-ray machine developed by Marie Curie and Sir Humphry Davy's miner's lamp. But research is expensive nowadays and such altruism is not compatible with institutional sponsorship. Only an individual would be free enough to give knowledge away and there is little autonomy available.

The essential nature of copyright

The other major property right created to protect and facilitate access to information, is copyright. Its function was originally to create an orderly market in mainly cultural products. In this orderly market, material would circulate to users while assuring income to the author(s) and protecting the investments of the producers and publishers. Concepts of copyright arose with the invention of printing, though modern laws began around 200 years later. The situation to be remedied was that if a work were popular, different printers would each bring out a version and none could make a profit. So the modern solution was that the author would choose who was to publish and no one was allowed to copy a work without the permission of the copyright owner, this being the author. The situation is complicated by the fact that copyright tends to pass to the publisher as a condition of publishing, and later publishers and other producers acquired additional rights to protect their investment in the presentation of a work. But the basic situation remains now as then, in that the author owns the copyright and no copying is allowed without permission (Laddie, 1996). In England the predecessor laws to modern copyright favoured the publishers in that they formed a Society, the

Stationers' Company, and shared out the works among themselves with the authors having no say.

There is no right to copy even once in general, but there is the right to use fully any document that is present. For non-electronic media, this is true of all the different aspects of copyright. Only copying is controlled, any other activity is permitted. This worked tolerably well as long as protected items were cultural and not 'useful' in the patent sense. However, it is the case that many copyright works are useful. Text embodies knowledge as well as pleasure. This implies that access to particular works is likely to be important to diverse groups of users and substitute works are unlikely to be acceptable. Also, there are works such as timetables and lists which are protected for the investment in their making but which are not cultural or creatively useful. These are protected by other means in many countries but are included under copyright in the UK.

For works of authorship, the prohibitions last for a very long time: the life of the author plus 50 years under the Berne Convention, and life plus 70 years in the EU. Given that most commercial activity takes place in the first few years of a document's life, this is virtually an eternal protection. For scholars dealing with important works, it is a considerable burden since their need for updated editions in the light of work being done is likely to be ignored as not being a commercially attractive proposition. This hampers cultural activity while having minor effects on the commercial issues.

There are exceptions to the no copying rule, known generally as 'fair dealing' in the UK and 'fair use' in the USA, where some copying is allowed in the public interest. In the UK examples include archiving documents due for export, news reporting, papers for judicial purposes or for public enquiries and for criticism and review. The best known is for research or private study. In the US the categories are very similar, but they are broadly stated to encourage these uses. In the UK, all the exceptions are narrowly interpreted with detailed explanations of what is and what is not allowed and a general feeling of grudging allowance. There are 49 sections dealing with exemptions in our current legislation (Laddie, 1996). This attitude has unfortunately affected the approach of the European Commission with its various Directives and discussion papers on this topic.

Copyright and the new electronic media

A significant problem exists in relation to electronic media where the entire basis for copyright control has changed. The use of any document electronically requires copying in order to take the image from its store and place it on the screen. This is the case whether the information is on a CD-ROM, on a tape, or on a remote computer and being sent across a network. This is because the digital symbols, whether stored as magnetic fields or etched pits, need to be converted to a screen image. If one says that no copying is permitted, following the law blindly, then one cannot even read a document and every single access to the item is possible only at a cost and at the discretion of its 'owner'.

In an Information Society, where a great deal of information is available only in digital form, there needs to be some equivalent of a pre-purchase inspection, a browsing right. It is unavoidable that one must pay for concentrated use of a work but there needs to be compensation for not being able to look and browse. To solve this there would need to be a specified amount of free time or maybe a delimited part of a work such as a contents page, abstract, title page and index. These could be free and the rest be paid for.

There is the related problem of fair dealing. It is not right that one can look at a work for certain purposes in one medium but not in another. If copyright management systems are being developed, then coding to recognize categories of use and let them through need to be built in. Because of the rising cost of newsprint and the falling costs of electronic delivery, electronic provision has become a popular option. Directories and encyclopaedias are coming out electronically because of the ease of updating. New multimedia products are appearing which allow different media to be integrated to produce new products which can only exist in electronic form. So an increasing proportion of cultural and informative material is becoming available only (or predominantly) electronically.

If one buys a printed product one can look at it in the shop. This is not so easy for tapes or CD-ROMs. But books and audio and video products can be borrowed or consulted in libraries. Some libraries are acquiring electronic products, but for people to use them there will be a charge to compensate the rights owners for a missed sale. There may also be a component for telecommunications, but not for CD-ROMs.

The third related problem is that of the substantial part. Copyright does not apply if only an insubstantial part is copied. However, substantiality has never been defined since the concept depends on quality as well as quantity. There are, however, quantitative rules of thumb which are approximately adhered to. This is acceptable for a printed product where one can see how much there is in total and select a portion. When something is in electronic form one sees only what is there, so what is needed is either a sensible code for quantity and quality or, better, an agreement of a certain amount that can be freely copied from any work. Very small works would suffer, but very large ones would gain. All users would gain by having certainty. Perhaps some combination of an agreed amount and a code for how much is there would be the best. For any work not offering this, there could be an indemnity for honest mistakes.

The 'quality not quantity' concept is also suspect. An idea might well be summarized in one sentence, but copyright protects expression and the expression is in the totality of the text. So the one or two sentences giving the bare bones may be better regarded as the unprotected 'theme' which may then be expressed in many variations and elaborations.

Creativity is normally cumulative; one needs to read and find out, to bring formerly unrelated ideas together and then create something new. Redundancy of information is vital. This is well known and yet copyright law requires a fresh start each time, as if ideas sprang out completely new from our consciousness.

A serious consequence is that libraries are seen by rights holders as competitors, allowing works to be borrowed rather than purchased. Yet these libraries provide the vital pools of broad information which authors need to create new works from which the rights holders then benefit. The access allows new fruit to grow. No one can tell which idea will spark, so that to study only known material in blinkers will cause true creativity to wither.

Two examples arise in software and in gene sequences.

- *Software*. As indicated in the section on patents, the main protection for software is as text in copyright law. However, this means that no incremental development can be sustained. Major inventions have been made in operating systems, which are particularly sensitive since these are reproduced in other computers if they are to be compatible. The EU Directive allowing interoperability has helped immeasurably here. Another difficult area has been with 'look and feel' cases, where what is copied is screen appearance and the underlying programs are likely to be different.

- *Gene sequences*. There has been some discussion of applying copyright to gene sequences rather than patents. This would protect long strings of genes and the component chemicals, giving them vast protection. The defence of an insubstantial part could presumably be used if only one gene were copied, but the copyright would have nuisance value. As copyrights do not have to be registered in most countries, only a court case could establish whether such claims would be allowed at all.

Meaning in patents and copyright

Looking at patents and copyright from another perspective, that of meaning, gives us no new material, rather another dimension to the preceding discussions. I refer to meaning transmitted via social relations concerning the contents.

With *patents* an invention is only complete if it can be expressed in a product or process as appropriate. This actualizes the meaning. Blanket patenting which catches discoveries where there is no known use ignores this sense of meaning. With *copyright* the importance of meaning is that virtually all knowledge is in a continuous web; one reads, sees, experiences and digests, and then produces something new which has a history nevertheless. Lawyers with an either/or mentality may refuse to take this history into account, but it is vital.

One positive aspect of electronic tracking systems is that they will help us to keep track of ideas and not allow false starts to be eliminated when they might prove useful again many years later. But these systems threaten to impose heavy development costs on users and they wipe out fair dealing. Complex and expensive access is bound to deter users and limit the range of their experiences. In due course the entire system will slow down and may fade away entirely.

The essential nature of personal information

The same trends that affect patent and copyright regulations also affect personal information, though in different ways. The situation with regard to personal information is in some respects the reverse of the intellectual property situation. Use is controlled by market forces, the need to sell newspapers or to carry out direct marketing. Control is by the individual subject of the information, but these subjects are the owners, while the users (newspaper editors, publishers, marketing staff) have no control in law.

This topic is raised because in its essential nature it follows the same trends and shows many of the same problems as those encountered in intellectual property rights. The desire of companies and of governments and local authorities to use information has little to do with the personality of the subject. It is a decision predicated by market forces.

Many of the ways that information is used are subjective and culturally determined. This is especially true of personal information where we are likely to have strong feelings about the importance of certain elements. Commercial evaluation of the data is likely to have a much narrower viewpoint depending on the functionality of the data. All other views are discounted. In this way the humanity of the data subject and the human uniqueness of personal information are ignored. However, these represent meaning, and the 'political correctness' movement arose from the perceived, but denied, power of words. Hence the cumbersome circumlocutions they put in place of important words.

Control versus use

One of the central themes concerning intellectual property rights was the imbalance between the control of rights owners and the needs of users. A similar imbalance is found in the case of personal information. In this case, control is related to privacy, and use to publication. The relevant pieces of legislation are highly varied.

Freedom of information (FoI) can apply to useful information from either the public or the private sector. Many countries have FoI laws which can cover the activities of individuals as well as those of organizations. In the UK there are a number of small-scale discrete pieces of FoI legislation. *Publishing* laws may address content directly, such as in libel law, and this is being updated for the electronic age. There is also the publication and use of factual information about people, such as health or educational records, or statistics of their lifestyles produced either for public sector planning or for private sector marketing purposes. These may be covered by FoI legislation or by data protection. In both cases this allows for accuracy and security to be monitored as well as data sharing and excessive monitoring. In most countries these would be covered by privacy legislation. In the UK the recently passed European Directive on data protection labels itself as a form of privacy law, the first such law in this country.

Rights to prevent publication are weak in areas such as the appearance of stories in newspapers, journals and books, though libel is a strong sanction for use after publication. But pre-publication action is much more powerful in areas such as use by marketing companies. Some use is, of course, explicit in the involvement of a subject in a service. Medical or educational records are kept as a natural part of day-to-day living. But the bulk of use of material picked up by investigators or given by the subject is without reciprocal gain except of publicity. The 'oxygen of publicity' is, of course, important in many careers and such people are generally thought not to need protection when the publicity is not quite as they like it. They take their chances. Other private individuals may be caught up in publicity not of their making, and they receive somewhat greater protection in practice. It does seem, though, that this is a distinction rather like that between the undeserving and deserving poor. Ideally, content needs to be true and non-sensational in all cases.

All arguments for the regulation of personal information are countered by the evident public interest in open reporting both of news and of the iniquities committed by industrialists and governments alike when they believe themselves safe from scrutiny.

Towards a more unified vision of information regulation

It emerges from this analysis that the regulation of intellectual property rights and that of personal information share many common features. They are not identical but follow similar trends and respond to external pressures in similar ways. It is important to treat all types of information in the same way if we are ever to understand information as one entity around which we can develop a more consistent approach and a more unified set of policy objectives.

I have noted the central concept of balance between competing interests with both intellectual property rights and personal information. Governments may wish to promote the interests of industry and commerce using the law, but this must be in the context of prosperity for all. In the long run, conditions that exclude or disadvantage the huge mass of ordinary people will be challenged and this is starting to happen with copyright (Laddie, 1996).

It is not only important to treat information in a way which is consistent internally, it may also be useful to treat it consistently externally within the approach of regulating other aspects of our lives. In this way we may observe links with earlier law and check for a consistent sustainable progression. Inconsistencies will create weaknesses and fault lines which will not hold under stress in the future.

Use versus ownership in other areas of the law

In this section I will attempt to draw an analogy between the way that information content is regulated under law and ways of handling use rights and ownership in other areas of property law. This paper will concentrate on English law, but similar frameworks in other legal systems allow the basic analogy to be transferred.

English land law

The right started with use. From the Norman conquest onwards villagers had grazing, harvesting and growing rights on 'common' land until landlords started enclosing this land for more 'profitable' exploitation and a need arose to define more closely which expectations could be held open by continued use and which would be brushed aside. The feudal lord could raise an army from his tenants and they had secure livelihoods on the land. This was an exchange of uses. When an army was no longer relevant, the landlords demanded ownership defined in terms of financial value. Tenants' value was then interchangeable with the value of other modes of exploitation and the tenants became expendable.

The dispute over how readily use rights may be overridden by property rights has not been settled. It continues to raise considerable passions. Ramblers assert known rights of way despite sporting, agricultural and military uses of the surrounding land. Motorway protesters wish to defend not just a specific route but the entire environment and way of life of an area experienced by the residents against the convenience of a new road for transient travellers. In both these cases the arguments involve finance but seem to be mainly about lifestyle, with convenience in pursuing more distant aims pitted against the enjoyment of the natural world at that particular location. There is, indeed, a movement to reclaim the roads for people and have street parties on major traffic routes. The aims have moved beyond subsistence husbandry as society in general has become richer. These movements create social unrest, resentment and pain, not an ideal state of affairs.

Parallels with the regulation of information content

We can identify in land law the progression from a proto-property use right to attempts to secure a fully controlled and secured piece of property. This same movement is currently going on in the information world. The balances struck now are likely to affect relations across the information society for a long time to come. It would clearly be in the interests of users and of the information industry if the disruptions occasioned by the application of land law, as outlined above, could be avoided. The following observations illustrate that information law shows parallel tendencies to the movements of landlords to monetary evaluation.

- *Patents.* Research and development can be extremely expensive and there are companies that specialize in producing 'me too' products where the R&D, testing and marketing have all been done. If they have been patented, then when the patent runs out it is cheap and easy to produce a product which is easy to sell and has lower start up costs than a fresh start product would have.

  These are fairly common in pharmaceuticals and exist in other areas, too. Of course, they have a place in the market in breaking the monopoly, but excessive copying drains investment from important but riskier new work.

- *Copyright.* In copyright the trend can be seen best by looking at the arguments against piracy. Copyright piracy occurs when a work is copied and sold without permission (Gurnsey, 1995). For example, the music industry felt that audio tapes would kill sales of records and CDs would kill audio tapes. The film industry thought that video would kill the cinema. In each case access to a copy boosted sales of other versions: 'see the film and buy the video'; buy a disc and record a tape for listening on a personal stereo. The possibility of copying is a reason for sales and stimulates the appetite for more products.

  A narrow focusing on sales figures allows rights holders to say they have lost sales even though an unknown number would translate to sales in practice. Rigorous enforcement and no copying would much reduce the sales of blank cassettes and recording equipment and also primary sales of the products.

For printed journals, those with high interlibrary loan rates also have high subscription rates. Those that copy a number of articles know later that these are the journals to subscribe to. In the short term, some sales are lost, but in the long term all these production industries are thriving, with copying and sales inextricably linked.

- *Personal information.* For newspaper and book publishing, the trend is seen in the way in which prior publicity robs a complainant of their right to privacy and justifies public interest. With administrative information the tendency has been to widen the concept of justifiable use as computerized techniques become ever more refined. At the same time informed consent is offered as the best means to ensure a let-out for objectors.

Notions of equity

Returning to concepts of English property law, we saw that land law was very rigid; ownership was an absolute, either one had it or not. A concept of trust started to grow in the middle ages by which land and other property could be owned by one person 'in trust' for another, usually a minor, to whom the rights would be ceded in due course. But these rights had no force of law, the trustee remained the full owner.

Wronged litigants demanded justice, equity, rather than law, and this new field grew up conferring rights grown from expectations (Gray, 1993). Even in this century, expectations are still being framed and new 'equities' developed. For instance, Lord Denning developed an equity to give common law wives a share of the joint home when relationships break up.

If such concepts were to be transferred to information law, one could see that expectations could grow into rights here, too. A possible starting point would be rights to users of multimedia products. If one buys such a product and it is interactive, the ingenuity of the user creates a new version of the work. Why should not the user acquire some rights in this work to distribute to friends or to exhibit in some way or perhaps even rights of commercial exploitation in certain cases (Turner, 1996a)?

The implications for public policy

It is important that we work out commonly understood criteria for assessing policy in the information field. We currently have neither common measures nor a common baseline of assumptions. The above ideas about information and its commercial and personal uses may offer some criteria for assessing the effectiveness of the given forms of regulation as tools of information dissemination.

Access

What was the original intention of the law in terms of who would have ready access, who would be disadvantaged and who left out of the calculations altogether? How and why has this changed? Is the original intention still being fulfilled or is there a new one?

Meaning

Although a copyright text or a patented invention are protected, the underlying ideas are not, they are free, and this needs to be built into the equation. Economies of scope and scale allow much stronger protection for works already in tangible form out of all proportion to the extra opportunities for access.

Given that different uses may depend on different meanings, the value of the information and the degree of protection required may be variable. This is especially true for personal information where respect for the truth and the human being behind any story need reinforcement. It is also conceivable in the intellectual property field that different user interests may value the knowledge differently. Consistent with the public interest in allowing access, variable pricing to reflect different values and resources would be useful and might indeed become mandatory one day.

Meaning is the crucial component in understanding measures of value, public interest and graduations of need for access. Like complexity it is difficult, but if ignored renders our overview virtually null and void.

Further research

The connections between information policy and information retrieval may be made by considering meaning. Creativity comes with making unexpected connections between unrelated topics. This aspect needs to be developed in information retrieval systems. Murat Karamuftuoglu (1996), a research student at City University, has indeed been looking at complexity and meaning in terms of their implications for the design of information retrieval engines.

The concept of information users acquiring rights via expectations, as in the branch of law called equity, is interesting and needs further development.

Just as property can be termed 'a bundle of consequences', so information can be seen to have different values related to different outlooks or paradigms. Value is not one monolithic entity and more work is needed on graduated pricing structures.

I have shown that value is linked to access and also to meaning. Broad policies can be linked to the balance of interests and changes in the balance traced as they occur. Paul Turner (1996b), my research student, is currently working on EU policy formulation in intellectual property rights in the multimedia industry.

One needs to be sensitive to different interest groups in order to broaden access to all information sources. The desirability of access is itself an article of faith but it is critical in an Information Society where information is a central asset.

So, when evaluating information laws and policies, we need to ask who will benefit, who is disadvantaged but still has access, and crucially, who doesn't get a look in at all? If we can look at these questions objectively and ensure access and room for the needs of as many people as possible, then we will have an inclusive rather than exclusive Information Society. This is important in order to avoid the mistakes in our present and recent history in creating 'haves' and 'have nots' with all the disadvantages and injustices that has entailed. It is in the interests of the information industry to have as large a market as possible and as many capable users as possible. This will not be achieved if groups are excluded simply because they do not have the money or the influence to persuade rights owners in the short term of their needs for access. We all need to take a much longer term view.

Real Policy or 'Virtual Policy'? A Case Study of Tradeable Information Policy

David R. Worlock

Abstract

This paper reviews ten years of debate in Europe on commercial rights of access to government information, starting with the UK's innovative Government Tradeable Information Guidelines of 1986 and ending with the European Commission's Draft Green Paper on Rights of Access in 1996. US market development and commercial rights of access are compared to the European situation, and the needs of the European information industry in this regard are reviewed in detail. The paper looks at access to legal and business information as critical case studies, citing access to the UK VAT Register as a recent case study. The decline in government copyrights and the increase in public domain data released onto the Internet is contrasted with the growing tendency to create new information monopolies through privatization and deregulation.

The tradeable information model

In ten years of active debate on commercial rights of access to public sector information in Europe, the situation has changed entirely and yet remained very much the same. It is possible for private sector activists to say, as one did recently, that 'government information is free, yet everywhere it is in chains', while a public servant could riposte 'government information was in chains, but now most of it is on the Internet'. Yet this debate was intended to provide a stimulus for the growth of the information marketplace and of the commercial sector in electronic publishing in Europe by emulating US experience and by providing a form of developmental support without subsidy. Government, by providing primary information without charge, would stimulate inventive entrepreneurs to add high levels of value in order to make such information more effectively available to targeted groups of users.

This notion of 'value added' was a vital one in the ideology of the private sector: it allowed companies to live with the idea of non-exclusive licensing by government to the private sector, since value added would be the competitively exclusive element, and it allowed government to at once license the core information non-exclusively and add value in its own context. This meant that the idea of non-exclusive access to core or primary information was not at odds with a government printer, like Her Majesty's Stationery Office (HMSO) in the UK, adding its own levels of value to government information for re-sale; or business information parastatal organizations, like CERVED or CAMERDATA, adding value to information for their user communities; or the German organizations, like the FIZ institutes or STN network, adding value to their own databases, by placing them in an appropriate retrieval and networking environment.

The essential problems with this apparently felicitous market development model emerged in practice. It proved extremely difficult to define source or primary information, to define value-added services and, indeed, to get governments to keep their side of the bargain and set up appropriate licensing procedures. Such raw primary data, which information market companies had simply seen as core statistical data, government announcements and administrative orders, statutes and secondary legislation, and databases of information collected from the public at large by reason of statutory requirement, have often proved to be difficult to track down in practice. Both government and the private sector have been guilty of deluding themselves that there is more value in these databases than there sometimes is, and where genuine attempts have taken place to catalogue government information holdings (the UK Department of the Environment Spatial Database Initiative is a case in point), private sector take-up has been disappointing. Where such take-up has taken place, negotiations have been drawn out into exhaustive contractual debates which frustrate the essential purpose behind the original UK guidelines of ten years ago (DTI, 1986).

The development of tradeable information policy

Many of the instances given in this paper concern practice in the UK. This is deliberate, on two grounds. In the first instance, the UK guidelines on tradeable government information of 1986 were the first development in Europe of this nature, and much of the thinking from that process was adopted into the European Commission's *Guidelines for Improving the Synergy between the Public and the Private Sector in the Information Market* (CEC, 1989). On the other hand, the UK's retention and use of Crown copyright demonstrates attitudes towards retention of control of government information which are amongst the most clear-cut in Europe and tend to throw up case studies of real interest. This does not imply for a moment that issues discussed are not fully relevant in all other parts of the European Union, or indeed that UK practice, because it is so obvious, presents a particular problem. Unwillingness to license utilization of government data does not need legal sanction to be effective. The number of instances in which database developers have been able to collect information from all member states in order to create integrated, cross-border, value-added products, which help and support trading activity and derive from non-exclusive licences granted by the member state governments, remain very few and far between. In some member states, it is clearly and legendarily impossible for commercial entities in other member states to even attempt to license government information, regardless of the equality of treatment issues which may be involved.

Let us go back, however, to the beginning and revisit some of the underlying principles to see what practical sense we have made of them over the last ten years. Pioneers of access to government information arguments in Europe ten years ago did not think that they were making particularly revolutionary suggestions. They believed that if the strategic goal was to create a free trade area in Europe with greater transparency and lower barriers, in order to promote and increase trade and therefore wealth and employment on a transnational basis, then the removal of barriers to trade caused by inadequate, insufficient or unreliable information was of prime importance. They identified government as the source, although not the only source, of information used in the trading process and, at a time when the prevailing notion was one of 'level playing fields', it seemed natural to seek common conditions of access to government information in the various states of the European Union in order to create conditions sympathetic to the development of pan-European databases. Insofar as the European guidelines were an attempt to do this, they are commonly reckoned to have failed. But the key markers that they laid down were as follows:

- Governments should license freely and non-exclusively to allow the information industry to grow through adding value through re-use of public sector database collections.

- Governments should be encouraged to create catalogues of licensable information and make them available to private sector developers.

- Having licensed private sector companies to invest in developing government data to serve markets better, governments should not normally go out and create other services with the tax-payers' money in order to compete with these licences.

- Re-use of primary source data by private sector organizations should normally be free, although the guidelines recognized the rights of governments in some instances to recover the cost of actually supplying the information to the private sector (as distinct from the costs of its collection).

- Article 2(4) of the Berne Convention should be utilized to allow governments to 'exempt from copyright all texts covering legislation, public administration, economic and social policy and activity, and norms and standards'.

These principles remain close to the heart of the private sector database industry in Europe and, indeed, are the most important elements within the nineteen which the European Information Industry Association has put forward to the European Commission as part of its expectations for a draft directive on commercial rights of access to government information (see Appendix to this Chapter).

With guidelines like this in place (and the UK national version even had a model contract produced by HMSO attached to it), it might be thought that matters would change rapidly. They did not, and it is instructive to see why. We identify the following major reasons:

- The guidelines were not effectively communicated to responsible individuals within member state governments and, indeed, few member state governments had officials deployed specifically to manage information policy. Where such policy coordination did exist, as for a time in the UK, it was simply coordination and not control. It did not, for example, prevent wayward departments from going in their own directions.

- Neither government nor the private sector were sufficiently aware of government primary source data holdings. No catalogues were produced in many countries and, where they were (as indicated above, in the UK), they were ineffectively deployed.
- In the late 1980s member state governments were becoming very concerned to reduce government expenditure in the face of industrial recession and began to see government information as a revenue source. Just as the private sector over-emphasized the economic opportunity on its side, so the public sector did the same. Hard-pressed bureaucrats sought budget relief from data sales, even though any revenue flows tended to go to central Treasury controls rather than individual operating departments.
- During this period, and increasing in strength throughout the period, the pervasive movement towards privatization of state functions and the removal of former government activities into parastatal or privatized organizations was a key policy feature. There was a tendency for organizations to be privatized with their information resources. British Telecom took the United Kingdom telephone directory with it, for example, and certainly regarded this as a commercially exploitable entity (selling annual licences for re-use for sums reputed to be in excess of £500,000 per annum) until Oftel proposed re-regulating this area in 1995.

There are countless other examples of this unthinking creation of information monopolies by government, and a certain amount of evidence that where government was conscious that it was creating new monopolies, it succumbed upon the grounds that the information concerned was a vital part of the asset base of the newly privatized organization, and could be one of its exploitable benefits. Besides taking more and more government servants off the payroll, the privatization movement has sharply reduced the amount of information within the scope of the guidelines, and this in itself might be taken as a critical reason for their failure.

The current situation

It is necessary to give this background in order to demonstrate why we are where we are. However, we need to keep on reminding ourselves that the arguments originally advanced in the guidelines had nothing to do with government policy or making better informed citizens. The arguments put forward then, as now, were commercial and economic, and they related to developmental opportunities which were as clearly in front of European Union citizens then as they are now. And since some of the opposing interests have at times expressed a view that this simply reflects the avaricious desires of private sector information service developers who wish to corner public sector information and re-sell it at a profit to tax-payers, who funded its collection in the first place, it is worth looking at some of the areas of opportunity that are created if access to government information without barriers is allowed:

- The potential for cross-border information services is enhanced. Private sector investment in the translation and harmonization of information resources becomes more realistic if the rules for release of information are the same in each member state, the point of availability is clearly known, the type of cataloguing that we have referred to above has taken place to allow relevant resources to be recognized, and the costs of obtaining the information are calculated on the same basis in each case.

- The opportunity is enhanced in network environments where information service developers are able to charge their customers not for the underlying information content, but simply for the value-added service superstructure located on top of it. Let us postulate, for example, a service that improved the European Commission's existing TED (Tenders Electronic Daily) service, and which drew deeply upon regional government tendering opportunities throughout member states. The added service value could be intelligent agent applications which allowed users to identify subject areas and be notified by the system when opportunities of interest to them were lodged on the database. Without arguing the virtues or lack of them of such a system, the point to be made is simply that current networking styles on the Internet create conditions like this where underlying information may be free, but users may choose to access information through a paid-for service that adds value to the interaction.

- Players in the information marketplace may be encouraged to promote access to information resources and more fully commercial information distribution in the one sector crucial to both government and the private information companies. This is in the

> area of information for small- and medium-sized enterprises (SMEs), and many now believe that this can only be achieved on an international value-added basis through the use of ubiquitous networking. The drive to get things right in this context has so far been ineffective. Countless programmes, funded by member state governments and the European Commission, have sought to create local resource centres and information dispersal points based on Chambers of Commerce and other entities. By and large, these have failed to change anything. A considerable body of opinion now believes that if the value of information products and services is to become effective within the business models of SMEs, then it will happen because the private sector information industry effectively markets to them. And if the private sector information industry is to be effectively re-energized to create the value-added services which SMEs will use, then radical easement of access regulations governing government information is urgently required.

Clearly, then, we can conclude that neither the economic opportunities nor the industrial growth requirement have gone away in the last ten years. Indeed, in the age of the information superhighway (a term now only used by politicians and civil servants), this all takes on a desperate relevance. Three case studies, drawn from the UK (once again, in the lead both as an information marketplace and as a regulatory environment under pressure in this regard) demonstrate how the effective dialogue between public and private sectors is now breaking down.

HM Customs & Excise

In regard to the release of the Register of VAT-Paying Companies in the UK, HM Customs & Excise has, over a ten-year period and in the face of the Government Tradeable Information Guidelines, promulgated by another department of the same government, deployed the whole range of possible reasons for obfuscation or delay. When initial claims that the Register was Crown Copyright were rebutted, the Department took refuge in the idea that the information was confidential. When the information industry indicated that it did not seek any confidential data, but simply the complete listing of the names and addresses of companies who currently pay the tax, shorn of details of their registration numbers and the amount of tax that they pay, the Department responded that these data were part of an implied contract between the tax-paying company and the tax collector, and to divulge them would be a breach of that contract. When this argument was demolished, the Department sought refuge in the idea that the data were covered by the Official Secrets legislation, and, indeed, indicated on one memorable occasion that the legal opinion that this was so was itself covered by such legislation. Finally, in 1995, the Department was cornered and forced to relent, and initiated a public consultation on the issue. In April 1996, this consultation came to an end and the Department wrote to participants indicating that 'the core of support for (public access to the VAT Register) came from the finance, credit and information sectors who felt that such access would benefit businesses, particularly those providing business information, assessing creditworthiness, or underwriting potential business risk ...'. Particular issues of concern (there were only 100 responses to this exercise) were privacy and security and 'the additional risk of exposure to unsolicited junk mail or nuisance phone calls'. On these latter grounds it has been decided to maintain the secrecy of the VAT Register. It is one of the beguiling ironies of this UK example that a country which has no central business register, no mandatory registration of trading entities who do not seek limited company status, and therefore no ability to say how many small- and medium-sized enterprises it actually has, feels unable to release to the information industry data which would improve the accuracy and effectiveness of business databases throughout its economy. And this on the grounds of privacy, security and the avoidance of junk mail in a country with a thriving direct marketing business, excellent business telephone directories, and Yellow Pages, and Data Protection legislation which does not extend to corporate entities. As elsewhere in the European Union, it sometimes seems to the information industry as if any argument is good enough to block access to information which can only improve the economic life of the Union as a whole.

Inland Revenue

A further example shows government acting on the other side of the equation. In the early 1990s the Inland Revenue in the UK, responsible for the collection of all business and personal taxes except VAT, decided to try to increase earnings from its information resources, and in particular from its tax manuals. These documents were internal guidance notes for tax inspectors which advised them on the Department's own view on the interpretation of statute and case law. The tax publishing market in the UK is highly competitive, with some four major groups sponsoring competitive services. For tax accountants and lawyers, only fully comprehensive services will do, and if the previously confidential Inland Revenue tax manuals were to become available, the information providers felt that they needed to be available in all services. The values upon which publishers were competing in this sector were cross-referencing and commentary, not underlying information. However, in order to get the best price for its product, the Inland Revenue chose competitive tender and awarded an exclusive electronic publishing contract to one of the four competitors. It was then sued and, in a settlement out of court, agreed that a further publisher could have access to the same data. Presumably, if the remaining two competitors wish to gain access, they too will have to bring a legal process (although, it is to be hoped, this reversal will prompt some re-thinking). However, the whole episode, finally resolved in May 1996, illustrates clearly the point made above regarding the increasing willingness of governments to trade information which is essential to key business functions in ways which could lead to the lowering of quality standards in the marketplace as a whole, even if they increase the revenue flow to central government itself.

Her Majesty's Stationery Office

A third example must be the ongoing privatization of HMSO in the UK. We noted above the creation of data monopolies through privatization, and the problems that this created. In the case of HMSO, Crown Copyright has been specifically removed from that organization prior to privatization, and a new licensing function will be created within the UK Cabinet Office. So, on the one hand, HMSO will be privatized without the benefit of its unique hold on UK government copyrights, which would seem to diminish its value, while on the other hand, where it does retain control of value-added services which it developed over the years and which UK private sector interests were unable to develop, it will be effectively privatized with its information monopolies intact. Since presumably the licensing regime will prevent those monopolies from being broken, many believe that this solution provides the worst of both worlds. This solution also does little credit to a generation of adept and diligent publishers at HMSO who have used their skills to create margins which are now worth the effort of privatization. On the other hand, the privatization of HMSO in this peculiar manner does not add a new competitive element, or increase the diversity and variety of the UK marketplace.

Conflicting policies and expectations

However, one thing clearly signalled by HMSO's repositioning is the determination of many units of government to get their information into shape and onto the Internet so that they can communicate directly with many classes of users. The latest organization in the UK to take this stand is the Select Committee on IT to the House of Lords, and the first legislation in progress to be treated this way, the Arbitration Bill, has now been published on the Internet. Yet it appears to be the case that governments still want their cake, and the ability to eat it. While making this information available in the cause of 'open government', the residual licensing body left behind by the sale of HMSO will undoubtedly continue to seek to sell Crown Copyright. In a recent submission to the European Commission from the General Council of the Bar, the governing body of barristers in the UK, the barristers noted that 'a crucial issue was whether the continuation of Crown Copyright protection in the law of the land can be justified'. The position in other countries varies, but there is some consistency in the overall picture, with the exception of the UK and certain other countries having British-type laws, including India, Singapore and Israel. In the USA there is no state copyright in legislation, and the same is understood to be the case in Japan. Some Commonwealth countries have moved, or are moving, away from state copyright protection for their laws; for example, there appears to be no such protection in Pakistan, and Australia seems likely to abandon it. In Europe, with the exception of Ireland (where there are indications that copyright in legislation is not enforced), enquiries conducted in recent months have not revealed any country in which the state enjoys copyright protection in legislation. Responses from some 13 out of 15 European Union or EFTA countries indicate that there is no such protection.

The irony of the situation in the United Kingdom is that the UK government has a 'Code of Practice on Access to Government Information', and widely advertises its 'Open Door Policy on Information'. The code of practice on Access to Government Information includes five commitments:

- to supply facts and analysis with major policy decisions;

- to open up internal guidelines about departments dealing through the public;
- to supply reasons with the administrative decisions;
- to provide information under the Citizen's Charter about public services, what they cost, targets, performance, complaints and redress;
- to respond to requests for information.

Here, indeed, the chronic schizophrenia of modern governments is fully exposed: on the one hand, an Open Door and, on the other hand, a retention of state copyrights and restricted licensing policy. The information industry at large is now totally confused by these activities. Is there any chance that a French or German database developer, seeking to translate UK legislative materials into the database in his own language for the support and guidance of cross-border traders, would have any hope of understanding the nuances of UK government information policy?

The indignation of the UK barristers is also noteworthy as a symptom of increasing user resistance to government information controls. Barristers will wish to adopt legislative texts of legal instruments into their own information systems and use them for their own reference purposes. They want to buy information services from publishers for the commentary and other value-added services that they provide, and not for the value of the underlying documentation. They believe that government should not restrict their access to that, and it is hard not to agree with them.

Conclusion

In the light of all of these issues, the burden of expectations upon the Green Paper on access to information is very heavy indeed. In early drafts, the Commission has indicated its interest in providing more transparency in this area, and the private sector information industry in Europe has consistently, through the European Information Industry Association, urged the adoption of a directive in this area to replace the ineffective guidelines promulgated over the past ten years. The nineteen key principles which information companies in Europe seek to have included in such a directive are attached to this paper as an appendix. They take the principles cited above and expand them into a matrix of information market measures designed to cover the key issues. While it is as yet unclear as to what stance the Commission will take in the final version of the Green Paper, the fact of the Green Paper itself indicates that rumbling discontent in this area is now widely recognized, and that the Commission believes that this is not a devolved issue of subsidiarity, but something upon which important economic interests in Europe rests. Given that the likely drafting and process time required for a directive will be up to five years, it is also clear that the hopes and aspirations of 1986 may have to be postponed a little longer and that we will have to seek a resolution beyond the millennium.

Appendix

EUROPEAN INFORMATION INDUSTRY ASSOCIATION (EIIA): TRADEABLE INFORMATION PRINCIPLES

The major sectors of the Directive would concern the following points:

1. Public organizations should, as far as is practicable and when access is not restricted for the protection of legitimate public or private interests, allow public database collections to be used by private sector companies and exploited by the information industry through electronic information services.
2. Member States should incorporate such a right of access into the conditions of release, use and exploitation of public sector data and information.
3. Member States should regularly review the data and information collected by their departments, and publish the outcome of such reviews in order to further the possibility of the re-use and re-exploitation of government-held information.
4. The principles of licensing and pricing such public data should be made clear by Member States to private sector organizations, and efforts should be made to harmonize these elements across public administrations.
5. The public sector should not place restrictions upon the type of customer or the territories to which newly-created services developed by the private sector from publicly held information sources are sold.
6. Public sector databases shall not normally be sold upon an exclusive basis if exclusivity distorts competition.
7. The public sector should encourage investment by the private sector in the development of information services based on public data.
8. Where public sector bodies provide electronic information services directly, such services should not distort competition and should not be created in order to compete with pre-existing private sector services.

9. Where the public sector currently supplies electronic information services, such services should be reviewed, with a view to deciding whether they are more appropriately provided by the public or private sector, and whether greater involvement in the development of such services by the private sector is desirable.
10. Electronic information service providers within the European Community should be treated upon an equal footing and have an equal right of access to the public information held by each Member State.
11. Public sector support for information services should be in line with articles 92 and 93 of the Treaty (on aids granted by the State).
12. Direct or indirect financial support may be provided by the public sector to encourage pre-competitive research and development and the emergence of new market sectors, but should not support the viability of mature services.
13. Public funding may support services which are necessary for the public interest, provided that such services could not be economically viable and could not be provided by private sector interests.
14. There should be encouragement for joint ventures between public and private sector interests where these are most appropriate for the development of the information marketplace.
15. Conditions governing application of public support to users of European electronic information services should not discriminate against these services on the basis of their European country of origin.
16. Public sector accounting and budgetary procedures and exchange controls should not prevent access by interested public departments to electronic information services throughout the Community.
17. The public sector should seek to remove legal and other barriers to the use of public information by the private sector.
18. The public sector should, to the highest extent possible, make use of the discretion given under article 2(4) of the Berne Convention to exempt from copyright all texts covering legislation, public administration, economic and social policy and activity, and norms and standards. Where government-held information does fall within the copyright convention, the public sector ought not to award exclusive rights of reproduction to a single organization, as this might hinder value enhancement by other commercial sector operators.
19. When public sector information or data is made available for private sector use or exploitation, any pre-existing citizens' rights of access to the original information as determined by legislation must be preserved.

ORGANIZATIONAL PERSPECTIVES

Overview

David Bawden

In some ways, it might seem that the organizational setting would provide the most straightforward environment for the development of information policies and consequently for their study and analysis. Organizations sit mid-way on the spectrum of scale from the individual (whose 'information policies', while they may well exist, are unlikely to be explicitly formalized) to the national and (even more) the international levels, in which information policy considerations are diffuse, heavily value-laden, and explicitly political. Organizations, after all, may be expected, much more so than individuals or nations and societies, to have explicit purposes and goals, with clearly defined structures and processes to support them. Furthermore, it is in organizations, specifically commercial organizations, that information management techniques were pioneered, and in which the newer field of knowledge management, with its close links to information policy, has been developed (see this volume, p.74). Perhaps this is not so unexpected, given that the three components generally taken to be the foundation concepts of knowledge management—content, culture and technology—emerge clearly in the Workshop papers as being of equal significance in information policy formulation.

It may appear somewhat ironic then, that information policy has been less intensively studied at the organizational than at national and international levels (Kajberg and Kristiansson, 1996). By contrast with the extensive literature devoted to related and analogous topics, Orna's (1990) seminal work remains the only comprehensive, and practically oriented, study of this area. While questions of commercial sensitivity must be a factor here, they are unlikely to be the whole story.

One clue to the difficulties inherent in this area is the very diverse set of entities included together under the heading of 'organizations'. Indeed, even defining quite where the boundaries of an organization lie is problematical. This makes it difficult to say with absolute certainty what information and knowledge can reasonably be said to be associated with a particular organization (Harrington, 1991). This diversity is likely to increase as organizations respond, in very different ways, to changes in their environment (see, for example, Handy, 1994; Baden-Fuller and Stopford, 1992). The papers included in this section show a wide diversity, of scale, purpose and culture, within a small circumference. They include: higher education institutions (themselves a highly diverse set, in terms of size, structure, culture and perceived mission); Advanced RISC Machines, a small, new and highly technical enterprise, with a culture to match; GlaxoWellcome, a large and multinational commercial enterprise; and a state-run health service, so far-reaching in scale as to have provoked the oft-repeated, if apocryphal, claim to have the largest staff headcount of any European organization since the Cold War Red Army. Given that these are but a fraction, and by no means a representative sample, of the variety of entities covered by the term 'organization', it becomes easier to see why drawing general information policy lessons from specific organizational settings is not a popular pastime.

One point which does emerge clearly from the papers in this section, and which must be a particular difficulty for studies of organizational information policy is the inconsistent, sometimes flatly contradictory, use and definition of terms. While this may seem somewhat pedantic, perhaps primarily of academic interest only, the difficulty of knowing quite what is meant by 'policy', *vis-à-vis* the other concepts related to it, has to be seen as a major difficulty in analyzing policy within organizations, and in making recommendations to pragmatic policy-makers, who will have little patience if there must be extensive ground-clearing of terminology first. David Allen and Tom Wilson (p.178) point out that the terms *policy* and *strategy* are closely related, to the point where they have effectively become synonyms, often used interchangeably. In a commendable bid for precision and clarity, they define policies—principles for courses of action—as antecedents of strategies—plans defining the means by which these courses of action are implemented. Margaret Haines (p.168), in rather similar vein, speaks of the development of guidelines, with subsequent development of strategies to facilitate implementation of these guidelines at a local level.

Again at the risk of appearing pedantic, it should be pointed out that a confusion between *information policy* and *IT policy* is more likely to arise in the organizational setting than elsewhere (*pace* the arguments about the 'I in IT' in national initiatives such as Information Technology Year). Most, if not all, of the new breed of Chief Information Officers in commercial organizations have come from an IT/computing background, and the assumption that an improvement in information provision equates to improvement in technical infrastructure will be familiar to any information professional. This is not to say that there is no relationship between technology and information policy; Harry East's paper (p.221), in particular, is entirely based around the results and consequences of such a relationship, with regard to enhanced access to electronic information sources within higher education, and David Pye (p.191) lays considerable stress on the same point, in the context of a small commercial enterprise with a peculiarly rich and well-developed technological communications infrastructure. Elspeth Scott (p.206) refers to several examples of developing technologies both as a stimulus to policy development and as a means of disseminating and publicizing policy formulations. Nonetheless, the distinction in the round between an overall information policy and a more narrowly scoped IT policy should be clear. There are some hopeful signs that some of the misunderstandings surrounding this issue may be lessening; Allen and Wilson, for example, note that the strategic plans developed by higher education institutions are now tending to focus on information, and on information systems, rather than on IT as heretofore. The emphasis is on exploitation, in their words, rather than implementation, which strikes a note with Scott's information management, as opposed to IT, mission—making information easy to find and easy to use. Haines' paper gives an example of how the two aspects may be combined within an overall policy statement, referring to 'effective management of information and appropriate use of information technology'. It is interesting to note that Allen and Wilson suggest that the move towards a more sharply defined emphasis on information *per se* may be accompanied by a more democratic, consensual form of policy and strategy development, and by a lessening of—probably unnecessary—detail in the policy statements generated.

Another fairly general issue to emerge, which one must suspect to be of particular importance in the organizational environment, is the question: what matters more—the formal policy statement, the document which is produced by the process of policy formulation, or the formulation process itself? Allen and Wilson show overwhelming support, at least in the academic environment, for the view that it is the latter—the improved communication and understanding engendered between the various parties—which is of greater importance.

This, in turn, brings up the issue of exactly how policies are formulated and implemented. Allen and Wilson suggest that the answer is not a simple one; an iterative process seems to be favoured in the private sector, but this approach was not followed by most of the higher education respondents. They show convincingly that the simple and 'rational' top-down model (intended strategy→deliberate policies→realized strategy) is being rejected (if indeed it was truly ever followed in practice) in favour of a bottom-up 'emergent' form of policy formulation (*ad hoc* decisions →emergent strategy→realized strategy) within the context of organizational learning.

It was noted earlier that the diversity in the nature and environments of organizational entities was likely to lead to a divergence in the methods for deriving and implementing information policies, indeed, in the understanding of the term itself. This is exemplified in the difference between the private sector, where a formal and logical policy planning framework may be feasible (though without support and input from the bottom up it will probably not be successful), and the higher education world, where it is clearly not (Allen and Wilson). This theme—the differences in methods, and indeed rationales, for the formulation and implementation of information policy, according to the environment of the organization—echo through the papers in this section: the highly and explicitly political (with large and small 'p') environment of Haines' NHS; Scott's international organization, newly merged from two mature entities, rather different in style and culture, with a rapidly developing and unstable environment, and a problem (for a commercial organization) of large size; Pye's small commercial organization, growing rapidly and developing its systems and policies in an informal and largely *ad hoc* fashion. Indeed, this variety raises the question whether it is even sensible to search for a common framework of understanding, still less recommendations for methodology, for information policies in settings bounded only by the fuzzy concept of 'organization'. It may be that some categorization or typology within this concept may be necessary, before anything detailed and more substantive can be said which would be generally applicable.

Nonetheless, perhaps surprisingly, some general points do seem to emerge from the papers in this section. Those noted here are those which impressed themselves on this commentator; readers will no doubt find others acceptable to their own backgrounds and preconceptions. One such point, obvious perhaps but worth stating explicitly, is the close link between information policies and the other policies and strategies of the organization, in line with Orna's (1990) view of an information policy as linking information resources with the strategic (i.e. highest) aims of the organization. We find this expressed in different ways: Haines' information policies being developed in response to major policy and structural shifts within a national service, and Scott's basing of an information policy within higher business goals and as an enabler of an 'intelligent enterprise', are perhaps the clearest examples. Despite the evidence from Allen and Wilson that this linkage may in some cases be more apparent than real, and intended more for political than practical purposes, it does appear that organizational information policies implemented without such a linkage must be doomed to irrelevance and failure.

Another general factor is a very close link between information policy and organizational culture, the latter a concept of great significance, if lacking an unambiguous definition (see, for example, Hampden-Turner, 1990 and 1993). The two seem to be symbiotic, each informing and influencing the other. Scott, in particular, notes that information policy has a key role to play in the development of a new corporate culture, as well as itself being determined by existing cultural factors. This is not so surprising, when one considers that an organization's culture is dependent on, and can be described in terms of, the way in which information and knowledge are transmitted and used within it. This point comes out most clearly in relation to Pye's 'open, non-hierarchical and bureaucratic culture' with rapid and informal business communication and decision-making, and with a consequent openness in information access.

A third general focus of commonality is the variety of ways in which information policy, in practice as opposed to theory, is formulated and implemented. Scott expresses most explicitly what appears to be common to all in describing the desirability of a coherent formal framework, or a specific methodological model (perhaps a formal change management programme). The need for a good understanding of what information content and processes are already there—through information auditing or mapping procedure—is described most fully by Pye, but again appears to be a common aspect. Thereafter, a general process of identifying issues→consensus building→obtaining approval→implementing→monitoring and evaluating appears to be the norm, allowing for differences in the political processes within different types of organization, but always allowing for debate and interaction. While none of the contributors goes as far as Ulrich (1994), who argues that policy formulation must include contributions, directly or via surrogates, from all those who will be affected, including those not yet able to contribute (including, in the extreme, the unborn), nonetheless all strive for inclusivity in the debate.

As a last general point, we may take as a common concern the perceived factors determining the success of information policies and strategies, and the ways in which the degree of success may be evaluated. While it would be unfair to regard the attention given to these aspects as disappointing, there is clearly a need for more work to be done. One aspect which emerges strongly through these papers is the sheer complexity of policy issues in any organization, particularly when the environment and technical infrastructure are rapidly changing; as more than one of these papers points out, policy may well be made virtually by accident, and may have quite unexpected results. All the papers, as we have noted, in one way or another, identify the need to involve as wide a variety as possible of those who will be affected by the policies as a *sine qua non* of success; in turn, this is likely to be associated with an approach to policy formulation and implementation which is, at least to some extent, bottom-up and incremental. This does not seem to conflict with the other factors of seeming general importance: nominating an individual or small group to take responsibility for policy issues, and ensuring explicit, and visible, support at the most senior level possible, with consequent assignment of adequate resources. An explicit linking of policy formulation with quality procedures and with the promulgation of standards also arises in several of the contributions. Information policy evaluation receives varied attention; the studies of the higher education setting provide broad-brush quantitative pictures, illuminated by qualitative insights, across a whole sector. The studies within individual organizations do not have much to say about evaluation, the processes of formulation and implementation being at too early a stage.

Although it is not a major theme in any of the papers, it is interesting to reflect that more than one mentions the avoidance of information overload as a purpose, or by-product, of information policy formulation and implementation. Perhaps future policy formulations will recognize that, alongside safeguarding, filtering, summarizing, and indeed discarding information ('corporate forgetting'), the minimization of information overload will be a major purpose of an information policy, protecting the organization and its people from information paralysis.

Finally, it is worth saying something about the processes of policy formulation, information policy included. Necessarily they are forward looking, to the medium- or long-term, and hence must be, to some degree, visionary in nature. An explicitly visionary approach is espoused here by Scott, and this may be expected to be a significant feature of all worthwhile attempts at information policy formulation. The vision must, of course, be kept in balance: a strong dose of pragmatism is still needed to ensure a degree of success in the implementation, development and eventual evaluation of the policy outcomes.

Library and Information Policy Development in the NHS

Margaret P.J. Haines[1]

Abstract

The National Health Service has undergone a series of major changes which have revolutionized the pattern of health care delivery in England, introducing a more managerial culture into the service. This paper examines the implications of these reforms for library and information policy and identifies some of the critical success factors in gaining high level recognition for library and information issues.

Introduction

The National Health Service has undergone a series of major changes which have revolutionized the pattern of health care delivery in England. The seeds for reform were sown in the late 1970s and early 1980s with the publication of findings from the Royal Commission on the National Health Service (NHS), the NHS Management Inquiry and government reviews of primary and community care, all of which showed unacceptable variations in patterns of health care delivery, sensitivity to patient needs, and application of clinical standards and management information systems (NHS, 1979; DHSS, 1983,1987, 1989).

The cumulative effect of these critical findings was policy changes which introduced a more managerial culture into the NHS through revised and strengthened management structures, improved information systems and mechanisms for closer monitoring of the care provided by

---

1. Margaret Haines was Library Adviser to the NHS from January 1995 until October 1996 when she joined the Library and Information Commission.

NHS professionals. However, the most significant revision of the NHS began in 1989 with *Working for Patients* which, whilst leaving untouched the basic principles of tax-funded health care and free care at the point of use, introduced a number of key changes, such as reducing the number of organizational tiers in the NHS, introducing an internal market of purchasers and providers, and devolving much of the authority for commissioning care and non-medical education and training to local authorities (Department of Health, 1989).

The purpose of the new NHS is to secure, through the resources available, the greatest possible improvement to the physical and mental health of the people of Britain. The main national policies for meeting this purpose are the *Health of the Nation*, the *Patient's Charter*, and a *Primary Care Led NHS*. These operate alongside other national strategies on *Research and Development, Information Management and Technology* and *Promoting Clinical Effectiveness*.

The specific objectives are to make the NHS a more responsive service by bringing decision-making closer to the patient through devolution of authority to local level, and to improve the clinical and cost effectiveness of services through supporting Research and Development (R&D) and promoting evidence-based decision-making.

Information challenges in the new National Health Service

All of the policy changes listed above have indeed had a tremendous impact on information provision and use in the NHS. The need for more precise management information has created demands for information systems and technologies to make the gathering and sharing of patient-related information more efficient. The focus on evidence-based decision- making has created the need for new sources of information such as databases of systematic reviews and for greater access to, as well as better filtering of, existing clinical knowledge in both print and electronic forms. In order to share in decision-making, patients need information in formats specifically tailored to their needs. New players in the NHS marketplace, such as Health Authorities and GP Fundholders, have information needs which must be investigated and addressed. In summary, the information challenges of the new NHS are more complex than ever before and to ensure that these are efficiently and effectively addressed requires a new approach in information policy development.

The following quotation from *Managing the New NHS* illustrates the government's understanding of this point (Department of Health, 1994):

> The effective use of relevant information will be more important than ever in the NHS to ensure the delivery and management of services ... The NHS Executive has a role in ensuring that information and research findings: the 'knowledge base of health care'—are effectively transmitted via libraries and other means.

Existing information policies

As indicated earlier, new information systems and strategies were introduced as part of the reforms in an attempt to provide better management information on progress towards the *Health of the Nation* targets and other policy goals and to support more efficient running of the health service and the wider Department of Health.

The Department of Health has three major information strategies: the Public Health Information Strategy, the Health Care Information Strategy and the Personal Social Services Information Strategy, as well as strategies which cover corporate and divisional information systems and infrastructure. These are coordinated through a Departmental Information Strategy Steering Committee which provides overall direction for the development and implementation of departmental information systems and infrastructure strategies and ensures that they are linked to and support overall Department of Health business and policy objectives. These information strategies were designed to gather and collate health information primarily to support policy-makers and senior managers in the health service.

The information needs of the wider NHS are delivered through the Information Management and Technology Strategy, *Getting Better with Information*, which was launched in 1992. This strategy sets out the vision for a better NHS through the effective management of information and appropriate use of information technology. Key objectives of the strategy are to develop a national information infrastructure and to develop an information skilled workforce for the NHS.

The NHS Executive has several other information strategies, including the Information Systems Strategy of the R&D Strategy, and, more recently, information components in the Promoting Clinical Effectiveness Strategy and the Patient Partnership Strategy. These focus more on resource development and dissemination rather than information infrastructure, network development or information to support policy making. The R&D Information Systems Strategy, in particular, has been designed to support the production of systematic reviews of evidence about the effects of health care and to disseminate information about the research work being funded or about to be funded by the NHS R&D programme.

Despite the prevalence of information strategies, by the mid 1990s there was widespread concern that there were still problems at local level within the NHS in accessing the knowledge base of health care and that more could be done at national level to facilitate this access. A series of national seminars on *Managing the Knowledge Base of Health Care*, chaired by the Parliamentary Under Secretary of State (Lords), Baroness Cumberlege, addressed some of the issues in 'transmitting the knowledge base of health care via libraries and other means'.

The Cumberlege seminars showed that despite the apparent opportunities to demonstrate their value in solving some of the information challenges in the new NHS, NHS librarians were not making as effective a contribution as possible. This was reflected primarily in duplication of effort and lack of coordination but also in the lack of visibility for the profession within the wider NHS. Reasons given for the failure of NHS librarians to meet their potential were: inadequate and complex funding mechanisms; lack of adequate training for new roles in supporting evidence-based health care; lack of integration with IT networks in parent organizations; lack of up-to-date guidance on libraries from the NHS Executive; and lack of mention of libraries in current information strategies (British Library, 1992; 1994).

Other problems which were highlighted at the seminars included the need for greater assistance from information professionals in quality filtering health information, especially resources on the Internet, and more access to information support for all NHS staff, not just for medical staff working in Trusts. Problems in accessing NHS libraries had been identified as a major problem for primary care staff, particularly those in rural areas, and for non-medical staff in Trusts.

The debate begun at the Cumberlege seminars resulted in four strategic objectives being identified as the basis for further action. The first two suggested that the knowledge base needed to be improved and more widely disseminated using new technologies such as the Internet and the NHS's own Intranet. The second two suggested that good library and information practice needed to be promoted and that local organization and access to libraries and thus to the knowledge base needed to be improved. Other specific recommendations included the development of a national health library strategy to coordinate delivery of NHS library and information services with other providers in the health information sector, increased training for NHS librarians to support their role in evidence-based health care and greater emphasis on standards and quality initiatives.

The role of the NHS Library Adviser in policy development

Following the Cumberlege Seminars, the Department of Health and the NHS Executive agreed to appoint an NHS Library Adviser to ensure that library and information issues were on their policy agenda. The post was seen to have an enabling function, i.e. to start discussions and to put items on the agenda of those concerned with developing and implementing policy in the NHS. Among the key tasks assigned to this post were:

- to study and assess the recommendations of the Cumberlege Seminars and to make proposals to the Department of Health and the NHS Executive on what could be taken forward within available resources; and
- to advise the Department of Health and the NHS Executive on a national policy to ensure effective coordination of health care information provision and dissemination of the knowledge base and in particular to devise a national library and information strategy.

Other specific tasks included:

- encouraging local library cooperative initiatives;
- considering and promoting standards and good practice;
- encouraging initiatives to signpost the knowledge base of health care;
- strengthening links between government and the health library community.

After a six-month period of analysis and research involving the NHS library and information community as well as colleagues in the Department of Health and the NHS Executive, the NHS Library Adviser prepared a report for the NHS Executive on a proposed way forward. This report suggested that good progress was already being made towards the first two Cumberlege objectives as a result of work being done by the R&D Directorate on developing research-based evidence databases, and by the Information Management Group in developing the NHS network infrastructure with links to the Internet. However, progress was slower on the other two objectives; local NHS access to the knowledge base was neither uniformly available nor adequately supported. The report concluded that solutions needed to be found to improve the local coordination of information access and provision.

After further consultation with all NHS library networks and regional librarians, the NHS Library Adviser was able to compile a list of problems relating to the utilization and impact of NHS library services which were common across all eight regions. This list resulted in a set of proposals for two different target audiences.

The first set of proposals involved working with local NHS librarians and their regional representatives, on:

- health library accreditation systems;
- signposting evidence on the Internet;
- cross-sectoral health library cooperation;
- guidance on professional development opportunities;
- research agendas relevant to health library and information provision.

The second set of proposals was aimed at encouraging the relevant NHS Executive officials at national and regional level to:

- simplify library funding and extend use of libraries to all NHS staff;
- provide training for librarians to support evidence-based health care;
- link NHS libraries to the NHSnet and the Internet;
- create regional library units to coordinate library service delivery;
- fund research into health information delivery;

- develop new policy on NHS library provision.

Progress towards library and information policy development

With respect to the first set of proposals, NHS librarians were extremely helpful and active in supporting the initiatives proposed by the NHS Library Adviser. They developed guides on evidence-based resources, both print and electronic, and produced Web sites on regional library networks, often in cooperation with their R&D information manager colleagues. The NHS Regional Librarians Group (RLG) worked closely with the NHS Library Adviser on a new accreditation system, on a training kit for NHS librarians and on developing a research agenda. RLG and other health library groups have been active in supporting the new LINC Health Panel which has been created to coordinate work on cross-sectoral issues, such as library accreditation and library support to the nursing profession.

With respect to progress on the second set of proposals aimed at NHS Executive policy makers, it is important to note that the NHS Library Adviser is, in essence, a one-person section located within the Information Services Division (ISD) of the Department of Health and not within a policy unit in the NHS Executive. This placement was due to the strong support for the post within ISD at a time when major staff reduction was occurring throughout the Department and the NHS Executive. This continued public encouragement of the post and postholder by senior ISD managers counteracted many of the disadvantages of not being seen by some NHS Executive staff to be a core NHS policy post.

Despite some initial delays in reaching key NHS staff in all directorates and regions, the NHS Library Adviser was able to make progress in the policy arena. Strong support for her policy proposals was given by the R&D Directorate which commissioned a paper on better integration of libraries within the R&D programme. This resulted in the commitment by the R&D Board to provide financial support for training for librarians to support evidence-based practice along the lines of the innovative Librarian of the 21st Century project which was funded by the R&D programme in Anglia and Oxford Region (Palmer and Streatfield, 1995). The regional R&D Directors also provided libraries with free copies of the Cochrane Database of Systematic Reviews and funded Internet links for many libraries. The NHS R&D programme has also funded information research relating to primary care and consumer health information needs and, together with the Health Care Directorate, has promoted the role of libraries in clinical effectiveness.

Much of the Adviser's time was spent working with regional officials on facilitating better coordination of library and information support at local level through the creation of NHS Regional Library Adviser posts. Postgraduate Deans and other regional officials were very supportive of the value of these posts and there will soon be at least one full-time Regional Library Adviser in every region.

On the whole, the NHS Library Adviser has made good progress in encouraging library related policy development within those NHS Executive Directorates with knowledge base related priorities. However, the funding issue and the lack of multidisciplinary library services in many NHS institutions remains a problem. There are still many NHS staff working in primary and community care who do not have access to library support and the issue of funding this support will need to be addressed. Even if funding can be found, these staff have problems in finding time to visit libraries and therefore libraries will need to develop innovative outreach programmes. Accreditation should help to improve and develop libraries but standards of information support need to be identified for all staff working in the NHS. Finally, there is still a need to encourage NHS managers, not just librarians, to be involved in making the knowledge base of health care accessible for all NHS staff.

The difficulty in solving most of these remaining problems is that they are not clearly the responsibility of any one Directorate within the NHS Executive. Library-related policy issues are owned by many different Directorates with no clear lead Directorate. The unit responsible for issuing the last general policy guidance on libraries, HM 70(23) in 1970, no longer exists. One of the NHS Library Adviser's proposals to work through some of these issues had been to create a cross-Directorate working party on library and information policy. This idea gained wider acceptance by NHS Executive Directorates when the Chief Executive of the NHS gave it and the work of the NHS Library Adviser his support. A senior manager within the Corporate Affairs Division of the NHS Executive who had agreed to chair the Working Party also agreed to work with the NHS Library Adviser on a paper on knowledge base access issues which the Chief Executive had requested.

It would appear that library related policy development is now on the agenda of the NHS Executive. Critical success factors in getting to this stage include: clear signals from the 'top of the office' that this policy area is a priority; support from direct line managers in facilitating meetings with key policy-makers; timing the delivery and style of policy proposals appropriately for government policy-makers; and being able to relate the policy area both to priorities of these policy-makers and to the priorities of 'grassroots' workers.

Postscript

The developments towards an NHS library and information policy which had taken place up to July 1996 were presented at the Cumberland Lodge 'Understanding Information Policy' Workshop. It is important to note (this paper is being written post-workshop), that further significant progress was made shortly after this event. In September 1996, the Cross-Directorate Working Party on Library Policy met for the first time and approved a paper which the NHS Library Adviser presented to the Executive Board on October 11, 1996.

This paper recommended that:

- the Cross-Directorate Working Party should investigate the funding of libraries and proposed solutions for streamlining the funding process and for ensuring the funding of multidisciplinary libraries;
- the Working Party should also develop new guidelines on access to the knowledge base and supporting information services for NHS staff;
- Regional Offices of the NHS Executive should lead on developing strategies to facilitate the implementation of these guidelines at local level.

The paper was received positively by the NHS Executive Board which requested that draft guidelines be presented again for Board approval by mid-1997. The Working Party met immediately to consider funding issues and to develop an outline for the guidelines. Work is now in progress on these issues and a new NHS Library Adviser, who took up her post in January 1997, will be taking a leading role in this policy initiative.

A subsequent development in the autumn of 1996 offers even more hope for the implementation of new 'knowledge base access' information policy in the NHS. The White Paper, *A Service with Ambitions*, was released towards the end of 1996 (Department of Health, 1996). This White Paper is intended to be the third part of an overall health and health care strategy, the other two being *Health of the Nation* and *Caring for People*. The Paper identifies five strategic objectives: a well-informed public; a seamless service, working across boundaries; knowledge-based decision making; a highly trained and skilled workforce; and a responsive service, sensitive to differing needs.

The White Paper will be followed by a wide consultation with patients, the public and people who work in the NHS in order to refine and improve existing policies in three important areas, and to ensure that these policies are part of a coherent strategy. The three areas are information, professional development and managing for quality.

With respect to information, the White Paper broadly defines the information requirements for the NHS, which include the need to:

- provide information to patients and the public so that they can make informed choices about their health and health care;
- provide professionals with relevant information about the latest clinical knowledge, research findings, health outcomes;
- ensure confidentiality of patient information;
- provide the necessary information about services and resources to support research, audit and the efficient running of the service.

The first two of these needs are the same as those which were identified at the Cumberlege seminars and which have been underpinning the work on library and information services policy. It is important to note that the NHS Executive recognized that much work on policy in the information area had already taken place or was underway and, indeed, the supporting material for the launch included references to the work on information networks and library services.

The Information Work Programme was launched in December 1996 at an event which included presentations by the then Secretary of State for Health, Stephen Dorrell, and John Horam, who was the Minister responsible for leading the Information Programme. Their presence and the calibre of the delegates invited to participate is one more indication of the growing awareness of the importance of 'knowledge base access' information policy within the NHS.

Information Systems Strategy Formulation in Higher Education

David Allen and Tom Wilson

Abstract

In organizations in business, industry and government, *policy* usually signifies the top-level vision statement, while *strategy* suggests the ways in which the policy or vision is to be brought about. However, the two terms have now become conflated as synonyms and the reality in organizations is that the previous, top-down image of a policy–strategy–tactics framework is being rejected in favour of a view of organizational culture and processes of survival, giving rise (from the bottom, upwards) to actions that have a strategic impact on the organization. This paper reports on research into information strategy formulation in UK higher education institutions. It reveals that the process encouraged by the Higher Education Funding Councils (as a policy decision) founders upon the reality of organizational cultures and politics.

Introduction

Kristiansson (1996) argues that information policy can be analyzed on a number of perspectives or levels, including: global, international, national, regional, industrial, organizational, individual and information system. While most of these areas have been comprehensively explored within the information policy literature (see, for example Trigo, Correia and Wilson, 1996; Bortnick, 1985; D'udekem-Gevers and Lobert-Maris, 1996; Dedrick and Kraemer, 1995; Moore, 1991), one key area that has not been explored in any depth (Kajberg and Kristiansson, 1996) has been the organizational level (Orna, 1990; St Claire, 1994). This paper focuses on information planning at the organizational level within the UK higher education sector.

The current interest in UK higher education information strategies stems from the recommendation by the Higher Education Funding Councils (HEFCs) that universities should produce them, and from the action taken by the Joint Information Systems Committee (JISC) to provide guidelines for their development. During the late 1980s and early 1990s most higher education institutions (HEIs) developed strategic plans which were information technology focused (our research suggests that over 90 per cent of HEIs developed these). However, over 73 per cent of these were perceived to have either failed or been only partially successful. HEIs are now, with the active support of JISC, developing strategies which focus on their information and their 'information systems' rather than the technology. The most common terminology used, and one supported by JISC and the Higher Education Funding Councils, is 'information strategy'.

This paper examines the relationship between strategy and policy, the practice of strategic planning, and some results of a survey of HEIs on aspects of strategic planning in respect of information technology and information systems generally.

Policy and strategy

The terms *policy* and *strategy* are clearly closely related. In dictionary terms the distinctions are clear: policies are courses of action developed by those in authority in any setting, although the following definition emphasizes national administrations:

> *Policy*: A course of action adopted and pursued by a government, party, ruler, statesman, etc.; any course of action adopted as advantageous or expedient (*Oxford English Dictionary*, CD-ROM version, 1995).

And another dictionary also offers:

> *Policy*: (2). a principle or set of principles on which to base decisions (*Chambers 21st Century Dictionary*, 1996).

Strategy, on the other hand, has its origins in warfare. Older editions of dictionaries rarely referred to any other meaning and one of the most recent gives this context as its first meaning:

> *Strategy*: (1). the process of, or skill in, planning and conducting a military campaign… from Greek *strategia*

> from *stratos* army + *agein* to lead (*Chambers 21st Century Dictionary*, 1996)

or, as the *Concise Oxford Dictionary* puts it: 'the art of war'. In business, of course, warlike metaphors abound—'killing off the competition', 'putting in a pre-emptive strike', and so forth—so it is not surprising that the notion of strategy as providing the rationale for dealing with the competition should have been seized upon.

Chambers, however, goes on to give the second definition:

> *Strategy*: (2). a long term plan for future success or development

which is probably the sense in which most people understand the concept today.

Believing that it is important to establish our usage of terms, we derive from these definitions an understanding that policies are the antecedents of strategies. Policies provide the principles for courses of action, while strategies are intended to define the means whereby those courses of action can be implemented, and the goals of those actions achieved. To demonstrate the relationship we can point to the government's *policy* to reduce the incidence of crime and to its *strategies* to accomplish this, namely, the introduction of more severe sentences, the demand that those sentences should be custodial, and the building of more prisons.

This clear distinction in our usage is all the more necessary because the two terms are often used indistinguishably, and because the term 'strategic planning' is often used where 'long-term planning' might be more appropriate, given the competitive connotations of the word *strategy*.

The Joint Information Systems Committee (JISC) survey

The study described here was commissioned by JISC and was intended to cover all 192 higher education institutions in the UK. The survey was carried out between June and September 1995 and resulted in a response rate of only 43 per cent—a rather disappointing figure but one which, perhaps, reflects the degree of enthusiasm for the idea of information strategies.

It was the intention of the survey to gain the view of a variety of institutional stakeholders in the strategy-making process, namely:

- chairpersons of the committees to which the strategy-making process had been delegated;
- academics involved in the process, either within the relevant committees or as spokespersons for particular groups;
- librarians;
- heads of computing services.

As we mention above, the survey results indicated that 90 per cent of HEIs had a formally documented IT-based strategy and that 62 per cent claimed to have an information strategy. Seventy four per cent of those that did not already have an information strategy claimed that they were considering developing one. It is significant that this survey was conducted between April 1994, when the HEFCs suggested that all HEIs develop an information strategy, and December 1995, when JISC provided guidelines suggesting how the HEIs should develop one.

Planning in higher education

Increasingly, all activity in academic institutions is being guided by strategic thinking: relating teaching to the declared aims of government policy on higher education; relating research to strategic directions that provide the best opportunities for achieving success in the Research Assessment Exercises; and exploring teaching and learning strategies that relate to initiatives of the HEFCs in the area of computer-assisted learning. The effect of this trend towards information strategy formulation is that institutions are becoming more aware of the need for strategic planning. This is a common factor throughout the public sector, as Knights and Morgan note (1995:196):

> In the UK the development of strategic management has been particularly encouraged by the State as a way of stimulating a more competitive and productive economy ... Governments throughout recent decades have sought to cajole managements to be more pro-active and strategic in their approach to business and competition.

Yet, in many cases, the strategic planning model that is being imported, in its crudest form, is from the private sector. This model has been described as the 'classical' or 'rational' approach to strategic planning.

It was pioneered by Ansoff (1984) and developed by Porter and Millar (1984), Porter (1985) and others. The approach taken in most HEIs has been the rational planning approach, the key features of which are that it is:

- undertaken by a small top management team within an organization;
- separated from the implementation process;
- not necessarily undertaken by those who will implement the strategy;
- focused on analysis not synthesis;
- perceived as a rational and logical process.

This view is described Figure 1, below. In this view an intended strategy is developed, from which flow a number of deliberate policies, which are then implemented to become the realized strategy. This rational view has been attacked by a number of researchers. Mintzberg (1993; 1994) attacks the deterministic, top-down nature of the classical approach, criticizing what he describes as its obsession with control, its simple-structured nature, its separation of those who develop the plan and those who implement it and, crucially, its reliance upon analysis to the exclusion of any form of synthesis.

Figure 1: The classical or rational approach

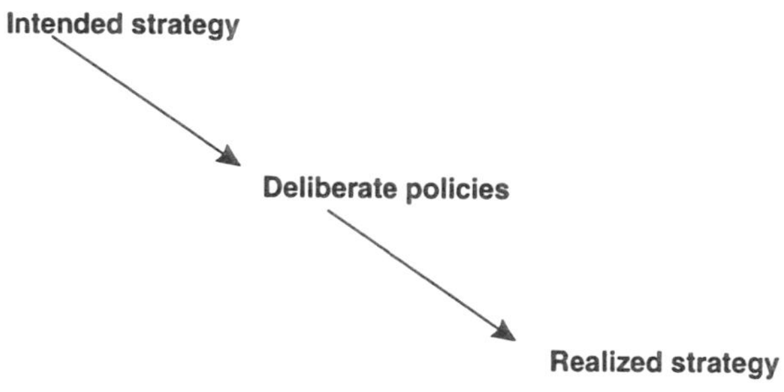

Alternative views have been developed which emphasize different aspects. Two of the more influential of these are logical incrementalism (Quinn, 1980) and the 'emergent' approach developed by Mintzberg (1994). Logical incrementalism focuses on the context and processes of strategy formulation rather than its content. Quinn argues that strategy formulation is primarily an internal political process, which proceeds in a number of logical steps rather than as a one-off process. Mintzberg argues that the crucial type of strategy is the 'emergent', which has 'evolved', rather than the formalized, intended strategy. This has led to a position where, as Reed (1992: 43) notes, 'the contributions of these writers indicated that the actual practice of organizational decision-making diverged sharply from that envisaged in the model of formal or instrumental rationality'.

The argument that the strategic planning process should be formal and logical may be supported from the viewpoint of the private sector, and some credence may be given to this idea. However, in the context of HEIs, it does not and cannot apply. Many HEIs have decision-making processes which are very different from those in business: they are more democratic, focusing on committee structures and consensus-building. This is true even in the less democratic, more centrally controlled, types of institutions, which recognize that in any HEI there are a number of powerful stakeholders who, if they are included, may affect the process positively, or, if excluded, may sabotage it. The process of formulating information strategies is intensely political since it can influence the structure of the organization, and therefore the power of every key stakeholder. Top-down, rational approaches adopted from business are likely to fail in HEIs, which are essentially political institutions, as they ignore this aspect of the process. A more realistic model of the process would accept the view that (Araujo and Easton, 1996:363):

> ... middle management and lower ranks are no longer conceived as mere cogs in the mechanisms of translation of strategic into operational objectives, but as individuals striving for personal autonomy and self fulfilment (c.f. Miller and Rose, 1990). Strategies can emerge from initiatives undertaken by enterprising individuals, following their own personal agendas and aspirations (Burgelman, 1988).

We therefore argue that the following model (Figure 2), is more applicable. In this view strategy is seen as emerging in the form of *ad hoc* decisions, as a result of organizational learning, the behaviour of interest groups or coalitions, and the interaction of power relations within the organization. This then merges with the deliberate policy to become the realized strategy.

Figure 2: The policy process (based on Mintzberg, 1994: 24).

In light of this model of information strategy and policy the question must be raised: what are the key issues which facilitate the success of such a process? When starting to look into this question, one is immediately faced with the problem of the lack of empirical research in this area. However, if one explores such related subjects as the strategic planning of information systems, a great deal of research has been undertaken. Galliers (1991) and Wilson (1989) have identified from the literature a number of key factors which influence the institution's ability to implement the strategy successfully:

- There is a need to align strategies, i.e. to link related organizational strategies, particularly business strategy and the information systems strategy (McLean and Soden, 1977; Martino, 1983).
- Key stakeholders (including senior managers and IT staff) should be involved within the process of formulating the strategy (Galliers, 1986; 1987).
- The process should allow opportunity for debate and consultation (Moscovivi and Doise, 1994; Checkland, 1981).
- The process should be reviewed on a regular basis (Hirschheim and Smithson, 1987) and this should preferably be an iterative process (Earl, 1989).
- The approach taken must fit the organizational structure and culture (Allen and Wilson, 1996).
- Motivational issues are important: the strategy should be developed in order to be implemented, rather than, as so many are in the public sector, to satisfy an external body.
- Those who implement the strategy should feel that they have ownership of the policies.
- The process should have a powerful champion.
- The strategy should be adequately resourced.

All of these issues were explored in the survey. However, in this short paper we will focus on results pertaining to the following: the alignment of strategies; the involvement of key stakeholders; the ownership of the strategy; the need for the process to be reviewed on a regular basis; and the motivation behind the process.

The need to align strategies

When asked, 'Was the IT strategy explicitly tied to the strategic goals of your institution?', the institutional response in 75 per cent of the HEIs was affirmative. However, when asked to give one example of such a link, many respondents left this section blank. The responses that were made tended to be very broad in their scope. However, when the stakeholders were asked to identify two or three of the most significant

IT developments in their HEI, only 12 per cent stated that these had been planned or anticipated within the IT strategy.

The importance of the link between IT strategy and business strategy has been recognized within the private sector: however, until recently, the problem within the HEI environment was that academic strategies tended to be bland and generic. The linkage between the two would be of more *political* importance in terms of *legitimizing* the strategy within the HEI than of practical relevance in terms of defining objectives and aims. This points to the importance of the process of strategy formulation rather than the final document.

Most of the of the HEIs had linked their information strategy to their IT strategy and the academic strategic goals or plans (see Table 1 below). This may reflect the fact that academic strategies are now becoming more meaningful, and less bland and generic. If an HEI already has 'meaningful' teaching and learning, IT or academic strategies, then explicitly linking the information strategy to these can be seen as a critical element in the success of the strategy.

Table 1: Frequency of responses to the question: 'Is the Information Strategy explicitly linked to ...'

Nature of response	Number of positive responses	Percentage of positive responses
Academic strategic goals or plans	47	85
The IT strategy	46	84
Learning strategies	45	82
Teaching strategies	43	78
Telecommunications strategies	32	58
Financial strategies	27	49
Estates strategies	26	47
Human resource strategies	24	44

Ownership and the involvement of key stakeholders

The inability to gain 'ownership' of the strategy was pointed to by a number of stakeholders as a key factor in the failure of the IT strategies. Stakeholders in a number of HEIs described the strategy as 'yet another piece of paper' because it failed to be 'owned' by key stakeholders. As one respondent stated:

> The strategy failed to be 'owned' by the institution and hence never 'engaged' financial mechanisms.

It can be argued that the failure to gain 'organizational' ownership of the IT strategies can be linked to the fact that they were often produced either by the IT Director or by a coalition of 'computer enthusiasts' who had a limited vision of the HEI's needs. The survey results showed that in 34 per cent of HEIs the strategy was *written* by the IT Director. In a further 55 per cent of these HEIs it was *produced* by an IT Committee, only 26 per cent of which had members drawn from most sectors of the HEI.

The information strategies are, however, being developed in a more 'consensual' manner than the IT strategies. The majority of the HEIs are producing the strategy through a committee. The data suggest that the committee members are usually appointed rather than elected, but are drawn equally from a wide basis and from a group of 'experts'. Indeed, the committees formulating information strategies do tend to be fairly representative. The library was represented in 93 per cent of committees, academic computing services in 90 per cent, academic staff in 90 per cent, and administrative computing services in 81 per cent. This communication across services and between academics, managers and services (who before the process often did not communicate on a regular basis) seems to be a lasting and important by-product of the planning processes. Those stakeholders who felt that their IT strategy had been successful described the process of formulating a strategy as enabling debate and communication across the HEI. Some stakeholders argued that it was successful *primarily* because it had played an important political role in facilitating communication. As one stakeholder noted, 'it has helped the centre and the departments to come to a shared understanding'. Another stakeholder pointed out that it had 'sparked a fuller debate' in his institution. This is a view supported by the data, relating to information strategies from this questionnaire: very few of the respondents (3 per cent) believed that it was primarily the information strategy document that mattered, while 88 per cent believed that it was the *process* of information strategy formulation itself that was important. Seventeen per cent of that 88 per cent indicated that it was the formal mechanism for facilitating communication with people in other departments or schools that they found most useful. The majority of the stakeholders indicated that they felt the process was both highly productive (47 per cent of respondents) and useful (63 per cent of respondents).

Ninety-seven per cent of those HEIs that had formulated, or were currently formulating, information strategies indicated that it would be put out for consultation before it was finalized: this is a larger percentage than for the IT strategies (86 per cent). This may reflect the fact that many stakeholders are realizing the importance of 'legitimizing' the strategy to gain support at the implementation stage.

The need for the process to be reviewed on a regular basis

It is perhaps obvious that, of all the HEI's strategies, the IT strategy will become obsolete most rapidly. The pace of change of IT can soon render technological decisions made in the IT strategy obsolete. The IT strategies produced were often criticized on these grounds, specifically that the length of their planning cycles was incompatible with their (often) detailed nature. Experience in the private sector suggests that the most effective process is an iterative one, but this was only the case in only 29 per cent of HEIs' IT strategy formulation process. The data suggest that the information strategy planning cycle was not particularly longer than the IT strategy planning process (in 37 per cent of cases the process was iterative).

Motivation

It can be argued that the motivation behind the process of strategy formulation will directly affect the level of commitment members of the organization are prepared to devote to it. The data gathered from the survey suggest that the main reason for the IT strategies was the 'requirement' of external funding bodies: 48 per cent of HEIs stated that this was the principal motivating factor. The next most frequently mentioned factor was to coordinate planning and investment policy for IT, which was mentioned in 21 per cent of the HEIs. The position is perhaps clouded by the fact that some HEIs had revised their strategies on a number of occasions whilst others had merely produced one version. However, it seems reasonable to postulate that many IT strategies were never meant to be implemented; they were merely intended to satisfy external requirements of the JISC Computer Board.

In light of the fact that JISC guidelines were only to be given in October 1995 it is interesting that 62 per cent of HEIs in the sample stated that they were currently developing, or already had, an information strategy as early as July/September 1995. Of those HEIs which responded that they neither had nor were developing an information strategy, 74 per cent indicated that they were considering developing one. It is significant that, although the initial impetus may have come from the external bodies, a number of stakeholders pointed to internal pressures for the development of an information strategy. One commented that his institution had been motivated to develop an information strategy because:

> As far as I am concerned, the University needs one to plan future priorities of IS/IT development. But I suspect the VC may have been persuaded by the HEFC requirement.

Thus the rapid uptake of the concept of an information strategy may be because it met an existing institutional need. The concept is certainly useful to stakeholders in HEIs in a political sense because it enables them to raise the pressing issues surrounding information provision with the authority of the funding councils. Thus one stakeholder noted:

> My reason—because we need a framework for Library/Computing convergence and the IT Strategy. The institution's reason? Because HEFC wants one.

Other motivating factors for the formulation of the information strategy included the need to review the HEI's IT strategy in light of perceived failings, as one stakeholder noted:

> .... recognition that the previous IT strategies had been technologically led. The coming strategy is now clearly focused on exploitation rather than implementation, and coordination of the support of information services for all staff groups.

The majority of the responses indicated that stakeholders were moving beyond IT strategies to focus on information provision, the importance of linking the key 'information' issues to academic goals and the reorganization of 'information' services.

Conclusion

Our conclusions from this analysis of the current situation and the past record of strategic planning in relation to information technology in HEIs are easy to state.

First, all experience of strategic planning in business and industry demonstrates that success depends upon involvement in the process from the bottom up and commitment to the processes of change on the part of all stakeholders in the system. Our prognosis for the information strategy process is more hopeful than for that of the IT strategies. However much depends upon the JISC guidelines which were issued after this survey had been conducted. Unfortunately the JISC guidelines suggest a reinforcement of the 'classical' approach to planning. Unless the top-down process is modified, and unless genuine participation from all levels of the organization is achieved, the idea of information systems strategies in higher education will barely outlive the rhetoric.

We would add to this the fact that if organizations are to change in the way they create and use information (and this is the function *par excellence* of universities), they must harness innovation wherever it manifests itself in the organization. Again, this requires the commitment of stakeholders at all levels and the participation and encouragement of anyone pursuing innovative methods within the university.

Changing the Corporate Culture: Information Policies for Business Excellence

David Pye

Abstract

Increasingly, organizations in all sectors are beginning to recognize that significant business advantage can be gained by managing and leveraging their information assets more effectively. This notion is a powerful one and it has captured the imagination of many senior managers. This paper reflects on the attempts of a young, dynamic British company to respond to the challenge. Unusually, it positions information policy in relation to quality management, business processes and corporate culture.

Introduction

In preparing a commercial input to the British Library Workshop, I was asked to write a paper to show how a young, energetic company, Advanced RISC Machines (ARM), is recognizing and confronting some critical business issues relating to the management and control of information.

Like all organizations these days we are swamped with information, generated from every transaction we make. Across the organization we hold a vast range of information in many different formats, recording just about every detail of our business. Increasingly, we are turning to sophisticated information technology tools to help us manage and control this data explosion. Unfortunately, and as we are discovering, providing the tools is not so much the solution as the start of the problem. What is the policy for data collection? How is information to be stored? How much is to be re-published and to whom? And, as the price of technology falls, and tools-led 'solutions' become more readily available, is there a danger that companies are losing sight of their real business needs: to leverage information assets effectively and wisely? Even if our information systems represent best current practice, what human and other factors should we be considering too?

My personal background and expertise lie primarily in the area of quality management. In writing this paper, I have been reflecting on the delicate balance between the company's need to be customer-focused, reactive, innovative and light on its feet; and those elements of management control (bureaucracy, if you like) which are needed to maintain effective communication and coordination. This tension between creativity and control represents something of a culture paradox for a small, dynamic and highly flexible company like ARM (Figure 1).

Figure 1: The culture paradox

Many successful small and medium-sized enterprises (SMEs) in the IT sector employ highly motivated, engineering-oriented managers who find it difficult to address some of the 'softer' people issues associated with rapid growth. Commonly, a gulf may emerge between management (who believe they are absolutely clear on policy and direction) and the staff, often young, who cannot fathom the tactics needed to meet management's expectations of them. No amount of technology replaces well thought-out 'people policies', with clearly stated roles and responsibilities. Conversely, no amount of people policy replaces good process policy, which can help generate useful management data for benchmarking performance to a particular standard. It is a combination of all these factors that provides the useful management information needed to steer the business better, rather than rowing it harder. This paper discusses the experiences of one such SME, and the ways in which it generates information and disseminates it around the organization. After giving some background to the company and its information infrastructure I will focus on three closely linked issues: quality management, information, and corporate culture.

Background to Advanced RISC Machines

Advanced RISC Machines Ltd (ARM Ltd) was founded in November 1990 as a spin-off from Acorn Computers. ARM, with its headquarters in Cambridge, has expanded rapidly and organically, from twelve people in 1990, 40 in 1994/5, to more than 140 in 1996. Its fundamental business is in intellectual property; designing microcircuitry for use in a range of advanced applications.

The new company was charged with transforming the ARM microprocessor from an Acorn Standard to an Industry Standard, challenging the dominant positions of Intel and Motorola architectures. Significant inroads have been made, with the ARM 'chip' family now forming the core of partnerships with such major players as Alcatel, Atmel, AKM, Cirrus Logic Inc., Digital, GEC Plessey Semiconductors, Lucky Goldstar (LG), NEC, OKI, Samsung Electronics Co., Sharp Corporation, Symbios Logic, Texas Instruments, VLSI Technology Inc., and Yamaha.

The mission of the company is to design and license competitive designs for small size/low-power-consumption/high-performance 32-bit processors and associated software tools to ARM Partner organizations, and through them to world-class original equipment manufacturers (OEMs) for incorporation into portable or computationally-intensive applications such as digital mobile telephones, computer games consoles, and television set-top decoders for cable and satellite TV reception.

Figure 2: The ARM Business Model

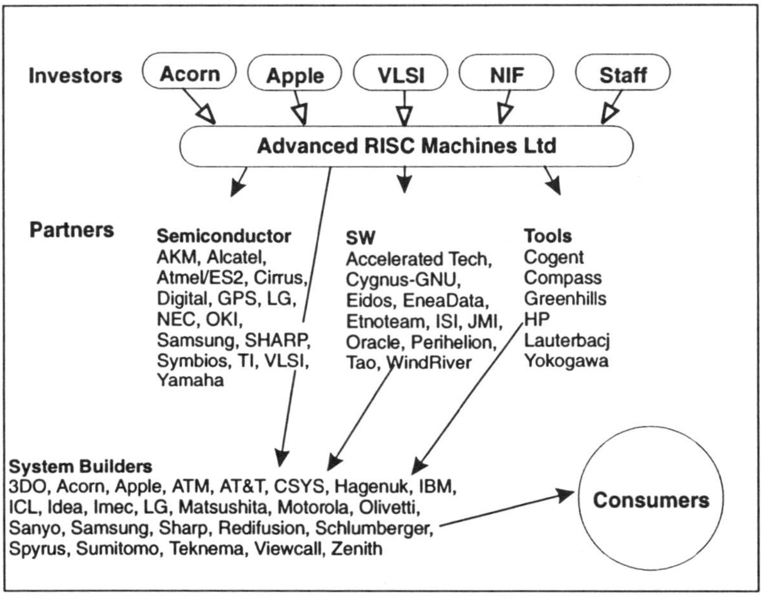

ARM revenues are generated from five streams:

- licence deals direct with Partners for use of the designs and their physical production;
- royalty income per chip sold in a device (e.g. a portable phone or games machine);
- consultancy;
- software tools and training;
- support and maintenance.

Turnaround times in the semiconductor industry, from design concept to working silicon chip, are getting ever shorter, with each successive family of chip being orders of magnitude faster that its predecessor, and yet smaller in physical size, and using less power. Commonly, more than one million transistors can now be embedded into one small square of silicon, measuring only 0.6cm x 0.6cm.

Some of the best brains in England are employed at ARM in the design of this fast-moving commodity, the average age being around 28, and typically with two technical and/or mathematical degrees from first-rate universities. International awareness is encouraged, with ARM employing many different nationalities to encourage the tenet: 'think global: act local'.

ARM's information environment

The corporate culture at ARM is 'open, non-hierarchical and non-bureaucratic, respecting people as individuals whilst striving for world-class excellence'. The style of the company is 'hard work and fun'. Almost complete freedom of information (*open*) is encouraged within ARM. Staff are trusted to treat appropriately (*non-bureaucratic*) large volumes of confidential ARM information (*respecting people as individuals*). There is no restriction placed upon acquiring information external to ARM (*striving for world-class excellence*). All forms of enquiry are used, but there is extensive use of online sources. Information acquisition is left largely to personal discretion, and sharing of information is by personal contact or diligent curiosity. Much current and historical technical information resides in the heads of the founder-members of ARM and other senior designers, and is shared through the (*non-hierarchical*) involvement of these staff in engineering projects.

ARM does maintain some restricted circulation lists for certain business-sensitive information (e.g. company financials, strategies, sales reports, Board minutes, etc.) This information is not 'secret', in that any member of staff may ask and be given the information. The policy is in place to ensure that the risk of accidental loss or misuse of this key information is minimized.

The range of means of discovering and disseminating information at ARM is very wide indeed, with broad channels of communication available to all members of staff. This is true both within the organization and outside it. Rich, multifunctional channels of communication are in place with all ARM's Partners and are installed at both project and Board level. Regardless of where the information is generated, it is shared across the organization using state-of-the-art tools.

Table 1 summarizes the main mechanisms for information discovery and dissemination at ARM. It is divided into four categories: hard copy resources; external electronic information resources; internal electronic information resources; and other information resources.

Table 1: ARM's information infrastructure (summary)

Hard copy information resources	**External electronic information resources**
• A small document library exists (<100 hard-bound volumes) with one part-time administrator. No indexing or cataloguing; listing by date order of purchase. • A simple book purchasing policy is in place with a generous budget; staff may purchase reference books with authorization. The *Financial Times* is available for information browsing. Much duplication of individual copies of various business, trade and professional journals. • Press cuttings services are used to monitor the company's media profile. • A controlled hard copy central filing system, indexed and organized by customer name and filed/retrieved by an administrator. The choice of whether or not to place documents within the system is left to individual discretion (an exception is signed contracts, which are filed separately for legal reasons).	• Unlimited World Wide Web access is permitted. • ARM maintains its own presence on the Web, offering general information about the company; current job vacancies; press releases; detailed technical information on ARM products in the form of datasheets. A record is kept of enquirer visits by number only. • Electronic mail is encouraged as the preferred medium for communication and information exchange at all levels of the organization. All staff have an individual e-mail address and are expected to use the facility to the full. • Unlimited access to subscriber-only Internet newsgroups. • Secure direct-dial UUCP links with ARM's partners and holdings company investors. • ARM subscribes to commercial online data services such as Dataquest.
Internal electronic information resources	**Other information resources**
• Unlimited Intranet Web access (known internally as the Staff Information System); mirrored via private Integrated Services Digital Network (ISDN) lines to ARM offices on three continents and auto-updated daily. Accessible by all staff, with general and company-specific information entered locally, unmediated, and viewable globally across ARM. • Organized company file-structures, maintained by ARM are open-access to all ARM staff for the deposit of reports, project information, and correspondence. Local access-control (to files) is the responsibility of every member of staff, to ensure reasonable access with adequate protection against loss or corruption. • Numerous ARM-maintained database applications, including a mix of proprietary databases and internally designed systems. • ARM maintained internal Newsgroups (special interest groups (SIGs) related to scientific interests and personal interests, e.g. ARM five-a-side football). An ARM-maintained Weekly Report mechanism, encouraging staff to share their projected short and medium-term goals, for the wider understanding of cross-project issues.	• Regular 'communication meetings' for all staff. • Formal presentations by senior managers from time to time, reporting on company results, new strategies, etc. • Repository of company presentation materials (in Microsoft Powerpoint format) to encourage re-use and uniformity. • Video and other training and instruction materials.

Information and business processes: an under-researched area

In a highly competitive market environment, understanding the customer's needs is very high on the Chief Executive Officer's (CEO) agenda. Steps are taken to understand customers' requirements in every detail, and to have this information pervade the whole organization. ARM's approach is to use customer input to drive company actions and for everyone to strive to achieve complete customer satisfaction. This is achieved through effective communication, by putting business processes in place to control the translation of customer requirement into quality product.

ARM's business processes are simple and lightly documented: this is typical of a high-tech SME in its early years of growth. Internal self-assessments, using a repeatable methodology, are used to identify the company's strengths and weaknesses in areas of technological and financial performance, and this supports a *kaizen* philosophy of continuous business improvement (a Japanese word now used to describe the small, cumulative steps which improve quality). Similarly, the results from the self-assessment exercises help to identify other issues that need to be addressed (such as management quality and leadership). ARM recognizes that its business success is inseparable from the capture and understanding of its external data, the exploitation of internal business process information, and the control of its intellectual capital.

On the face of it, the introduction of formal quality management techniques and procedures should allow any organization to improve its performance. In practice, these techniques have to be applied with some sensitivity, with the amount of process acceptable to the organization being linked to its ability to understand and intellectualize the information that flows from the collection of new data (these data being an automatic output of any newly installed process). Moving from enthusiastic start-up to a quality-repeatable mature organization involves not only changes in physical size and the introduction of formal written process, but also changes in intellectual outlook and behaviour. In the case of ARM, the technical 'can-do' attitude is underpinned with a parallel growth in knowledge and accumulated wisdom that can be applied to advantage through controls of just sufficient weight, so designed and placed as to keep the organization high on the cusp of maximum energy, without tipping over into the twin chasms of bureaucracy or bankruptcy.

A severe limitation of existing quality management tools and models, however, which may reflect their origins within manufacturing environments, is that they are not well-tuned to the needs of service industries, especially those where human creativity is the key productive resource. They do not pay sufficient attention to the linkages between control, the use and development of information management, and the people-centred 'empowerment' processes necessary to meet the dynamic requirements of business excellence in the late twentieth century.

Information audit exercise

For this reason, ARM embarked on a small-scale information auditing exercise. This was carried out at the UK premises of ARM during the summer of 1995 by two MSc Information Science students from City University's Department of Information Science: Kathryn Foden and Erika Hornby. The exercise consisted of two phases: the compilation of an information resource inventory, and then a series of more qualitative approaches to understanding aspects of ARM's information culture.

In preparing the information inventory, a very broad interpretation of what constituted an 'information resource' was adopted: one which embraced physical documents, electronic numbers and text, voicemail and knowledge embedded in human memory ('brainware').

The second part of the audit consisted of an information resources questionnaire to record the qualities (timeliness, relevance, ease of integration, etc.) that define an information resource's utility. A supplementary questionnaire was developed to gather qualitative insights into the context of information use in the company, to find answers to such questions as the role of information in ARM, and ideal information scenarios as expressed by members of the ARM staff. A further questionnaire survey examined the quality of ARM's processes in terms of the information flows supporting its 'customer-supplier chains' (of which many more are internal than external), and related the findings explicitly to the end-customer.

It quickly became clear that the ARM culture was in conflict with the aims of the classic information audit. ARM's culture, where most business is conducted electronically or verbally and *fast,* tends to encourage local information concentrations. Information resources therefore tend to be held in small pockets, local to the point of use, and rarely considered 'complete'. This finding tends to limit the capability of the information audit.

A second, important phenomenon is that due to its great flexibility and 'can-do' approach, ARM's features, systems and processes change very quickly. Issues are recognized, resourced and fixed by small teams with wide powers. A good example is the complete refurbishment of ARM's WWW pages; specified, staffed, designed, tested, documented and launched globally by a team of three in the space of two weeks! In this flexible environment, the audits were set up to discover, locate and evaluate information resources of relevance to ARM and ARM's Partners. The objectives were to:

- inform ARM of existing information-related systems and practices;
- identify problems or shortcomings in existing information-related systems and practices;
- provide an initial assessment on the appropriateness of existing systems in relation to ARM's goals and mission;
- begin to examine possible solutions to known information-related problems at ARM;
- make recommendations for improvements to information-related systems at ARM.

The broad-brush conclusions of the information audit may be summarized as follows. Important information, though in existence, is not disseminated to the appropriate people at the appropriate time. This, in turn, directly affects the company's ability to be customer-responsive. The rapid growth of information is seen to be having an effect upon ARM's ability to store and manage it. As the company grows, yet larger amounts of hard-copy information need to be stored while in use, and then archived to statutory timescales greatly in excess of those envisioned only a short time ago. This, in turn, throws a new load on the organization, relating to the traceability of versions, to ensure that only current versions are stored, while old versions can be safely destroyed. This same issue affects the storage and backup of computer files and the intensity of the backup regimes. It is probably universally true that organizations using IT extensively have found that the new technologies have delivered daunting volumes of information without providing, *per se*, the techniques to manage that information effectively.

The published literature on the subject does not deal well with information auditing in fast-moving SMEs, where commercial considerations and organizational flexibility overshadow conventional information science training and methodology. That more time is needed to perform additional analysis on information gathered in the initial audit, is not doubted; yet due to the fast-moving nature of the organization, when that time can be found, the data are out of date. The conclusion from this is that a lighter-weight information auditing mechanism is needed from the information science community, the better to make available the benefits of auditing to dynamic, creative, commercial organizations.

Management Information Systems developments

It was recognized, partly as a result of the information auditing work and partly through the increased efficiency being demanded by the ARM Directors, that improvements in ARM's Management Information Systems (MIS) must be put into place. Success breeds success in quality improvement initiatives. As one part of the organization makes an improvement in *its* processes, that part of the organization will begin to exert pressure on its neighbours (the internal customer-supplier chain) for improvements in the quality of inbound information being supplied. Only when this phenomenon is observed can Total Quality Management be said to have arrived. A large company-wide database is to be implemented and the intention is to narrow down to a series of options which can be assessed against the framework of the existing company culture.

The task force goals are to:

- make recommendations on how and when ARM might implement MIS to improve its operational efficiency;
- oversee the implementation of chosen systems (and by implication, any associated processes);
- achieve timely (and measurable) results;
- allow prototyping, controlled risk-taking, orderly disposal of failures;
- grow towards a unified and coherent MIS.

The task force methodology is to:

- form a small task force comprising two Directors, two Operations Managers, the IT Manager, one IT Engineer, one Sales Engineer and one Technical Support Engineer;
- meet regularly;
- identify owners to provide detail and drive to completion solutions graded by importance and likelihood for success;
- identify key company data, their users in each area, and any potential or actual overlaps;
- investigate current underlying technologies; look for standards or standardization possibilities (to ease future convergence);
- develop action plans to implement recommendations.

Constraints and considerations are that:

- consideration is needed over company-wide visibility and usage of data;
- the amounts of raw data poorly understood at this time;
- international multi-user remote access is required 24 hours a day;
- international multi-user remote update capability is preferred 24 hours a day
- heterogeneous documents have to be handled successfully;
- the international acceptance and integration of any 'home-grown' solutions must be ensured.

ARM's 'can-do' culture still provides for quick and flexible local responses to locally identified problems. Little formal restraint is acceptable to govern creative solution-fixing and no heavyweight 'approval committee' structure has ever been part of the ARM culture. The high ambient IQ and wide-ranging computing skills of the workforce, together with the open culture, permit a predisposition to inventing tools and mechanisms in-house. This is seen to be speedier (or more intellectually challenging/satisfying?) than doing the research/testing needed when undertaking a *make or buy* decision. It also conceals the real cost of developing tools in-house as many are developed in the staff's spare time, using company resources whilst they might otherwise be idle. The legacy is large amounts of untracked company data of greater or lesser (i.e. unknown) value, residing unsupported and unsystematically arranged in pockets where the problem was first identified. Duplication of information is high.

The variety of tools and applications in use is wide, each performing manipulation of similar source-data in many different ways. Resource usage (i.e. disc-space) is hard to evaluate properly, but may always stay ahead of the problem owing to the falling costs of storage and the increasing performance of the hardware.

Advantages of 'spot fixes' are that they:

- provide cheap, fast, creative solutions at the point of need;
- give the implementing staff a strong sense of empowerment and achievement;
- need no hierarchy of bureaucracy for approval or close control;
- play to the 'can-do' company culture.

The disadvantages are:

- the value of company information is unknown;
- there is no central control of information;
- information is exposed to risk of espionage, corruption and loss;
- duplication of data, with many information-owners unknown or only known *by chance* to a few;
- excessive time-wasting when merging of information is needed (i.e. for mail-shots) with great potential for embarrassment when internal sloppiness becomes externally visible.

Routes to business excellence

I have briefly touched on the array of issues and challenges connected with information management, MIS, information storage and retrieval, and information technology procurement within a single company. It is evident that Business Process Engineering and other quality initiatives tend to focus upon what can be easily described and measured. This is clearly reflected in their documented outputs: business process descriptions, flowcharts, reports, management indicators and metrics. The role of information of all kinds in supporting (or even being a precondition for) business processes is barely acknowledged within these methodologies. The existing tools of Information Resource Management, notably information mapping and auditing, have proved to be very valuable within ARM in raising an awareness of bottlenecks and dysfunctional information flows.

The two concepts have to be interlinked and to proceed at a complementary pace, or resource spent upon either is likely to be wasted and the initiative fall into disrepute. Both Quality Management and Information Resource Management aim to deliver improvements, but a corporate-wide strategy of linking both seems to be required, ('Information Quality Management' ?).

What perhaps both sets of tools miss out on is the unique human ability to link and contextualize disparate pieces of data as usable information. A recent internal study within ARM underlines the most important point about information provision and dissemination: the human dimension. State-of-the-art mechanisms and tools do not of themselves improve information flows and company performance. Placing information online and providing 'wacky' front-end graphical user interfaces does not in itself motivate staff to read the information and grow wiser. The torrent of online information available both externally and internally—available, but not necessarily *understandable* in the precise moment and in its precise ARM context—poses a great challenge.

Good leadership identifies issues early, increases cooperativeness, improves information sharing, and keeps morale high and discipline aligned to the organizational culture. Superior leadership includes an additional concentration on information classification and the assessment of its commercial implications. Without this understanding, information overload threatens to leave information (as a resource), a poor cousin to the three traditional elements of production: labour, costs, and materials.

The provision of company-provided Intranet services to some extent reduces overload, as there is an implied element of control over what can be viewed. Sound leadership and motivation of the staff to use this new medium, and to share information across projects or functional groupings, will over time assist in providing competitive edge. It is fair to suppose that easily accessible, up-to-date and reliable information results from having good process in place. Process yields recordable information, and process requires access to good information, a virtuous circle that provides a neat paradox to be solved by the active SME which may see process as bureaucracy to be avoided like the plague.

A new order of organized information control, skills-sharing and cooperative working must prevail to keep information chains as short and yet as rich as possible. Making more information available is not enough. Understanding the information that *is* available has a far bigger payoff. ARM is putting into place measures to increase commercial awareness and to improve the ability of all staff to take action in advance of challenging situations instead of remaining victims to events seemingly beyond their control. This requires a plan of training and mentoring for specific individuals that is not left to chance. A new skill of knowledge management is needed to filter, control and protect the company's intellectual property. This is the challenge for ARM Ltd in the latter part of this century and the dawning of the Information Age.

Acknowledgements

Some of the ideas and activities described in this paper arose partly out of the findings of an EU-funded collaborative research project, IMPROVE, funded under the ESPRIT Programme's Technologies for Business Processes (TBP) initiative. ARM led and managed the consortium, which included the following individuals and organizations:

EC Project Officer	Dr Giorgio Basaglia (DG-III, Brussels)
Coordinating Partner	Peter King (ARM Ltd, Cambridge)
Partner	Roberto Galimberti (Etnoteam SpA, Milan)
Partner	Emilio di Cristofaro (Galgano e Associati SrL, Milan)
Partner	Manfred Kreutle (pdv Unternehmensberatung GmbH, Bremen)
Associate Partner	Ian Rowlands (City University, London)

I would like to thank them for their contributions, more complete details of which can be found in the Definition Phase document 'IMPROVE Project 20450: Extract of Results for Public Dissemination' which can be viewed on ARM's Web server at http://www.arm.com/.

Evaluating Information Policy in a Multinational Organization

Elspeth J. Scott

Abstract

This paper describes the process of information policy-making in a newly merged multinational organization. The purpose and objectives of policies and their relationship to overall information and corporate strategy are reviewed. The approach to date has been essentially pragmatic and driven by business need rather than a coherent framework or a specific methodological model. The processes of identification of issues, consensus-building, policy drafting, user buy-in mechanisms for decision-making, and activities surrounding implementation are still in a state of evolution. Compliance monitoring and evaluation of the policies *per se* remain a future challenge. However, it is useful, one year on from integration, to consider what has been achieved, what lessons have been learned, and what changes should be made in the next phase.

Introduction

On 23 January 1995, Glaxo announced its intention to merge with the Wellcome Foundation Ltd. The new company, GlaxoWellcome plc, is the largest pharmaceutical company in the world and among the top three companies in the UK in terms of market capitalization.

A merger of this nature presents both threats and opportunities. The climate of upheaval provides a fertile breeding ground for change and a chance to implement visionary strategies. I like to think that the establishment of a small team to address information policy issues within R&D was a manifestation of that creative vision, but time will be the judge of the effectiveness of this initiative.

As background to the information policy-making process, I want first to fill in a few more details about this multinational company, its business goals, its organizational structure and its corporate philosophy. I shall describe the policy team, where we sit in the organization, our role, and our *modus operandi* before going on to discuss some key information policy issues in greater detail. Finally, I shall examine the circumstances impacting the policy process and distil some of the lessons learned over the past year.

The GlaxoWellcome context

GlaxoWellcome plc is a research-based company whose business is bringing innovative medicines and services to patients and the health care providers who serve them. Early in the integration process it established clear business goals, among which is the following:

> To build a learning organization that fully realizes the potential of all our resources—our people, technology, information and capital.

Any R&D-based organization is by its nature information-intensive. It is gratifying, however, that the importance of information has been recognized at the top level of management and this has fostered a corporate climate where information is treated as a key contributor to business success; this is what, for so many years, LIS professionals have been campaigning for. This is not just lip service to an ideal, but a very real understanding of the value of information and the need to be an 'intelligent enterprise' which is reflected in substantial resource allocation not just for IT, but for managing content-based information services from both internal and external sources.

The Group IT Director reports to a main board Director, and his direct report, the Director of R&D's Worldwide Information Resources (IR), sits on the R&D Executive. The Information Policy group sits within IR in a group called Information Management & Analysis (IM&A). The driving force which underpins information strategy is the group's objective to increase R&D effectiveness in bringing new drugs to the market. Liz Orna (1990) has described information policy as 'linking information resources with the strategic objectives of the organization', and this is precisely what we aim to do. However, issues which are important for R&D quite often need to be addressed globally and so, increasingly, the policy unit is operating corporately rather than purely in R&D. An example of this is the development of GlaxoWellcome's corporate Intranet policies and standards which have global applicability.

The team itself is small; we are just five people:

- Head, International Information Policy & Standards (IIP&S);
- US Policy Coordinator;
- UK Policy Coordinator;
- International Information Contracts Manager;
- Policy Administrator.

Small is beautiful! It allows us to keep in close contact and act as a focal point for policy issues. In reality there are two triangles: two and a half of us working on information policy issues, and two and a half concentrating largely on copyright and contracts.

The mission of Information Management & Analysis (which broadly equates to the information services as opposed to IT functions) is to 'make information easy to find and to easy use'. This mission is entirely within the spirit of our corporate and R&D objectives. In order to make information easy to find and to use it must be:

- acquired (purchased externally or collected internally);
- made accessible to the business;
- held in an appropriate format, so that it is
  - » reusable
  - » and retrievable.

The benefits of ready accessibility to the organization are manifold, since information:

- supports decision-making;
- aids discovery;
- speeds up the development process;
- promotes internationalization;
- cuts duplication of efforts and reduces costs.

But ready accessibility is not everything; we also have a duty to protect information from the dangers of unauthorized or inappropriate disclosure (or deliberate misuse) as well as ensuring the integrity of the corporate knowledge base for the future.

Information policies and standards help to lay down rules and methods for managing information consistently across an organization. They also protect the company from risks such as the loss of intellectual property and (potential) accusations of the neglect of assets. The pharmaceutical industry is, of course, heavily regulated with tough codes of practice, including Good Laboratory Practice (GLP) and Good Clinical Practice (GCP). These codes ensure that information relating to our products is correctly handled at all stages of both the product and document life cycle.

We therefore modified the Information Management & Analysis mission statement to 'make information easy to find and easy to use and compliant with legal and regulatory requirements'. Our vision is to contribute to the building of that learning organization by creating an information-conscious workforce.

Both partners, Glaxo and Wellcome, had their own ways of doing things prior to the merger. Glaxo tended to favour discrete Standard Operating Procedures (SOPs) which governed the creation, distribution and storage of documents, whereas Wellcome had a combined Document Policy whose development had been instigated by the need to compile and publish electronically the extensive documents associated with regulatory submission for drug approval.

Information policies can also help bring about cultural change which is vital in an industry which is undergoing radical and endemic restructuring at the moment, and even more so in a newly merged company where a new corporate culture has to be established. It is not simply a case of having to rationalize different procedures; there is an opportunity to take a visionary approach. I must stress the need to balance the desirability of taking a long-term view with providing a prompt response to urgent business issues.

Methodology

The first step is to identify what issues require a policy statement in order to resolve a business dilemma. Our approach to date has been highly pragmatic and driven by business need. For example, one of the first problems we were asked to deal with was to establish a unique identification scheme for R&D reports (different systems were in place in the two former companies and there were further differences between the

US and the UK). This was not rocket-science but it did provide a revealing insight into the whole process of policy-making and implementation which may be summarized in the following stages:

- identify the issue (and scope it);
- build consensus;
- get approval;
- implement;
- monitor compliance.

Issue identification

At the first meeting of the IIP&S team following establishment, around September 1995, we drew up a list of issues which would have to be tackled. We attempted to prioritize these according to their impact on the business and on information flows. By and large, that list has proved to be fairly accurate, although occasionally the scope of an issue has changed, or the business itself has raised a priority. For example, from the work that we had been doing on defining the policy for confidentiality of, and access to, R&D reports, we became involved in the development of corporate policy on IT security (incorporating information classification).

Ideally, one should seek *sponsorship* from the business for an issue at this early definition stage. The sponsor should be as senior as possible in order to lend weight to the importance of the issue in question.

For each issue we allocate a Lead Policy Coordinator who will have responsibility for defining the Terms of Reference, convening and chairing meetings. The 'Terms of Reference' document sets out the scope of the issue under consideration, the proposed membership of the group to be involved, the timescale and deliverable(s). Deliverables usually take the form of a draft policy proposal or 'Green Paper' for circulation and comment by the wider business community.

Building consensus

This is a tough one! Bearing in mind the adage that you cannot please all of the people all of the time, and that there is not enough time anyway to consult all of the people, the best approach is to use one's knowledge of the business coupled with asking around, to identify those groups who are most affected by the issue concerned and to identify representatives who can speak for those groups. This is not always easy! The sort of person who is likely to want to be involved very often has a strong personal interest in the topic and that personal agenda can sometimes be an impediment to consensus-building. On the other hand, if the representative has no real interest in the topic in hand, then attendance at meetings can lapse and an unbalanced view results. It is therefore advisable to try to keep numbers to the minimum compatible with adequate representation. This helps to avoid the inevitable problems of scheduling meetings with large numbers of people.

Pervading the entire information policy process is the need to *communicate* with the business. Our role, after all, is not to create policy out of thin air but to be facilitators and to act as a focal point for ensuring that the business has in place the policies that will help it function smoothly. So how do we communicate and promote debate on information policy issues in such a large organization? We use a range of techniques, including:

- policy fora;
- the GlaxoWellcome Intranet;
- presentations and discussions.

Policy fora

I have already mentioned that we seek representation from key business groups on specific issues. In addition, we are aiming to establish standing committees for each Division within R&D (Research, Development, Medical, and Regulatory). The representatives on these committees have to be 'empowered' individuals who act as multipliers of information, relaying policy proposals to their own areas and channelling feedback to the forum and the Policy Coordinator (who acts as convenor and sometimes even chair). The Divisional representative must be senior enough to accept this responsibility as conduit but not so high in the chain of command that they are removed from the day-to-day business issues. These policy fora have been slow to get off the ground. Senior management is supportive of the idea, but ideal representatives are not easy to find. At cross-divisional level, the hope is that consensus can be reached without the need for a formal committee, but meetings could be arranged to settle any conflicts should the need arise.

The GlaxoWellcome Intranet

Like many other large companies, GlaxoWellcome has an extensive Intranet (which is in itself generating lots of information policy issues!). A large proportion of US and UK employees and others in local operating companies (LOCs) have access to Netscape and to a vast amount of internal information. This seemed like an excellent way to reach people and keep them up-to-date with current policies and policy issues under discussion; we also hope to obtain feedback from users whom we would not normally reach.

We further intend to set up a newsgroup for the discussion of copyright problems around the world. As awareness of the need for education on intellectual property rights grows, so there will be a need to share experience with our colleagues in local operating companies and to provide guidance on corporate policy in this area.

Discussions and presentations

How we acquire and absorb information is to some extent a matter of individual taste. Personally, I find there is no better way to learn than to listen to a presentation and to take part in a discussion. This is a powerful form of communication for most people. At GlaxoWellcome, we try to maximize opportunities for making presentations to selected business groups, sometimes to senior management, sometimes to small Departmental meetings, sometimes one-to-one. Wherever there is a willingness to listen, we will go. As a team, we have prepared a set of standard overheads about our policy team (since people are still curious about our role) and about our aims and objectives. These can be augmented with material about the issues of most relevance to that particular group. The very preparation of these materials helps to focus our minds on the long term aims and short term objectives. It is important that we preach the same message whether in the UK, the USA, Italy, or wherever we may be. The feedback and questions raised at meetings are invaluable in helping to shape policy and how we communicate.

The approval process

This is also a hard one!—and not just for us but for the new organization as it begins to settle into its new structure and culture. The aim of the approval process is to empower people, but the reality is that for important issues one still wants to seek top management blessing. These senior managers are extraordinarily busy people; while they take the issues seriously, given time, there is nevertheless a host of priority business issues to attend to when the Executive meets. So, it is quite hard to get a hearing. Then, quite rightly, when presented with policy proposals, they want to know whether the various business groups have accepted the recommendations. It is easy at this stage for the process to be derailed because one individual has not had time to be briefed or has a particular view on an issue which is contrary to the general consensus. It is also quite hard to know how to proceed if some recommendations receive only qualified approval. However, an appropriate level of sponsorship can obviate some of these problems.

Another difficulty is knowing how much or how little detail to present to busy senior managers. The general opinion is that two A4 sheets is about as much as they have time for, but that is usually insufficient to present complex issues or careful background consideration. On the other hand, it does no harm to be forced to express policy and guidelines very succinctly as it encourages clear thinking and more efficient communication to the end users who must implement any forthcoming directive.

Let me illustrate the sort of problem one can encounter in getting policy agreed, with just one example. The issue in this instance was securing agreement on a policy to access the R&D reports database. The original proposal had combined two issues, namely levels of confidentiality of reports and access rights. Previously the different companies had had different approaches, and the US and UK practices for each had also differed somewhat. In order to launch the new joint R&D reports database, a policy for access had to be agreed. Managers readily recognized the benefits of allowing approved R&D staff to have access to all but highly confidential reports. However, the range of approved R&D staff tended to vary from manager to manager. Those concerned with the management of the database are still trying to rationalize the situation.

Implementation

Once a policy has been approved at the appropriate level, it then has to be communicated to those whom it will affect. The communication method chosen will depend on:

- the nature of the message (its complexity);
- the importance to the business;
- the number of people affected.

Everybody recognizes that we are all suffering from information overload and care must be taken not to compound that problem. The challenge is therefore to communicate *effectively* so that people receive the message and understand their responsibilities. Let me use the example of Information Protection here. The 'policy' is quite simple. Information is a vital asset and must be managed and protected appropriately according to its value and sensitivity. How does that translate into guidance for an organization of 10,000 people worldwide in R&D alone? The aim is to make the workforce aware of the importance of protecting sensitive information and to provide guidelines on what is 'appropriate protection'. We have classified information at four levels:

Level 1:	Highly confidential
Level 2:	Company confidential
Level 3:	Internal use only
Level 4:	Public domain

There has been much discussion about how to present the guidelines/instructions for handling information at the various levels and for different formats, e.g. electronic, paper, fax or voicemail. One is torn between the desire to keep everything very simple and concise and the need to present sufficient guidance to ensure that people understand how to handle the information appropriately. For example, few people would send sensitive information on a postcard, yet sending sensitive information or intellectual property over the Internet has been likened to just that (the release of pre-patent information into the public domain can seriously prejudice the company's patent position).

Even very senior people send and receive faxes in hotels and other public places. There are some real horror stories about such breaches of security, such as the one where a single wrong digit in a fax number caused a company's strategic plan to be sent to a local newspaper!

Security is an issue which merits a paper in itself. Suffice it to say that in the pharmaceutical industry it is critical, and all employees must take responsibility for the information they handle. Even apparently innocuous documents, such as the internal telephone directory, could be sensitive in the hands of an animal welfare activist.

The first step is to draw up the draft guidelines. This has been done by a cross-functional international team with representatives from IT Security, Information Policy, Human Resources, Legal Department and Internal Audit. Once these have been agreed, they will be posted as a Green Paper on the GW Intranet and tested for usability by piloting in two selected business areas, namely Research and Human Resources. Research was chosen because staff here tend to be intolerant of any rules or bureaucracy which might be perceived as restricting their creativity: in this environment it is largely intellectual property which must be protected. In Human Resources, it is employee information which may be sensitive. The usability pilot, which is expected to last about six weeks, will also provide information on the cost of implementation which may be considerable on a worldwide basis.

The final document will be submitted to top management and, if approved, the current plan is to issue a small glossy booklet, attractively presented, which will act as a quick guide to protection of information based on the four levels described. These will be tailored for individual countries; thus there will be US spelling for North America, it will be in French for France, and so on. Ideally, the distribution of these should be done in conjunction with short, mandatory presentations so that people have a chance to ask questions and hear some of the background reasons for the policy and its consequent implementation.

The implementation of new policies and standards may cause such a significant change in working practices that it may be necessary to introduce a special change management programme. We are not yet at that stage of evolution in the new company but we did institute such a programme at Wellcome in the case of our Document Management project. The new templates and technologies associated with the creation, management and publication of regulatory documents revolutionized not just the actual process but the whole corporate culture. I have to admit that the latter originally seemed a visionary target but I believe that having a common document policy actually had a significant impact on the internationalization of the company. It was one of the features that made Wellcome attractive to Glaxo (I am pleased to say that the new company is embracing best practice wherever it is found and internationalization, or rather globalization, is considered an important goal).

How was this remarkable benefit achieved? In a large multifunctional organization, it is very easy simply to concentrate all one's energies on local objectives and to fail to appreciate the wider goals of the whole enterprise. Thus one department or division may decide on a certain style, unaware of the impact of that style on others who must later re-use these documents for another purpose. If there is no standardization, the sharing and re-use of documents may be very difficult and may even result in the need for re-typing.

The DOCMAN project (as it was known) put the spotlight on the whole drug development process and compilation of the regulatory submission, especially in terms of the interactions between the various groups involved. As people came to understand their contribution to the common end, rather than seeing the process as an unwarranted intrusion on their creative freedom, they began to accept and take ownership of the problems and became enthusiastic participants in change. The project caused new working relationships to be forged as people made connections with their transatlantic counterparts: once the dialogue had started, information flowed more smoothly.

I don't mean to imply that this was a quick or easy process! It happened over a number of years, but it did happen and it was worth all the effort.

Evaluation

The last section, looking back at past experience, has brought us imperceptibly to evaluation. It is early days to evaluate the small number of policies which have gone through to the implementation phase but by and large they are working tolerably well.

Some examples of these are:

Laboratory Notebooks	New notebooks and practices following a change in US patent law
Document Identification	Unique identification of R&D documents worldwide
INDI (INternal Document Index) Access	Access rights to the combined R&D Reports Database
Standard Operating Procedures	A new numbering system for the merged company

Likewise it is too early for compliance monitoring which I expect will be a challenging future issue.

Factors influencing policy-making

It is unlikely that the conditions prevailing inside a large multinational company, particularly a newly merged one, have much applicability to the process of information policy-making in general, but I shall briefly raise those factors which have had an impact within my company.

Corporate culture

At the time of the merger it was said, rather unkindly, that Wellcome thought a lot about things and then did little, whereas Glaxo didn't think so much but just got on and did things. Surely this alone is a challenge for a merged organization; to strike that balance between the extremes of paralysis of analysis and ill-considered action. In defining policy and seeking to build consensus it is necessary to take enough time to consult widely and allow people to recognize the benefits of change, rather than focusing exclusively on finding solutions so that user-acceptance is sacrificed. Equally, if one waits until everyone is happy, one could wait for too long and perpetuate conditions of confusion and divergence. Once again, it is a question of balance and the particular circumstances prevailing.

National differences

Whole books have been written on this subject and I don't propose to deal with this in any depth except to reaffirm that there *are* differences and policy-makers would be wise to recognize them.

Size

GlaxoWellcome is by any standards a large company and its sheer size compounds many of the difficulties associated with the policy-making process, from choosing adequate representation to communicating and implementing policy decisions. The problems associated with size are exacerbated in a newly merged organization as existing networks and 'ways of getting things done' are disrupted and the decision-making mechanism becomes more uncertain. It is rather like an organism which has suffered a traumatic injury: it takes time to re-establish the neural connections which allow it to operate fully and effectively; likewise, it takes time to get to know and understand the new structure and key players.

A mitigating factor here is that there is a well-developed communications infrastructure. Within a very short time of the merger it was possible to communicate electronically across the two companies and this had a powerful impact on the speed with which the new company has been able to establish itself.

Competing initiatives

This might also be considered a function of size. In a company so large it is inevitable that parts of the business will tend to function autonomously, and indeed in the old Glaxo world there were many separate companies. An example of parallel initiatives can be seen in the area of the Internet/Intranet where, in keeping with its anarchic origins, many little groups sprang up to deal with Internet issues. Now that the technology is accepted as a corporate tool, a more corporate approach is being taken to policies surrounding its use.

Again, considering the size of the organization, one wonders what such a small team can possibly achieve. I said earlier that small is beautiful, but is tiny ridiculous? I don't think so. Visibility and recognition are undoubtedly a problem for us, but if we were to expand we might risk trying to create policy ourselves rather than relying on the business to tell us what it needs. Credibility can only come with time.

The lessons learned

So what are the lessons learned—the 'takeaways'—from this past year?

- *Recognize complexity*

  Not all solutions are easy or elegant. Sometimes the pathway to convergence is difficult and will require interim solutions. That is acceptable provided they don't prejudice the desired final outcome.

- *Preserve balance*

  I have already mentioned the importance of achieving balance in several different contexts in this paper. Policy-makers should strive to remain neutral where there are strongly opposing views.

- *Brevity and simplicity*

  Communication should be as brief and concise as possible. Try not to 'muddle the message'.

- *Think international*

  With the best will in the world it is all too easy to think parochially and forget the international differences. We are used to 'thinking US/UK', but must now concentrate much more on Europe and Japan where our other research centres are located. It does help if policy-makers have had international experience as well as a wide knowledge of the business.

Last but not least,

- *Hold the Vision!*

  This would be at the top of my list! It is perilously easy to be daunted by the magnitude of the task, to feel insecure about one's grasp of the complexities, to suffer from lack of recognition, to experience frustration with difficult people and generally to get so close to problems that it is hard to see the wood for the trees. The answer is to step back and reconfirm one's original allegiance to the vision of a learning organization using information really effectively.

Conclusions

The process of establishing information policies in this newly merged organization is quite obviously still evolving. Whilst the pragmatic approach adopted to date has been necessary given the upheaval of integration, it is now appropriate to lay down a more formalized methodology for creation and implementation of information policies. We must focus our efforts on these areas where information and information systems can have the greatest value and impact; too often large organizations have so much information at their disposal that they have difficulty managing and exploiting it and this is where policy can play a key role in ensuring improved flow of information and access to knowledge.

We must always bear in mind that policies should be there to *help* the business not impede it. Nor should policy become a holy grail in its own right. We would do well to maintain a balanced and pragmatic attitude, never taking ourselves too seriously. I will conclude with a quote from Douglas Bader in *Reach for the Sky*:

> Rules are for the obedience of fools and the guidance of wise men.

The Limitations of 'Free' Access in Academia: Making Commercial Databases Available

Harry East

Abstract

There is a long-standing and widely accepted tradition of providing access to the resources of academic libraries free of charge to the members of the institution. However, academic libraries operate in a real external market; there is a price to be paid for source material, and the richness of their collections has always been limited by the resources made available by their parent institution, but this market has been essentially transparent to the users. Several factors are now putting the assumptions behind this tradition under stress.

There are many reasons for this, but growth, in terms of the number of information sources available and in the size of the academic community, is an important one. The provision of a national networking system (JANET) has been made available on a public good basis, so that the end-user has no direct charges to pay for data transmission, although there is a significant investment centrally (i.e. via the Higher Education Funding Councils and ultimately the Treasury).

But networked delivery of databases of commercial origin does present new problems in terms of cost, price and charging. Large databases of this type are now being supplied, in principle, 'free to the user at the point of use' through JANET. Partly subsidized ('top-sliced') centrally, with some of the cost recovered through an annual institutional subscription, this present mode of distribution is, in practice, tending to disadvantage certain sectors of the academic community. This results from the contradiction between the accepted policy of parity of access and the current strategy of partial cost recovery. This paper examines the nature of these inconsistencies and the policy background in which they operate.

The ethic of free access to information survives in academia despite the increase in the university population and the enormous growth of sources of information, however defined, now available. It is true that there is a minority that challenges this assumption, but it is generally held that *bona fide* users within a university should not be charged directly for information services. These assumptions aside, it is difficult to contemplate how significant cost recovery could be imposed for what are now known as end-users in a community which is proverbially short of money.

The provision of information and communications services is likely to remain a public good objective in academia. This is well illustrated by the use and growth of electronic mail services which have flourished since the installation of the Joint Academic Network (JANET). With hindsight we can see that wide-area networking was inevitable, not just as a national phenomenon but as a process that led to the interconnections of networks on a worldwide basis in what is now called the Internet. One of the principal benefits of creating JANET presented to the Treasury, and ultimately the government of the day, was as follows. As the demand for computing power was increasing in universities, the need for extending data processing facilities was being expressed on each academic site. The possibility of interconnection between individual university computers offered not only the prospect of transfer of large existing data files between sites, but also of computing at a distance. These were major selling points to the funders.

In the event, when JANET was implemented the predominant (but largely unpredicted) early use of the network was for e-mail activities, essentially communication on a one-to-one or one-to-many basis. It is difficult to imagine that a facility for academics to talk to each other, for free, would have been particularly persuasive for funders. Indeed, the enormous growth of e-mail traffic has been examined in the past as a area that might be supported by some cost recovery process (at the institutional, departmental or individual level). Such debates have come to no conclusion as to how this might be implemented and e-mail remains a free good, financed by central funds.

The processes by which database resources have been made available to the academic community give some indications of the difficulty, complexity and sometimes the contradictions of implementing a 'free' access policy within academia. In this paper the term 'database' is used in a limited manner and refers to bibliographic and text-based databases that are the intellectual property of their producers. They are generally distributed as priced products directly by them, or by their agents, through commercial channels.

Changes in the supply of the long-standing scholarly abstracting and indexing (A&I) services, which comprise a large component of current academic online searching, can be used to illustrate how the market developed and how academic libraries responded.

A&I services were not created with the notion that they required librarian-mediators. Originally these printed outputs were a benefit of membership of the learned and professional societies producing them, distributed free or at low cost. The early A&I journals were in evidence as much in the end-user's office or laboratory as they were in the library. Increasing publication costs, associated with growth in the literature, led to a situation where institutional subscriptions became the main source of income for database producers, with the institutional library acting usually as the sole subscriber and repository.

In such a market the demand (in relation to print) of corporate subscribers was relatively inelastic compared with that of individuals. As a consequence, when electronic versions of A&I services (i.e. databases) began to be marketed through online hosts, and later through CD-ROM publishers, the corporate rather than the personal subscriber offered a conspicuous target. The library became the place from which most of these new services were first accessed.

Most academic libraries had introduced mediated online search services by the early 1980s. Despite the interest that such facilities promoted, mediated searches (i.e. those conducted by library staff on behalf of the users) remained, on the whole, a marginal activity in terms of the library's resource allocation. Mediation was seen to be desirable in terms of both effectiveness and economy but it nevertheless increased the workload on library staff. The main difficulty arose, however, in reconciling the pricing of these services within established library practices. The 'pay-as-you-go' tariffs of the commercial hosts produced charges that were difficult to predict and control. Moreover, this charging method was regarded as troublesome to operate within fixed annual budgets and not consonant with how libraries traditionally employed their resources (East and Tilson, 1993).

By the early 1990s many of the established databases, and an increasing number of new ones, became available on CD-ROMs. They were marketed on the basis of a fixed annual subscription. Even when the subsequent complications of networking and loading the database on to hard discs emerged, the price for doing so was at least predictable (actually, to some extent negotiable). Given the additional benefit that these products were designed to be essentially end-user devices, the rapid switch of library resources to this medium was virtually assured. Figure 1 maps the changes in the mean annual expenditures of a fixed panel of universities 1988–1995.

Figure 1: Mean annual expenditures, by database medium, of a constant panel of universities, 1988-95

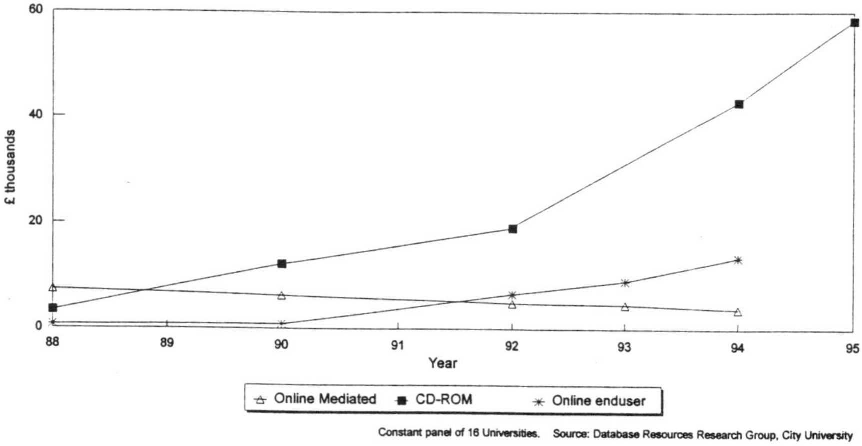

While it was early suggested that CD-ROMs represented a transient technology for access to the larger, more heavily used databases that are traditional resources for the academic community, their popularity clearly remains (McSean and Law, 1990).

Up to the early 1990s the following situation obtained. Database access was largely a prerogative of local institutional supply via library services. Librarians clung to the traditional policy that access should be free and had misgivings about the charging methods of the commercial hosts. Some libraries, however, responded by passing on some of the direct charges, justifying it in a rather apologetic way by claiming they were supplying a 'value-added' service. Few if any could bring themselves to charge true cost recovery. Others made no charges. In both cases the services were not widely advertised and there was effectively rationing. The arrival of CD-ROMs allowed libraries to subscribe to what was essentially a print surrogate available at a predictable annual subscription. Because databases in this medium were equally available to all users, there was no charge. But at this stage there was no collaboration between libraries on database acquisition and supply.

The concept of central provision of end-user access, operated across the academic community as a whole and, using JANET as a facilitator, emerged in 1989 and took shape in the BIDS-ISI service launched in 1991 (Law, 1994). Initially supported by the Computer Board, and subsequently endorsed by its successor the JISC (Joint Information Services Committee), the aim of the service was to provide an end-user service 'free at the point of use'. The 'deal' which secured community-wide access to the ISI database was negotiated by CHEST (Combined Higher Education Software Team) initially for five years and subsequently renewed. This method of providing database access has proved to be very popular: by mid 1996 nearly 100 universities were subscribing to this database and the mean number of daily connects to the service was in excess of 9,000 per day (East *et al.*, 1995).

The success of BIDS-ISI was followed by a number of JISC/CHEST acquisitions available on a similar basis. The more significant ones are listed in Table 1 overleaf and more are planned. These databases are supplied to *institutional* subscribers on the basis of an annual subscription. This payment accounts for approximately 50 per cent of the total cost of the service, the remainder being funded centrally by 'top-slicing'.

Derek Law, a member of JISC and a librarian, has been characteristically frank about how the policy behind these changes came about (UFC/ISC, 1992).

> The officials of the Computer Board showed great flexibility in allowing policy to develop anarchically, with confidence that the rules could be clarified later. When it

Table 1: JISC/CHEST dataset acquisitions, 1991-1996

Database	Launch date	Annual subscription	Number of subscriptions
BIDS (Bath (University) Information & Data Services);			
ISI	91	7000	98
EMBASE	92	4000	22
COMPENDEX	94	5000	44
IBSS	95	Free	108
Royal Society of Chemistry	96	1200	
EDINA (Edinburgh University Data Library):			
BIOSIS	96	7000	35
Periodicals Content Index (PCI)	96	200	44
Palmers Index to the Times	96	200	43

> was made clear that not only was this a dramatic leap in the dark but one that would be repeated at regular intervals, the Board felt the need for an *ex post facto* justification for what they had done, and to establish a policy framework for what had been, in effect, a piece of naked opportunism. The Board set up the National Datasets Task Group, as a vehicle through which policy could be developed. It was hoped that this would provide the justification and methodology for future action ...

In 1991 the Computer Board was replaced by the Information Systems Committee (ISC). This Committee had been given a wider brief to include library and administrative computing. By autumn 1992 it had produced an important document: *ISC Policy for Dataset Service Provision to the Education and Research Community* (UFC/ISC, 1992).

Two of the significant aims of the policy were to:

- establish the ISC policy framework for its participation in the provision of vital information datasets and associated services to the wider education and research community as a whole;
- act as a major funding agency alongside Research Councils, Government Departments and Professional Institutions and Societies and the sites themselves through libraries.

Recognizing growing demands for access to datasets, the document noted that, as the higher education system expanded through the 1990s, increasing pressures on resources would reinforce the need for a policy to achieve *economies of scale* in the provision of costly information services, particularly to expensive external databases. Further, the ISC recognized that it has a national role in the provision of such *common good services*:

> ISC will expect that access to any national dataset service will be available to any HE user authorized by his/her local service, and will normally be free for academic use at the point of access.

The Policy Document did not, however, state unequivocally where the money to support datasets provision would come from, but made some proposals:

> To ensure the best value for money in the context of overall funding, an inter-agency group of all funding bodies should be established to negotiate priorities and resource contributions ... ISC funding will include normally only capital for acquisition and transformation of the dataset, and the provision of essential hardware and software delivery platforms ... Funding for the provision of services ... will normally be expected to come in conjunction with other funding agencies or through subscription paid by user sites ... bibliographic datasets are likely to be appropriate for ISC investment (as a service) or for funding via libraries.

Law (1994) later observed that it was realized that the cost of sites acquiring twenty datasets at £4,000 to £5,000 each, would be well beyond the reach of the budgets of most libraries which were then (and now) paying the bills for ISI. This was quite deliberate, 'since it [the committee] wished the issue of services to end-users in general, and dataset services in particular to be seen as an institutional issue and not a library issue'.

Effectively this issue was fudged: the institutions have, on the whole, left the issue of database service funding in the hands of the libraries—in Law's felicitous phrase 'landing the library with the bill'. Worse, the policy somewhat tied the hands of the libraries by ruling that the service should be free at the point of use. One of the results of this policy was that subscription to services has been uneven: of the three subscription services started before 1995 (ISI, EMBASE and COMPENDEX), 66 per cent of the sites are at old universities, 27 per cent at new universities and 7 per cent at colleges of higher education (see Table 2).

Table 2: Database access and session cost by type of institution

Database	Old Universities	New Universities	Other HE Institutions
Number of subscribing sites:			
ISI	54	29	10
COMPENDEX	29	12	1
EMBASE	20	0	0
IBSS	54	33	30
% population having access (a,b):			
ISI	92	71	38
COMPENDEX	61	30	6
EMBASE	38	0	0
IBSS	92	65	62
Mean cost/session:			
ISI	£0.28	£1.99	£12
(a,b) Old universities populations based on 1993/4 figures; new and other HE based on 1992/3 figures.			

The institutional charging policy that was adopted is one of an across-the-board annual subscription regardless of levels of use or the number of actual or potential users. This had one obvious advantage: a simple accounting and revenue collection scheme. The Policy Document had endorsed the flat rate charge approach because 'usage of ISI ... does not correlate with institutional size'.

This is neither strictly true nor particularly relevant. If usage is segmented into groups according to the age/status of the subscribing sites, there are clear patterns of usage. These patterns can be seen in Figure 2 overleaf.

Moreover, by arranging the sites in descending order of BIDS-ISI use, it becomes fairly apparent that the heaviest users are those institutions that have a reputation for a competent research performance. Fortunately there is a fairly objective measure available for this: the four/five-yearly Research Assessment Exercise (RAE). In this exercise the research outputs of university departments are given a score on a 1 to 5 scale. By adding these scores together for each university and plotting them against the institution's corresponding BIDS-ISI usage, a clear correlation is obtained. The regression line of this plot is shown in Figure 3 ($R^2 = 0.7$, indicating a fairly high degree of correlation).

Figure 2: BIDS-ISI usage 1995: number of sessions by institutional type

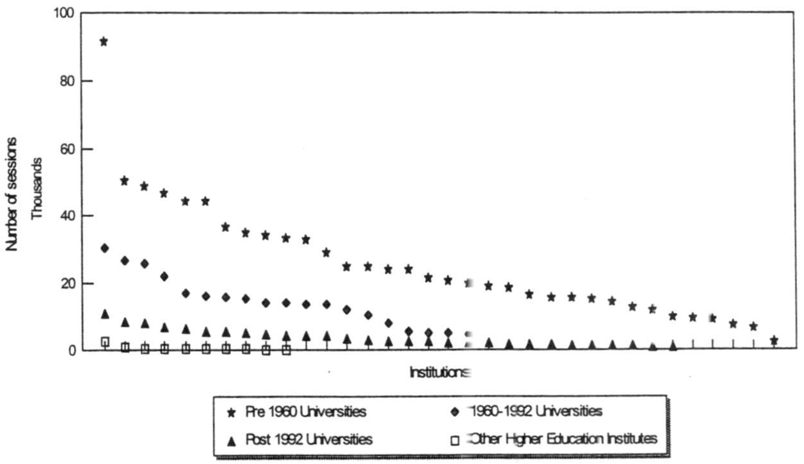

Figure 3: Relationship between BIDS-ISI usage and Research Assessment Exercise scores

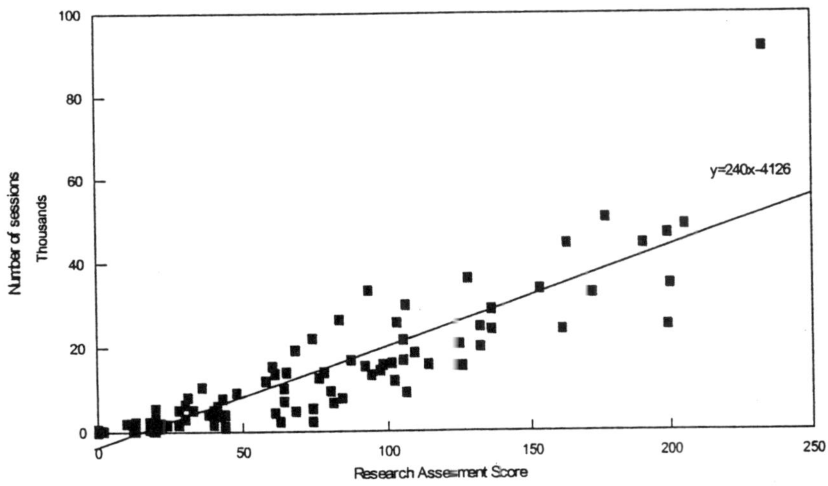

There seems little doubt that flat-rate charges tend to penalize and/or exclude low-volume use institutions. Leaving aside the fact that large, heavily-connecting institutions get good value (i.e. low unit costs per connection) compared with modest users, flat-rate charging excludes all potential *users* in those *institutions* that do not elect to subscribe. (The institutions do in effect contribute to the cost, which is assumed to be met partially by top-slicing, itself related to the institutional population.) It is difficult to suppose that any higher education institution has decided not to subscribe simply because the ISI databases would be of no interest to its users. More likely the predicted level of use is seen not to justify the subscription cost. This circumstance is not, however, imposed by the nature of online delivery, but by the current mode of revenue recovery. Moreover, this strategy does not fit easily with a stated aim of JISC (1995) that 'in providing production and development networks, [JISC] must seek to promote initiatives clearly focused on helping the community in meeting these challenges and remain relevant to the needs of the whole sector from smaller HE colleges to the largest university'.

One of the reasons for adopting a flat-rate subscription approach was that, quite understandably, it is simple to understand and cheap to administer. It has been an established approach to revenue collection by CHEST, whose first task was to arrange deals for software packages on behalf of the academic community. CHEST has a well deserved reputation for negotiating cost-effective arrangements with software suppliers, in which the universities get good value for money and the suppliers save considerably on marketing costs.

Ideally, the flat-rate subscription might be abolished and the service supported entirely by top-slicing. This does not seem to be a feasible alternative in the current climate. There is, however, some early evidence to show that the existence of a 'free' database service as contrasted with one which is 'free at the point of use' does have a considerable impact on both access and usage. The International Bibliography of Social Science has been made available through BIDS for a five-year period by means of support from the Economic and Social Research Council. It is free of any site subscription. In its first year of operation 117 sites registered for use and the absence of a flat-rate subscription has resulted in a more balanced distribution of availability: old universities (46 per cent); new universities (28 per cent); other HE (26 per cent).

Using hindsight and subsequent performance statistics, it is all too tempting to criticize strategies which were made in good faith and with constructive intentions about a policy framework which aims to provide vital information datasets to the wider education and research community as a whole. The strategy adopted has enjoyed a marked degree of success but has some latent flaws. Our own investigations on site registration indicate that it would be better to employ a two-tier system of pricing based on the level of usage, somewhat similar to tariffs adopted in the licensing of CD-ROMs.

Nevertheless, provision of 'free' services is not cheap to the provider and its continuation from central funding is by no means assured. A recent strategy paper from JISC (1996) was understandably cautious about the future:

> As the role of information systems becomes ever more crucial to meeting the aims of institutions it is likely to cost more. The JISC has facilitated many areas of IS deployment but it can make no funding assumptions; as the costs of meeting network and electronic information provision rise is not safe to assume that the JISC can continue to meet all these costs.

One mechanism that may well be brought into play is budget devolution. First popular with the polytechnics, this approach seems to be spreading slowly through the body politic of academia. In it, departments are responsible for contributing, among other things, to the cost of services from libraries. While they cannot opt out of this imposition, academic departments are given power to decide on how the libraries will spend their contribution to the budget. In recent surveys on CD-ROM databases, we have observed an increase in libraries acquiring specific subject-related databases by means of a direct or indirect subsidy from an academic department.

Whatever future changes in funding may be, an earlier paper by JISC (1995) studied the trends in the next ten years and took it for granted that:

> The student of the future will obviously be computer literate as such skills are already taught in schools. ... Students will also become 'information literate' in that they will expect to find information online and will know how to find it.

CONCLUSIONS

Summary and Reflections on the Workshop

Michael W. Hill

Introduction

The explicit intention of the Workshop was to gain a clearer understanding of information policy problems and issues; to debate the most appropriate frameworks, tools and methodologies for information policy analysis and evaluation; to inform a more critical approach to information policy analysis; and to provide some useful insights for those engaged in 'real-world' policy design and implementation. This was a very demanding set of objectives but, even if they were not wholly achieved, there is no doubt that substantial progress was made.

This paper summarizes and reflects upon some of the main concepts, ideas and approaches to understanding information policy that were generated at the Workshop both in the papers presented and in the reactions of Workshop participants. In its conclusion an attempt is made to relate these ideas and concepts to the original objectives set out by the organizers.

Defining information policy

David Bawden tackled head-on the fundamental question of what do we mean by 'information' when we talk about information policy? His answer was that part of the information spectrum to which the term 'knowledge' is applied. As he says:

> Knowledge can be seen as that form of information characterized by compression, abstraction and categorization, and which is thereby endowed with meaning and significance and transformative power. Information with lower levels of structure, and raw data, may be managed by

> systems ... and procedures. Knowledge ... can only be managed by policies.

There was some disagreement with this point, especially where raw data are concerned. Perhaps the majority of information polices may be concerned with knowledge management but certainly not all of them, data protection being a good case in point. There may be, as Bawden responded, a difference of understanding but, if so, it needs to be resolved. A broader definition of the term 'knowledge' may lead one back to a term as vague and all-embracing as 'information'. The political philosopher, Michael Oakeshott, gives an interesting discussion of the meaning of 'information' in his book *The Voice of Liberal Learning* (1989). He also makes the equation:

INFORMATION + JUDGEMENT = KNOWLEDGE

After discussing why information policy formulation must deal with complexity, Bawden then tried to match information policy with the semiotic framework of empiric, syntactic, semantic and pragmatic levels, concluding that the last is the dominant one. He finally concludes that effective information policy is:

- [intrinsically] complex;
- not concerned with technical solutions;
- dependent upon an appreciation of the meaning and significance of knowledge in its context.

Though there was a consensus that information policy formulation is a complex process and that studies already undertaken into the possible applicability of chaos theory would be worth pursuing further, some participants felt that Bawden's approach needed to be tested against the realities of institutional policy-making. The realities of some of the *ad hoc* policy-making and evolution, discussed *passim,* might be difficult to accommodate within his framework.

The meanings of 'policy' and 'strategy' also attracted discussion and dispute. David Allen and Tom Wilson reminded us that the *Oxford English Dictionary* defines 'policy' as 'a course of action adopted as advantageous or expedient' and 'strategy' as 'a plan for successful action based on accommodating the moves of opposing participants'. They argued, therefore, that policies are actions to implement the strategy. Most participants felt it to be the other way round. Elcock's (1991) account of a city council trying to implement its policy of avoiding cuts by a strategy of brinkmanship probably illustrates the difference in practice between the two terms.

There was agreement that in any paper on information policy it is essential to make clear one's use of the terms. Ian Rowlands quotes Weingarten's (1989) definition of information policy as comprising 'the set of all public laws, regulation and policies that encourage, discourage or regulate the creation, use, storage and communication of information'. Cochrane *et al.* (1993) define national policy as 'an *intentional* [my italicization] course of action followed by a government institution or official for resolving an issue of public concern'. They also say that 'making policy requires choosing among goals and alternatives, and choice always involves intention'. Add the qualification that to have no policy is also a policy (as in the case of the UK's information policy in the early 1980s) and one has a fair definition of governmental information policies.

Obviously such a definition does not apply to information policy in a private sector organization, nor for that matter to the internal management of information in government organizations. For these a better definition would be policies to meet the Board Agenda as set out in the report of the Hawley Committee (1996). As was commented, and is apparent from the papers, there is not and cannot be a single all-encompassing information policy. As was also commented, when they are exposed to the reality of being applied to actual situations, policies may conflict with one another and new policies may be required to resolve that conflict. Conflicting policies and their consequences lie at the heart of Harry East's and David Worlock's contributions. Complexities of this and other types were a recurrent theme during discussions.

Information policy frameworks and models

Ian Rowlands and Paul Turner began their oral presentation by revisiting the matrix of policy studies approaches developed by Trauth (1986) (see Figure 1).

The majority of articles on information policies, they claimed, fit into the bottom left hand segment, too few into the top half, especially the top right. They argued that there is a need for case study material which is both prescriptive and integrated (top right), though they acknowledged that it may be difficult to persuade policy-makers or 'think tanks' to open

Figure 1: Information policy studies matrix

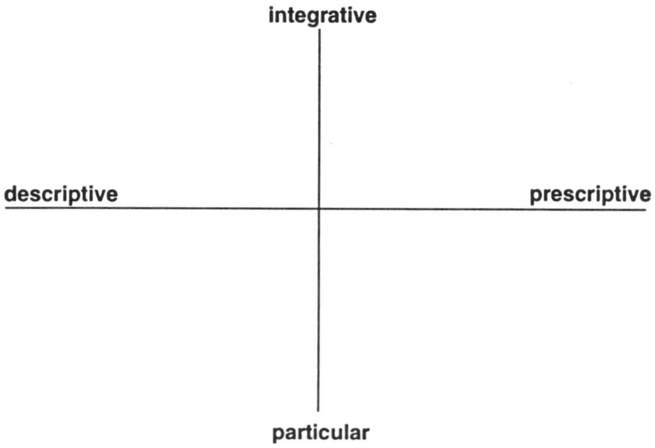

up their thinking at the key moments. The importance of the prescriptive element was noted by Elcock (1991:65) who wrote:

> ... fundamental ... is an assumption that policy analysis is both a descriptive and a prescriptive activity. It is concerned both with the extension of knowledge about how public policies are made and with their improvement.

Research into information policies must have in mind that the ultimate aim is better policy-making.

Rowlands and Turner highlighted the problems of complexity and scope in information policy studies and opened Lasswell's (1970) linear 'functional staged model' of policy-making to three re-interpretations to generate an approach 'to begin to isolate some of the main sources of complexity surrounding information policy'. There was agreement that the concept of the three stages—design, implementation and evaluation—was the basic framework for any study and that an elaborated version of this model takes account of feedback from evaluation and iteration during each of the stages.

The three re-interpretations of Lasswell's model develop 'an overall framework for generating value- and paradigm-critical research strategies'. They are:

- the rational actor (or planning approach);
- the bureaucratic approach (incrementalism);
- the garbage can.

The garbage can approach is adapted from an idea initially proposed by Cohen, March and Olsen (1972) and further extended by Kingdon (1984). Kingdon depicts policy-making as:

> ... a primeval soup [in which] ideas float around, confront one another and combine. The soup changes in a process of natural selection, survival, demise and recombination.

In discussion this seemed to be the preferred interpretation, probably because it fitted with the complex and often chaotic situations in which policy has to be formulated.

Information policies in reality

Nick Moore examined the merits of setting national information policies in the context of the political environment of the state. He had been struck by the fact that 'just about every country of significance has produced some form of information policy or is making an attempt to position itself as an information society'. The goals are indeed remarkably similar and in each case the policies (presumably in each country a set of policies) are aimed not merely at ensuring a place in the telecommunications world but also at the much broader social and cultural issues of the burgeoning information society. At the same time he noted the remarkable differences in effectiveness between the policies in the economically dynamic states of South East Asia and those of economically less dynamic Britain and was led to explore the comparison further. He offered two policy formulating regimes or models: 'neo-liberal' and 'dirigiste'.

The former is market-led, regards the state as at most a facilitator (often not even that) and leaves the private sector to get on with establishing the infrastructure and providing the necessary finance. One requirement the state cannot escape is that of producing a suitably educated workforce but even that is left, especially where continuing education and training is required, as much as possible to private sector initiatives. On the positive side the state tries to ensure that the financial and market environment is open for international activity. On the other hand with laws, regulations and even official regulators it endeavours to curb any anti-social or otherwise undesirable excesses of an entirely uncontrolled free market.

The dirigiste system is one in which the state acts in accordance with pre-determined objectives. This is a partnership between government and the private sector in which both are active in one way or another in providing investment, the information infrastructure (both technical and appropriately educated and trained personnel) and services. In this case the state shapes very definite information policies and can adopt strategies which ensure that local industries play a major, if necessarily protected, part in creating the information services and market. Moore was clearly convinced that the dirigiste system was the one most likely to cope with the rate of change that is happening and in particular to handle effectively and expeditiously the consequential political, social and cultural issues.

Since UK political principles, at the time of writing, lie at one extremity of the neo-liberal/dirigiste spectrum, it is useful to examine the situation in other western countries as well as making comparisons with the countries of the Pacific Rim. It seems that there is scope within the dirigiste model for wide variation in the private–public sector balance. In discussion, much was made of cultural differences and the difficulty of making comparisons between different political systems.

In the case of the UK where an extreme *laissez faire* approach has been adopted, there have been a number of reasonably imaginative government initiatives all of which have quickly run out of steam. It may be that government feels that leaving developments to market forces is the only way of bypassing the built-in inertia of officialdom. The wish to keep the UK hospitable to the headquarters of multinational companies may be another factor. In fairness to the government, it must be said that it appears to be trying to produce a more highly educated workforce for the future, even if efforts are partially negated by inability to fund more lecturers, demonstrators and tutors.

The factors that ought to be taken into account are many and range widely. Moore listed in his oral presentation a number of goals and motivating factors. Kristiansson, one of the participants, lists many in his FID paper, 'A framework for information policy analysis based on changes in global economic forces' (Kristiansson, 1996). Other lists appeared during other presentations and should perhaps be consolidated.

Barry Mahon's highly critical exposé of the information policy process in the European Commission gave added emphasis to the need, when analyzing information policies, to take account of power structures (for example, DGIII in Brussels versus DGXIII in Luxembourg) and the motivations of the civil servants who implement policies. Some of Mahon's comments reminded me of a member of the Commission who told me that her principal aim was to spend her budget. Her policies and strategies were designed to achieve just that! Another factor is personal commitment: the departure of a Minister or senior civil servant too often means that the policies he or she espoused will be dropped (the disappearance of the information policies in the Delors Plan is an example). Will Martin Bangemann's policies survive his eventual departure, I wonder?

Case study papers

Problems of implementation

David Allen and Tom Wilson produced the Workshop's first case study. They had examined two types of information strategy formulation in universities: one relating to information technology, the other to content. Typically, the IT strategies were formally documented, being written by the IT Director or an IT Committee in each university. The 'top-down promulgated' IT strategy proved to be unpopular, being perceived as unrelated to departments' real needs and giving rise to conflict, especially over resources. On the other hand, the content strategies tended to arise from a much wider process of consultation. As a result, they seemed to be more widely accepted and easily implemented.

Of course, the university environment, with its anarchic cast of highly dedicated, individualistic and articulate members, is very different from that within which national policies are formed. It is also very different from government departments or agencies and commercial organizations. Yet many similarities to the factors revealed by Allen and Wilson emerged in the contributions of Margaret Haines (on the National Health Service) and Elspeth Scott (from GlaxoWellcome).

In the NHS all policies and strategies are fundamentally about health and health care. There is a vision of a 'knowledge-based' NHS and a desire to ensure that medicine is 'evidence-based'. In GlaxoWellcome there is an organizational goal (among others) of building a learning organization that fully utilizes all its resources, including information. In both, Orna's (1990) dictum that information policy is concerned with linking information resources with the strategic objectives of the organization, is followed. In GlaxoWellcome the basic aim of the information service function is to make required information easy to find and easy to use. It is explicit corporate policy to evaluate the policies and their consequences against the benefits claimed.

The NHS has developed a range of policies to improve the quality and accessibility of knowledge-based resources, using new information technology to disseminate information widely, to promote better information practice and to improve access, cooperation and organization at the local level. The NHS has its thinking determined by the needs of health care providers throughout every part of the country. It needs to exploit its 600 libraries to the full. GlaxoWellcome is a multinational company and therefore has to consider the different social, political and cultural environments within which it operates or sells products.

The successful introduction of an information policy, which will have been initially drafted by an information specialist, was highly dependent in both organizations on successfully identifying a top level sponsor. Whether the product of the Hawley Committee, a consultative document (on managing the asset that is information) for chairmen, chief executives and boards of directors, will make getting that essential top level support any easier it is too early to tell.

Other factors to which attention must be paid if policy is to be successfully implemented include involving all those, or at least as many as practicable, who will be affected by it, ensuring relevance to priorities and that grass roots problems are addressed, getting the timing right and ensuring that the policy accords in all respects with corporate style and ethos. The imposition of IT strategies seems to be resented in many organizations, whereas a strategy to improve access to information content seems more readily supported. This is no surprise since the former is too often perceived as a threat to job security. Extra care is needed, therefore, at the formulation stage and at the implementation stage to listen to comments from those affected and to adjust the policy to incorporate reasonable ideas. At the stage of explaining the policy it is vital to emphasize the benefits of the system rather than its technical features.

Elspeth Scott drew attention to a number of factors which have special relevance to commercial organizations, though they are certainly not unique to them, not least security. Security is not merely a question of avoiding the external leakage of company secrets but also setting levels of internal confidentiality which correlate to levels of management.

There is also a need to educate staff in the risks to confidentiality of technologies like fax and e-mail.

Scott also draws attention to the fact that implementing a new policy, especially one involving IT, may necessitate changes at management level as well as in the way staff work. There is an implication that the scope for revising policy in the light of experience is likely to be limited to minor adjustments, even if feedback suggests a major reassessment is required.

As Tom Wilson remarked, big companies and big institutions can afford information policy units. Smaller organizations cannot and need the services of a consultant to act as a facilitator. This point was brought home to the Workshop by David Pye's highly entertaining account of trying to introduce management into the 'free for all' information environment of a small but rapidly growing IT company. This company has many highly creative technical staff who are used to exchanging ideas and information between themselves without restraint or formal requirements. Pye noted that the information and communication interface between ideas-driven technical staff and business-driven managers is often less than ideal. This needs to be addressed, although it may mean changing the corporate culture. Another need, now that the company has grown well past its original size, is an information system to manage internal and external information flows.

Essentially, the company's information policy is to allow staff almost complete freedom to seek information and ideas from colleagues and from external sources (including the Internet) and to trust the staff to handle information responsibly. It is proposed to hold and communicate information in electronic form only. To avoid alienating the technical whizzkids, a project-based approach will be used to introduce the new process, involving everyone in the company. To ensure that the essential freedom to generate ideas is not spoiled by accidental, unthinking leakage, e.g. on the Internet, education on security is proposed.

The Workshop discussion at this point focused on the information environment that would be best suited to the 'ideas staff' who work at high pressure and under considerable stress. The work culture, especially obvious in this case, is very different from, say, fifteen years ago. Time should be built into the day for play, for thinking and for allowing subconscious inspiration to come to one's consciousness. It is also essential not to clog the inventive process with too much information, a problem awaiting resolution in most organizations.

Information law

Tamara Eisenschitz discussed the implementation of copyright and patent laws, while Francis Aldhouse reflected on data protection law. These three areas of information law provide excellent examples of policies which are intended to strike a reasonable balance between incompatible interests. Each has had to be revised to take account of developments in information technology and business practices.

In the case of patent law, which was originally drafted to cope with physical, chemical and engineering inventions, new policies are being sought to cope with biological inventions. Apart from the US plant patents, the patenting of genetic material has not been allowed. Improved breeds of animals and of plants have to be protected, if at all, in other ways (the UK has plant breeders' rights). Now, however, it is possible to invent other forms of biological matter which have no equivalent in nature, e.g. by gene sequencing.

Since the basic principle of the patent is to allow a monopoly right to stop someone else making and marketing the invention but not a right to stop anyone making a copy for research purposes for a limited period in return for publishing details of the novel features of an invention, the principal problems are on what basis to include biological products. Until this issue arose the only ethical factor in patenting was a ban on inventions which might be used for an immoral purpose. Now other aspects of ethics are involved. Since the 1988 Copyright, Designs and Patents Act, the UK official policy seems to be to participate in the efforts of international bodies (the EU, the European Patent Office and the World Intellectual Property Organization) to develop internationally acceptable solutions and to adopt them here.

It is worth noting at this point that in each of the three areas a government committee was appointed to examine the situation and to report on feasible solutions. Data protection has a particularly interesting history. International trade issues gave rise to the need to legislate to protect what, at that time, was only a relatively small amount of personal data held in electronic format. Data protection was not primarily intended to protect privacy, rather to restrict the transmission of personal data and, by requiring those holding it to register with the Registrar, to keep tabs on the data holders' actions. However, the Courts have recently decided that the Data Protection Act should be seen as having a bearing on personal privacy and, of course, the EU draft instrument specifically mentions privacy. Another problem of implementation has been that the

Act has now to be interpreted in an environment of all-pervasive information technologies. The Calcutt Committee felt that data protection was relevant to the activities of the media and the Registrar has expressed a similar view. A further aspect was raised by Nick Moore who drew attention to cultural differences between nations in regard to privacy.

Evaluating information policies

The need for information policy evaluation has already been touched on several times. Elspeth Scott made the point that in a commercial firm there is a purpose for a policy, so the outcome of pursuing it must have benefit for the firm. Therefore, the policy is evaluated against the benefits claimed for it. This is less true for intellectual property and data protection policies but the Annual Reports to Parliament of the Comptroller-General of the Patent Office and the Data Protection Registrar do provide a review of how well the Acts are working and what problems have arisen.

Harry East looked at a particular problem where two policies conflict. Universities have a policy, normally called a principle, that library use should be free to students. The library pays for the books and journals and, therefore, logically should pay for the use of electronic sources. However, whereas, once bought, the use of books costs virtually nothing, each student search of an outside database has to be paid for. Since library budgets are limited and students are traditionally hard-up, the policy of encouraging students to become fully 'au fait' with modern IT gives rise to a conflict, the battleground being library stock and gadgetry.

Another problem arises from the Higher Education Funding Councils' (HEFCs) policy that there should be a flat charge to each university for access to datasets. The result is that the cost to major universities is about 10 pence per search, whereas for the former polytechnics, who make much less use of data than the research-oriented universities, it works out at more than 50 pence. A flat rate per search would penalize the research-oriented universities, while a rate calculated as a fixed percentage of university grant does not solve the problem.

David Worlock's paper evaluates national policies against the criterion of whether they are working as their sponsors intended. In the cases of the EU Guidelines on the *Synergy of Public and Private Sectors in the Information Marketplace* and the Department of Trade and Industry's *Tradeable Information Guidelines* he finds that they are not working and that the policies are a failure. The reasons, however, do not seem to be that the policies are necessarily wrong. Rather the reasons are that another policy, to exploit means of raising revenue, is now in conflict with the guidelines and, secondly, the officials responsible have no interest in making the policies work. In *The State We're In,* Will Hutton (1995) points out that:

> Unlike France or Germany, Britain has made no systematic attempt to train a class of officials competent in commerce and finance. So the state has no apparatus for making British industrial policies work and its efforts were undermined by a latent value system always ready to return to an earlier relationship between state, society and economy.

Perhaps if there were a Commissioner who had to report annually to Parliament on progress in implementing the various information policies, there would be action.

In conclusion

Let me now try to relate some of my conclusions to the explicit aims of the Workshop.

1. 'To gain a clearer understanding of information policy problems and issues'

The policy-making process is complex:

- This is due in part to the wide variety of inputs needed, including in an organization, consulting as many as possible of those likely to be affected, noting and feeding back significant new points and winning key staff over. At the national level success is unlikely unless those to whom the policy applies accept it.
- It is in part due to the need to take into account the potential impact on and from policies in other sectors (i.e. the information sector interacts with social, cultural, political and economic sectors).
- It is in part due to the fact that it is not possible to forecast correctly all subsequent events likely to affect the policy.

- It is partly due to the fact that at national level policies are made in a continuum of time and space. Each new policy causes a disturbance which has to be accommodated by the other occupants of the policy space. In the extreme case there is conflict and yet another policy is needed to resolve how to deal with it. As time goes on not only do new policies disturb existing ones but also events (for example the rapid developments in IT equipment and patterns of use) require policies to be modified or supplemented.

Human, social and political factors are very important:

- Policies will not be implemented in the way intended if they are not in tune with the wishes and desires of those whose task it is to implement them.
- Policies arise in different ways: an old policy needs updating to meet modern needs. Social changes require a new policy or supplements to an earlier policy. A crisis may arise which calls for a new policy or the abandonment of a former one.
- Some policies are expected to last a long time and are carefully prepared. Others are intended to be short term and receive less careful preparation.
- Information policies have to be seen as a component of the battle for authority and status. Governments and organizations, with the exception perhaps of some small and medium-sized enterprises (SMEs), seek the power to feed individuals with selected information, the power to demand information from individuals, and the power to police individuals' use of information (all reasons why the Internet is so popular).

2. *'To identify the most appropriate frameworks, tools and methodologies for information policy analysis'*

- At its simplest the information policy process can be regarded as a linear progression from aims through a tangled bush of inputs to formulation, implementation and evaluation. However, the model is complicated by the need to incorporate feedback loops at each stage including revisions at the evaluation stage.

- The flow line must lead on not only to meet new situations but also to allow for branching into supplementary policies.

- Three frameworks for re-interpreting the information policy process model were proposed: rational, bureaucratic or garbage can. There is a danger of oversimplifying to fit one or other re-interpretation to reality but, provided any study is in depth, trying to decide the extent to which each applies is helpful.

- Setting national policies against the political environment is valuable but, as was clear, this approach needs to be tested against a wider variety of political philosophies and practices.

3. 'To inform a more critical approach to information policy analysis'

- The range of inputs and factors that, as the papers and discussions revealed, should be taken into account in the policy formulation process mean that any analysis needs to be sure that it has included and evaluated every conceivable one. If any are omitted, for whatever reason, this should be made clear in the report.

- It is especially important and at the same time difficult to evaluate the importance of personal motivations.

- Account must be taken of the power base of policy-makers and of any supporters they may have.

- The aim of any analysis should be prescriptive, i.e. leading to lessons which can be applied the next time round.

- The outcome of implementing a policy should be determined by evaluation against the benefits claimed.

4. 'To provide useful insights for those engaged in information policy design and implementation'

- Policies, to be successful, must contribute to the general aims of the organization. In the case of national policies this means the party manifesto as at the last election or as modified since. Aims can and do change, thus providing another example of the changing situations policies have to endure.

- Formulation of a policy must accord with 'house' style and ethos.
- The timing of a policy is critical.
- Policies which are constructed by a 'bottom-up' approach to those involved are likely to fare better than those imposed from the top without adequate consultation.
- Policy formulators, other than those at Board level or equivalent, need to find a high level sponsor to help get new policies considered seriously. At national level a policy needs to be wholeheartedly endorsed by the relevant Permanent Secretary or it is likely to founder on the transience of Ministers and of grade 5 and 6 staff.
- A policy is not likely to be successful unless all the other policies necessary are in place (e.g. a policy of encouraging the greater use of IT requires that there shall be appropriate educational policies in place).

Directions for Future Research in Information Policy

David Bawden, Tamara Eisenschitz and Ian Rowlands

The contributions to this volume have identified information policy as an area of considerable interest, not just for academics, but as a practical response to a wide range of problems and issues in organizations and in society. These Proceedings conclude with a few suggestions and pointers for further research.

The theoretical basis of information policy studies

The conceptual foundations of information policy

Work is needed to establish and develop the ontological and epistemological foundations supporting information policy research. In particular, there is a need to develop a richer understanding of basic terms, concepts and paradigms, and how these are perceived by policy-makers, as well as how they are used by the policy studies community. Complexity and scope are significant methodological issues in information policy studies and new ways of looking at these problems are required.

Tools and methodologies for information policy studies

Considerable potential exists for appropriating tools, techniques and experience from other, more mature, spheres of policy analysis: how useful and relevant are these in the context of information policy? The question of how we create knowledge in information policy studies is an important one, especially bearing in mind many of the caveats expressed in this volume about how research findings may be coloured by values, norms, power relations, professional traditions, cultural expectations and other 'subjective' factors. The development of research strategies which are more value- and paradigm-critical is of crucial importance.

The dynamics of information policy and policy-making

It is evident from the published record that there is a shortage of case study material bearing on the design, implementation and evaluation of information policy, at whatever level. Where possible, case studies should aim to be prescriptive and to identify critical success factors in the implementation and delivery of information policies. Studies evaluating information policy outcomes, in particular, are very thin on the ground. This suggests that more work is needed to develop a richer and more appropriate range of indicators to evaluate the human, social, economic, commercial, cultural and political impacts of information policies. The relationship of information policies to 'real world' needs and expediencies of those impacted by these policies needs more explicit recognition and inclusion in studies. Links with other specialities may help here.

Studies of a comparative nature are also required, to help to point up some of the differences that may be attributable to political and social factors or to national or corporate culture. Case studies of successful corporate information policies and examples of 'best practice' would be especially valuable.

A more colourful interpretative palette is also required: case studies should include an examination of how different analytical frameworks (e.g. rational actor, bureaucratic, garbage can) may be used to yield richer insights, while remaining alert to other, possibly more rewarding, frames of reference.

Finally, there is a need for studies of an historical nature (possibly using oral history techniques) to chart the development and evolution of policy and policy-making institutions.

Building bridges between information policy and other specialities

Information and knowledge management

The linkages between information policies, information strategies, and information and knowledge management are not well understood: this issue urgently needs to be explored and clarified. Where and how do existing information management tools, such as information auditing and mapping, sit in relation to organizational information policy? Can information policies be used to combat and contain the phenomenon of information overload?

Information technology policies and strategies

Similarly, how do organizational and national/international information polices relate to information *technology* policies and strategies? Is it possible to link systems analytic tools into a more unified framework for information content policies and strategies? Is information content and information technology work carried out by the same people? If not, whose opinions and influence carries greater weight? Is it possible to make explicit links between information policy and strategies for business process improvement and Total Quality Management? In each case, conceptual frameworks and case study materials are urgently needed.

Public policy

What can we learn from public policy studies in other issue areas such as welfare, housing and the environment? How do policy-makers perceive information content and technology issues? How do their constituencies perceive information content and technology issues? How do various information policy regimes (e.g. data protection and freedom of access to information) interact: is the relationship synergistic or antagonistic?

What are the impacts of large-scale information policy in terms of their ability to leverage economic, social and cultural development? What kinds of indicators and measures can be developed to evaluate these policy goals?

Education and training

Where does information policy currently sit in the library and information science curriculum? What should be taught and how? There is a need for curriculum development in this area and for teaching and learning materials. Is there a requirement for continuing professional development courses in this area? Finally, is there a place for an information policy perspective on other, non-LIS courses, such as journalism, social administration, business computing, systems analysis, and IT management?

The role of information *in* policy-making

Moving away from the study of information policy specifically, what are the information needs and preferences of policy-makers? To what extent and how does information and research support the needs of policy decision-makers? What sort of mechanisms can and should be delivered by the LIS community to respond to the particular needs of policy-makers? Evaluations of existing information and research delivery systems for policy-makers are required.

WORKSHOP DOCUMENTATION AND PROGRAMME

City University Information Policy Unit
British Library Research & Development Department

UNDERSTANDING INFORMATION POLICY

A Residential Workshop to be held at
Cumberland Lodge, Windsor Great Park,
22-24 July 1996

Introduction

The Information Policy Unit at City University is organizing a high-level residential Workshop on information policy which will be held this summer, 22-24 July, at Cumberland Lodge in Windsor Great Park. This Workshop will bring together academics, consultants, policy-makers, and senior information managers to discuss and react to a series of presented papers. The intention is to focus on the tools, concepts and frameworks which the LIS community uses to understand and research information policy issues. Attendance at the Workshop is by invitation only. However, we hope to publish edited Proceedings of the Workshop for the attention of the wider LIS community.

The Workshop is supported financially by the British Library Research & Development Department who will meet the costs of food and accommodation (but not travel, except in the case of participants from outside the UK).

The need for the Workshop

Information policy is currently receiving unprecedented attention within the library and information community; as Michael Hill (1994) rightly points out, the literature is literally overflowing with articles, reviews, reports and books. The scope of this literature is very wide, embracing such diverse concepts as the creation and regulation of information markets, information for citizenship, information as a lever of national and regional economic development, and information as a critical resource in organizations. Each of these perspectives on information policy shares a common assumption that coherent measures are needed in relation to 'information' in order to realize higher-level goals such as wealth creation or greater social justice.

The information policy construct therefore stretches right across the broad canvas of modern life and its analysis can be seen to have political, social, economic as well as legal implications. In many ways, information policy appears to belong to a class of complex policy problems such as industrial or welfare policy that, despite their evident importance, defy easy analysis or 'solution' (Burger, 1993). It is perhaps no longer necessary to justify 'why?' information policy is such a rich area for study and analysis, but the more difficult question of 'how?' such studies should best be carried out is still highly problematic. It is this latter question which offers the starting point for the Workshop.

The aims and objectives of the Workshop

The intention of the Workshop is to focus attention on ways in which the LIS community can arrive at a clearer understanding of information policy problems and issues; despite all the rhetoric, relatively little attention has been paid so far to developing the *theoretical foundations* of the subject. If we are to make progress, a debate about the most appropriate frameworks, tools and methodologies for information policy analysis and evaluation is urgently needed (Rowlands, 1996). The results should inform a more critical approach to information policy analysis and hopefully provide some useful insights for those engaged in 'real-world' policy design and implementation. Within these broad aims, the Workshop would attempt to meet the following objectives:

(a) to explore current approaches to understanding information policy problems, from both theoretical and more pragmatic perspectives;

(b) to encourage dialogue and closer links between the world of ideas (the research and consultancy communities) and policy-makers;

(c) to disseminate the findings to a wider national and international audience, in the form of a proposed publication in the British Library Information Policy Issues series.

The structure of the Workshop

Rather than structure the Workshop around the traditional divisions of information policy indicated by scale (international-national-organizational-individual), a more integrated approach is suggested which should enable common themes and strands to emerge. The Workshop structure reflects the fact that information policy is a *dynamic process.*

Problem identification and agenda setting
Policy formulation and planning
SESSION 1

⇓

Policy adoption
Policy implementation
SESSION 2

⇓

Post-implementation evaluation of policy
SESSION 3

The above is a widely accepted model of the policy-making process and it shows how the Workshop is divided into three coherent sessions embracing policy design, implementation and evaluation.

The Workshop is based around 13 presentations by leading academics and practitioners reflecting basic theoretical concepts as well as issues of practical concern in policy design. Papers will be circulated in advance of the meeting and considerable time will be allocated for discussion of the various issues raised; this interaction would form an important outcome of the Workshop. We are particularly keen to make sure that the Workshop is run in such a way that both practical and more theoretical perspectives are integrated into the discussion. In each session, speakers will be encouraged to address some of the key questions outlined in the next section.

The Workshop programme

Monday 22 July

Arrive at Cumberland Lodge from 4pm onwards. Dinner at 8pm will be followed by a talk given by Professor Charles Oppenheim.

Tuesday 23 July

SESSION 1: DESIGNING INFORMATION POLICIES

What are 'information policies' and how do they evolve? From what traditions does information policy draw? How do certain ideas find their way onto information policy agenda and not others? What kinds of information and research support are needed to design successful policy? Is policy-making a 'rational' process? Is information policy neutral or driven by ideological values? How important are institutional factors in information policy design?

Nigel Macartney	Chair's Introduction
Ian Rowlands & Paul Turner	Models and Frameworks for Information Policy Research
Nick Moore	Planning Information Policies for the Information Society
Barry Mahon	European Information Policy: the Shaping Role of Institutions
David Allen & Tom Wilson	Information Systems Strategy Formulation in Higher Education
Michael Hill	Summary

SESSION 2: IMPLEMENTING INFORMATION POLICIES

What are the ingredients of a 'successful' information policy? Who is responsible for implementing policy? How do they secure the commitment of key stakeholders and ensure compliance? To what extent do different policies interact or even possibly compete with one another? What power structures underlie the adoption and implementation of information policies? Does information technology shape information policy, or vice versa?

Maureen Grieves	Chair's Introduction
Tamara Eisenschitz	Information Policy: Legal and Regulatory Frameworks
Francis Aldhouse	Implementing Information Policy at UK National Level
Margaret Haines	Coordinating Library and Information Policies in the NHS
David Pye	Changing the Corporate Culture: Information Policies for Business Excellence
Michael Hill	Summary

Wednesday 24 July

SESSION 3: EVALUATING INFORMATION POLICIES

How effective is policy X in relation to meeting its objectives? How can information policies be monitored and evaluated? What sort of feedback information and mechanisms are needed to generate better policy responses? What are the wider social and economic impacts? Who are the 'winners' and 'losers'?

Clive Weeks	Chair's Introduction
David Bawden	Information Policy or Knowledge Policy?
Elspeth Scott	Evaluating Information Policy in a Multinational Organization
Harry East	Limitations of 'Free' Access in Academia
David Worlock	Real Policy or 'Virtual Policy'? A Case Study of Tradeable Information Policy
Michael Hill	Summary

List of delegates

Francis Aldhouse	Office of the Data Protection Registrar
David Allen	University of Sheffield
David Bawden	City University
Claire Beasley	City University
Mairéad Browne	University of Technology, Sydney
Jacqueline Cropley	Clifford Chance
Harry East	City University
Tamara Eisenschitz	City University
Maureen Grieves	British Library Research & Development Department
Margaret Haines	Department of Health
Michael Hill	Fédération Internationale de Documentation (FID)
Michael Kristiansson	Royal School of Librarianship, Copenhagen
Nigel Macartney	British Library Research & Development Department
Barry Mahon	Eusidic
Nick Moore	Policy Studies Institute
Dave Nicholas	City University
Charles Oppenheim	de Montfort University
David Pye	Advanced RISC Machines Limited
Ian Rowlands	City University
Elspeth Scott	GlaxoWellcome plc
Paul Turner	University of Namur
Clive Weeks	Derwent Information Limited
Tom Wilson	University of Sheffield
David Worlock	Electronic Publishing Services Limited

Bibliography and References

Aiyepeku, W.O. (1982) Mapping the information environment of policy-makers: some empirical findings from Nigeria. *Social Science Information Studies*, 2(2), 79-91.

Aldhouse, F. (1996) Electronic government: a UK perspective. *International Review of Law, Computers and Technology*, 10(1), 160-168.

Allen, D.K. and Wilson, T.D. (1996) Information strategies in UK higher education institutions. *International Journal of Information Management*, 26(4) 239-251.

Allison, G.T. (1971) *The essence of decision: explaining the Cuban Missile Crisis*. Boston, MA: Little Brown.

Anderson, J.E. (1990) *Public policymaking: an introduction*. Boston, MA: Houghton Mifflin, 2nd edition.

Ansoff, H.I. (1984) Implementing strategic management. Englewood Cliffs, NJ: Prentice Hall.

Araujo, L. and Easton, G. (1996) Strategy: where is the pattern? *Organization*, 3(3) 361-383.

Baden-Fuller, C. and Stopford, J. (1992) *Rejuvenating the mature corporation*. London: Routledge.

Ballantyne, P. (1995) *Information capacity development and environmental policy-making*. Maastricht: European Centre For Development Policy Management, Working Paper 7.

Bates, B.J. (1990) Information systems and society: potential impacts of alternative structures, *Telecommunications Policy*, 14(2), 151-158.

Bawden, D. (1990) Value-added information systems and services, *Perspectives in Information Management*, 2, 157-179.

Bearman, T.C. (1988) Uses of scientific, technical and societal information by policy makers, *Knowledge in Society*, 1(1), 27-53.

Bellotti, V. and Sellen, S. (1993) Design for privacy in ubiquitous computing environments. In: de Michaelis, Simone and Schmidt (eds.), *Proceedings of the Third European Conference on Computer-Supported Co-operative Work*. Amsterdam: Kluwer Academic Publishers.

Bennett, J.R. (1987) *Control of information in the United States: an annotated bibliography*. Westport, CT: Meckler.

Bezold, C. and Olson, R. (1986) *The information millenium: alternative futures: a report for the Information Industry Association*. Washington, DC: Information Industry Association.

Blagden, J.F. (1980) *Do managers read?* Cranfield Institute of Technology Press and British Institute of Management.

Bortnick, J. (1985) National and international information policy, *Journal of American Society for Information Science*, 36(3), 164-168.

Braman, S. (1988) *Information policy and the United States Supreme Court*. University of Minnesota, PhD thesis.

Braman, S. (1989) Defining information: an approach for policymakers, *Telecommunications Policy*, 13(3), 233-242.

Braman, S. (1990) The unique characteristics of information policy and their US consequences. In: Blake, V. and Tjoumas, R. (eds) *Information literacies for the twenty-first century*. Boston, MA: Hill, 1990: 47-77.

Brier, S. (1996) Cybersemiotics: a new interdisciplinary development applied to the problems of knowledge organisation and document retrieval in information science, *Journal of Documentation*, 52(3), 296-344.

British Library (1992) *Health care information in the UK: report of a seminar held on 1 July 1992 at the King's Fund Centre, London*. London: British Library R & D Report 6089.

British Library (1994) *Managing the knowledge base of healthcare: report of a seminar held on 22 October 1993 at the King's Fund Centre, London*. London: British Library R & D Report 6133.

Browne, M. (1996) Personal communication, 14 November 1996.

Browne, M. (1997a) *The field of information policy: (1) fundamental concepts*. (Unpublished MS).

Browne M. (1997b) *The field of information policy: (2) re-defining the boundaries and methodologies*. (Unpublished MS).

Buckland, M.K. (1991) Information as thing, *Journal of the American Society for Information Science*, 42(5), 351-360.

Burgelman, R. (1988) Strategy making as a social learning process: the case of internal corporate venturing, *Interfaces*, 18(3), 74-85.

Burger, R.H. (1988) *The evaluation of information policy: a case study using the SATCOM report*. University of Illinois at Urbana-Champaign, PhD thesis.

Burger, R.H. (1993) *Information policy: a framework for evaluation and policy research*. Norwood, NJ: Ablex.

Burke, M.E. (1994) Introduction to scenario forecasting, In: *Proceedings of the European Business Information Conference 1994, Paris, 23-25 March 1994*. London: TFPL Publishing, 225-231.

Burkert, H. (1992) The legal framework of public sector information: recent legal policy developments in the EC, *Government Publications Review*, 19(5), 483-496.

Burns, T. and Stalker, G.M. (1961) *The management of innovation*. London: Tavistock Publications.

Bushkin, A.A. and Yurow, J.H. (1981) The foundations of United States information policy. In: Gassmann, H.P. (ed.) *Proceedings of the High Level Conference on Information, Computer and Communications Policies for the 80's, Paris, 6-8 October, 1980*. Amsterdam: North-Holland.

Calcutt, Sir D.C. (1993) *Review of press self-regulation,* Cm 2135. London: HMSO.

Carley, M. (1994) *Policy management systems and methods of analysis for sustainable agriculture and rural development*. Rome: UN Food and Agriculture Organization / International Institute For Environment and Development.

CEC (1989) *Guidelines for improving the synergy between the public and private sectors in the information market*. Luxembourg: Office for Official Publications.

CEC (1994) *Europe's way to the information society: an action plan.* Brussels: Commission of the European Communities.

CEC (1996) *High level group of experts in the social and societal aspects of the information society* [http://www.ispo.cec.be/hleg/hleg.html].

Chalton, S. and Gaskill, S. (1988) *Data protection law.* London: Sweet and Maxwell.

Chambers, R. (1994) All power deceives, *IDS Bulletin*, 25(2), 14-26.

Chartrand, R.L. (1986) Legislating information policy, *Bulletin of the American Society for Information Science*, 12(5), 10.

Checkland, P.B. (1981) *Systems thinking, systems practice.* Chichester: Wiley.

Cochrane, C.E. *et al.* (1993) *American public policy: an introduction.* New York: St Martin's Press.

Cohen, J. and Stewart, I. (1995) *The collapse of chaos: discovering simplicity in a complex world.* London: Penguin Books.

Cohen, M., March, J. and Olsen, J. (1972) A garbage can model of organisational choice, *Administration Science Quarterly*, 17(1), 1-25.

Compaigne, B.M. (1988) Evolving technology and blurring boundaries: new perspectives for evaluating media competition. In: Compaigne, B.M. (ed.) *Issues in new information technology.* Norwood, NJ: Ablex.

Council of Europe (1981) *Convention for the protection of individuals with regard to automatic processing of personal data.* Strasbourg: Council of Europe, European Treaty Series.

Council of Europe (1984) *Convention for the protection of human rights and fundamental freedoms.* Strasbourg: Council of Europe, European Treaty Series.

Coveney, P. and Highfield, R. (1995) *Frontiers of complexity: the search for order in a chaotic world.* London: Faber and Faber.

Crain, I.K. (1994) New approaches to information management for very large resource assessment databases. In: Singh, A. (ed.) *Proceedings of UNEP and IUFRO International Workshop in Cooperation with FAO on Developing Large Environmental Data Bases for Sustainable Development.* Nairobi: United Nations Environment Programme, 40-49.

D'udekem-Gevers, M. and Lobert-Maris, C. (1996) The non-profit applications of the information highways: comparison of US and EU policies. In: Dias-Coelho, J. *et al.* (eds) *Proceedings of the 4th European Conference on Information Systems: Lisbon: July 2-4, 1996.*

Dahlin, T.C. (1990) *Books and documents on government information policy: a selected bibliography*. Moniticello: Vance Bibliographies.

Davies, S. (1994) Information, knowledge and power, *IDS Bulletin,* 25(2), 1-13.

Dawes, S.S. (1991) *A theory of interagency information sharing: policy coordination.* State University of New York at Albany, PhD thesis.

Dedrick, J. and Kraemer, K. (1995) National technology policy and computer production in Asia Pacific countries, *The information society*, 11(1), 29-58.

Department of Health (1989) *Working for patients*, Cm 555. London: HMSO.

Department of Health (1994) *Managing the new NHS*. London: NHS Executive.

Department of Health (1996) *The National Health Service: a service with ambitions*, Cm 3425. London: HMSO.

DHSS (1983) *NHS management inquiry*. London: NHS Inquiry Team.

DHSS (1987) *Promoting better health: the government's programme for improving primary health care*, Cmnd 249. London: HMSO.

DHSS (1989) *Caring for people: community care in the next decade and beyond*, Cmnd 849. London: HMSO.

DiMento, J.F. (1981) Making usable information on environmental stressors: opportunities for the research and policy communities, *Journal of Social Issues*, 37(1) 172-204.

DNH (1993) *The Secretary of State's speech to the Library Association Umbrella Conference on 9 July 1993.* London: Department of National Heritage Press Office.

Downs, A. (1957) *An economic theory of democracy*. New York: Harper and Row.

DTI (1986) *Tradeable information.* London: Department of Trade and Industry. [Revised as *Government-held tradeable information: guidelines for government departments in dealing with the private sector.* London: Department of Trade and Industry, in 1990].

Durrance, J.C. (1989) Information needs: old song, new tune, *School Library Media Quarterly*, 17(3), 126-130.

Dye, T.R. (1972) *Understanding public policy.* Englewood Cliffs, NJ: Prentice-Hall, 2nd edition 1984.

Dye, T.R. and Ziegler, L.H. (1990) *The irony of democracy.* Monterey, CA: Brookes/Cole.

Earl, M.J. (1989) *Management strategies for information technology.* Cambridge: Prentice Hall.

East, H. and Tilson, Y. (1993) *The liberated enduser: developments in practice and policy for database provision to the academic community.* London: CCIS Policy Paper 4 / British Library R & D Report 6100.

East, H., Sheppard, E. and Yeal, Y. (1995) *A huge leap forward: a quantitative and qualitative examination of access to database services by British universities, 1988-94.* London: CCIS Policy Paper 5 / British Library R & D Report 6202.

Easton, D. (1979) *A systems analysis of political life.* New York: Wiley, 2nd edition, University of Chicago Press.

Eisenschitz, T.S. (1985) The value of patent information. In: Philips, J.J. (ed.) *Patents in perspective.* Oxford: ESC.

Eisenschitz, T.S. (1993) *Information transfer policy.* London: Library Association Publishing.

Elcock, H. (1991) *Change and decay? Public administration in the 1990s.* London: Longman.

Elton, M.C.J. (1991) *Integrated broadband networks: the public policy issues.* Amsterdam: Elsevier Science Publishers.

European Parliament (1995) *Directive 95/46/EU on the protection of individuals with regard to the processing of personal data and on the free movement of such data.* Brussels, 24 October 1995.

Galliers, R.D. (1986) A failure of direction, *Business Computing and Communications,* July/ August.

Galliers, R.D. (1987) Information systems planning in the United Kingdom and Australia: a comparison of current practice, *Oxford Surveys in Information Technology*, 4, 223-255.

Galliers, R.D. (1991) Strategic information systems planning: myths, reality and guidelines for successful implementation, *European Journal for information Systems,* 1(1), 55-64.

Galvin, T.J. (1994) Rights in conflict: public policy in an information age. In: *New worlds in information and documentation. Proceedings of the 46th FID Conference and Congress 1992*. The Hague: FID.

Garnham, N. (1994) What is multimedia? In: *Legal aspects of multimedia and geographical information systems: Proceedings of the European Commission's Legal Advisory Board Conference, Lisbon, 27-28 October 1994*. Luxembourg: CEC Legal Advisory Board.

Grant, J.A. (1990) Making policy choices: local government and economic development, *Urban Affairs Quarterly*, 26, 148-69.

Gray, J. (1988) *National information policies: problems and progress.* London: Mansell.

Gray, J. (1989) National information policy: myth or magic? *Alexandria,* 1(3), 21-30.

Gray, K.J. (1993) *Elements of land law.* London: Butterworths, 2nd edition.

Gray, R. (1993) *Towards a framework for a national information policy: discussion paper for LISC(E) meeting to be held at the Department of National Heritage on 4 November 1993.* London: Rosemary Gray Associates.

Greenstein, S.M. (1992) Invisible hands and visible advisors: an economic interpretation of standardization, *Journal of the American Society for Information Science*, 43(8), 538-549.

Griffiths, T.A.G. (1977) *The politics of the judiciary.* Manchester University Press.

Guba, E.G. (ed.) (1990) *The paradigm dialog*. Newbury Park, CA: Sage.

Gurnsey, J. (1995) *Copyright theft.* London: Aslib.

Habermas, J. (1972) *Knowledge and human interests.* London: Heinemann Educational.

Hammond, K.R. *et al.* (1983) The use of scientific information in public policy making, *Technological Forecasting and Social Change*, 24(4), 287-297.

Hampden-Turner, C. (1990) *Corporate culture*. London: Hutchinson.

Hampden-Turner, C. (1993) *The seven cultures of capitalism*. New York: Doubleday.

Handy, C. (1994) *The empty raincoat*. London: Hutchinson.

Harrington, J. (1991) *Organizational structure and information technology*. London: Prentice Hall.

Hawkins, D.T. *et al.* (1992) Forces shaping the electronic publishing industry of the 1990s, *Electronic Networking*, 2(4), 38-60.

Hawley Committee (1996) *Information as an asset: the board agenda, checklist and explanatory notes*. London: KPMG IMPACT Programme.

Hernon, P. and Relyea, H.C. (1968) Information policy. In: Kent, A. and Lacour, H. (eds), *Encyclopedia of library and information science 48 II*. New York: Dekker.

Hill, M.J. (ed.) (1993) *New agendas in the study of the policy process*. New York: Harvester Wheatsheaf.

Hill, M.W. (1994) *National information policies and strategies: an overview and bibliographic survey*. London: Bowker-Saur.

Hirschheim, R. and Smithson, S. (1987) A critical analysis of information systems evaluation. In: Galliers, R.D. (ed.) *Information analysis: selected reading*. Maidenhead: Addison Wesley.

Hirschmann, A.O. (1970) The search for paradigms as a hindrance to understanding, *World Politics*, 22, 329-43.

Hoel, I.A.L. (1992) Information science and hermeneutics. In: Vakkari, P. and Cronin, B. (eds), *Conceptions of library and information science: historical, empirical and theoretical perspectives*. London: Taylor Graham.

Hogwood, B.W. and Gunn, L.A. (1984) *Policy analysis for the real world*. Oxford University Press.

Howe, E. (1991) The United Kingdom Data Protection Act, *Government Information Quarterly*, 8(4), 345-357.

Hutton, W. (1995) *The state we're in*. London: Cape.

IDRC (1994) *Information and agenda 21: report of an informal consultation on environment, development, and information*. Ottawa: International Development Research Centre.

Jacobson, R.E. (1989) *An 'open' approach to information policy making: a case study of the Moore Universal Telephone Act*. Norwood, NJ: Ablex.

Jenkins, W.I. (1978) *Policy analysis: a political and organisational perspective*. London: Martin Robertson.

JISC (1995) *Exploiting information systems in higher education: an issues paper*. Bristol: Joint Information Systems Committee.

JISC (1996) *Five year strategy*. Bristol: Joint Information Systems Committee.

Julien, E., Robinson, D. and Tinline, J. (1992) *Bibliography for the national summit on information policy*. Ottawa: National Library of Canada.

Kajberg, L. and Kristiansson, M. (1996) An overview of the field of information policy, *International Forum on Information and Documentation*, 21(1), 5-9.

Karamuftuoglu, M. (1996) *Semiotic approach to information retrieva*. City University PhD thesis: nearing completion.

Karni, R. (1983) A methodological framework for formulating information policy, *Information and Management*, 6(5), 269-280.

Keynes, J.M. (1936) *The general theory of employment, interest and money*. (London: Macmillan.

Kiesler, S.B. and Hinds, P. (1993) Technology, information and social behaviour. In: *The knowledge economy: the nature of information in the 21st century: annual review of the Institute for Information Studies 1993-94*. Nashville, TN: Institute for Information Studies, 117-135.

King, J.L. and Kraemer, K.L. (1996) Information infrastructure, national policy, and global competitiveness, *Information Infrastructure and Policy*, 4(1), 5-28.

Kingdon, J.W. (1984) *Agendas, alternatives and public policies*. Boston, MA: Little Brown.

Kochen, M. (ed.) (1975) *Information for action: from knowledge to wisdom.* New York: Academic Press.

Knights, D. and Morgan, G. (1995) Strategy under the microscope: strategic management and IT in financial services. *Journal of Management Studies*, 32(2), 191-214.

Kristiansson, M. (1996) A framework for information policy analysis based on changes in the global economic forces, *International Forum on information and Documentation*, 21(1), 19-29.

Kuhn, T.S. (1962) *The structure of scientific revolutions.* Chicago University Press.

Laddie, J. (1996) Copyright: over strength, over regulated, over rated? *EIPR*, 5, 253-261.

Lasswell, H.D. (1970) The emerging conception of the policy sciences, *Policy Sciences*, 1(1), 3-14.

Latham, E. (1965) *The group basis of politics.* New York, Octagon Books.

Law, D. (1994) The development of a national policy for dataset provision in the UK: a historical perspective, *Journal of Information Networking*, 1(2), 103-116.

Liebenau, J. and Backhouse, J. (1990) *Understanding information: an introduction.* London: Macmillan.

Lindblom, C.E. (1959) The science of muddling through, *Public Administration Review*, 19(1), 78-88.

Lindblom, C.E. (1979) Still muddling, not yet through, *Public Administration Review*, 39(6), 517-26.

Lindblom, C.E. and Woodhouse, E.J. (1993) *The policy-making process.* New Jersey: Prentice Hall, 3rd edition.

Lloyd, I. (1993) *Information technology and law.* London: Butterworths.

Machlup, F. and Mansfield, U. (eds) (1983) *The study of information.* New York: Wiley.

Mahon, B. (1996) The future of LIS research in Europe. *Information UK Outlooks*, 16, February.

Malley, I. (1988) *National information policy in the United Kingdom*. Shepshed: IMPC.

Martino, C.A. (1983) *Information systems planning to meet objectives: a survey of practices*. New York: Cresap, McCormick and Paget.

Martyn, J. (1992) UK government policy on the electronic information industry, *Journal of Information Science*, 18(4), 269-272.

Martyn, J., Vickers, P. and Feeney, M. (1990) *Information UK 2000*. London: British Library/Bowker-Saur.

McCrone, J. (1994) Don't forget your memory aide, *New Scientist*, 5 February 1994.

McIntosh, T.J. (1990) *Federal information in the electronic age: policy issues for the 1990s*. Washington, DC: Bureau of National Affairs.

McLean, E.R. and Soden, J.V. (1977) *Strategic planning for MIS*. New York: Wiley.

McSean, T. and Law, D. (1990) Is CD-ROM a transient technology? *Library Association Record*, 92(11), 214-215, 217 [see also letter entitled 'We should be praising CD-ROM not burying it' in *Library Association Record*, 92(12), 909].

Menou, M.J. (ed.) (1993) *Measuring the impact of information on development*. Ottawa: International Development Research Centre.

Milevski, S. (1986) Information policy through public laws of the 95th-98th Congresses, *Proceedings of the American Society for Information Science Annual Meeting*, 23, 21 -219.

Miller, P. and Rose, N. (1990) Governing economic life, *Economy and Society*, 19(1), 1-31.

Mintzberg, H. (1993) The pitfalls of strategic planning, *California Management Review*, 36(1), 32-37.

Mintzberg, H. (1994) *The rise and fall of strategic planning*. Hemel Hempstead: Prentice Hall International.

Moore, N.and Steele, J. (1991) *Information intensive Britain. A critical analysis of the policy issues*. London: Policy Studies Institute.

Moore, N. (1992) *Information policy: a discussion paper on the scope of the Policy Studies Institute*. London: Policy Studies Institute.

Moore, N. (1993) Information policy and strategic development: a framework for the analysis of policy objectives, *Aslib Proceedings*, 45(11/12), 281-285.

Moscovivi, S. and Doise, W. (1994) *Conflict and consensus: a general theory of collective decisions.* London: Sage.

National Heritage Committee (1993) *Fourth Report: press and media intrusion.* London: HMSO.

Nelson, C.E. *et al.* (1987) The utilization of social science informtion by policy-makers. *American Behavioural Scientist*, 30(6), 569-577.

NHS (1979) *Report of the Royal Commission on the NHS,* Cmnd 7615. London: HMSO.

Oakeshott, M. (1989) *The voice of liberal learning.* Yale University Press.

ODPR (1986) *Second Report of the Data Protection Registrar.* (London: HMSO.

ODPR (1988) *Fourth Report of the Data Protection Registrar.* London: HMSO.

ODPR (1994) *Tenth Report of the Data Protection Registrar.* London: HMSO.

ODPR (1995) *Eleventh Report of the Data Protection Registrar.* London: HMSO.

ODPR (1996a) *Twelfth Report of the Data Protection Registrar.* London: HMSO.

ODPR (1996b) *Our answers: Data Protection and the EU Directive 95/46/EU.* London: HMSO.

OECD (1980) *Guidelines governing the protection of privacy and transborder flows of personal data.* Paris: Organsiation for Economic Co-operation and Development.

Orna, E. (1990) *Practical information policies: how to manage information flow in organisations.* Aldershot: Ashgate.

Overman, E.S. and Cahill, A.G. (1990) Information policy: a study of values in the policy process, *Policy Studies Review*, 9(4), 803-818.

Palmer, J. and Streatfield, D. (1995) Good diagnosis for the twenty-first century, *Library Association Record*, 97, 153-4.

Parsons, D.W. (1995) *Public policy: introduction to the theory and practice of policy analysis.* Aldershot: Edward Elgar.

Pierce, J.C. *et al.* (1987) Environmental policy elite's trust of information sources, *American Behavioural Scientist*, 30, 578-96.

Popper, K. (1959) *The logic of scientific discovery.* London: Hutchinson.

Popper, K. (1973) *Objective knowledge: an evolutionary approach.* Oxford: Clarendon Press.

Porat, M. (1977) *The information economy: definition and measurement.* Washington, DC: Office of Telecommunications.

Porter, M.E. (1985) *Competitive advantage: creating and sustaining superior performance*. New York: Free Press.

Porter, M.E. and Millar, V.E. (1984) How information gives you competitive advantage, *Harvard Business Review*, 63(4), 149-160.

Quine, W.V.O. (1964) From a logical point of view. Harvard University Press, 2nd edition.

Quinn, J.B. (1980) Strategies for change: logical incrementalism. Homewood, IL: Irwin.

Reed, M.I. (1992) *The Sociology of organisations: themes, perspectives and prospects.* New York: Harvester Wheatsheaf.

Robertson, A. (1988) Social policy-making and the use of research. In: Davidson, R. and White, P. (eds) *Information and government: studies in the dynamics of policy-making*. Edinburgh University Press.

Roling, N. (1994) Communication support for sustainable resource management, *IDS Bulletin*, 25(2), 125-133.

Rose, R. (1976) *The dynamics of public policy.* Beverly Hills, CA: Sage.

Rowlands, I. (1995) Towards public-private synergy in the European electronic information services market, *Journal of Government Information*, 22(3), 227-235.

Rowlands, I. (1996) Understanding information policy: concepts, frameworks and research tools, *Journal of Information Science*, 22(1), 13-25.

Rowlands, I. and Vogel, S. (1991) *Information policies: a sourcebook.* London: Taylor Graham.

Saracevic, T. (1992) Information science: origin, evolution and relations. In: Vakkari, P. and Cronin, B. (eds), *Conceptions of library and information science: historical, empirical and theoretical perspectives.* London: Taylor Graham.

SATCOM (1969) United States National Academy of Sciences SATCOM Committee, *Scientific and technical communication: a pressing national problem and recommendations for its solution.* Washington, DC: National Academy of Sciences.

Sillince, J.A.A. (1994) Coherence of issues and coordination of instruments in European information policy, *Journal of Information Science*, 20(4), 219-236.

Simon, H.A. (1983) *Reason in human affairs.* Stanford University Press.

Slater, M. (1989) *Information needs of social scientists.* London: British Library Research Paper 60.

St. Claire, G. (1994) *Power and influence: enhancing information services within the organization.* London: Bowker-Saur.

Stewart, R.K. (1990) *Access and efficiency in the Reagan-era information policy: a case study of the attempt to privatize the national technical information service.* University of Washington, PhD thesis.

Suprenant, T.T. (1987) Problems and trends in international information and communication policies, *Information Processing and Management*, 23(1), 47-64.

Trauth, E.M. (1986) An integrative approach to information policy research, *Telecommunications Polic*, 10(1), 41-50.

Trigo, M.J.A., Correia, A.M.R. and Wilson, T.D. (1996) National information policy; the Portuguese legal framework (1980-1992), *Journal of Information Science*, 22(3), 219-227.

Turner, P. (1994) *Mapping and measuring the information industry.* MSc dissertation, City University, London.

Turner, P. (1996a) Personal communication.

Turner, P. (1996b) *Information policy in Europe : a case study in multimedia.* City University PhD thesis: in progress.

UFC/ISC (1992) *ISC policy for dataset provision to the higher education and research community*. Bristol: Universities Funding Council.

Ulrich, W. (1994) *Critical heuristics of social planning*. Chichester: Wiley.

US Domestic Council (1976) *National information policy—the 'Rockefeller Report'*. Washington, DC: US Government Printing Office for the Committee on the Right to Privacy.

Walsh, J. and Simonet, M. (1995) Data analysis needs for health sector reform, *Health Policy*, 32(1/3), 295-306.

Webber, D.J. (1987) Legislators' use of policy information, *American Behavioural Scientist*, 30(6), 612-31.

Webster, F. (1994) What information society? *The Information Society*, 10(1) 1-24.

Weingarten, F.W. (1989) Federal information policy development: the Congressional perspective. In: McClure, C., Hernon, P. and Relyea, H. (eds) *United States Government information policies: views and perspectives*. Norwood: NJ: Ablex.

White, D.A. (1986) Information use and needs in manufacturing organisations: organisational factors in information behaviour, *International Journal of Information Managemen*, 6, 157-170.

White, D.A. and Wilson, T.D. (1988) *Information needs in industry: a case study approach*. Sheffield: CRUS Occasional Paper 16. British Library R&D Report 5954.

Wilson, T.D. (1981) On user needs and information needs. *Journal of Documentation*, 37(1), 3-15.

Wilson, T.D. (1989) The implementation of information strategies in UK companies: aims and barriers to success, *International Journal of Information Management*, 9(4), 245-258.

Woolgar, S. (1996) Psychology, qualitative methods and the ideas of science. In: Richardson, J.T.E. (ed.), *Handbook of qualitative research methods for psychology and the social sciences*. London: BPS Books.

World Energy Council (1996) *Climate change 1995: the intergovernmental panel on climate change - second assessment report reviewed*. London: World Energy Council Report No. 5.

Index

Page-numbers in **bold** type denote main entries.